My Lucky Stroke

Sarah Brooker

16pt

Copyright Page from the Original Book

Published by Affirm Press in 2019
28 Thistlethwaite Street, South Melbourne, VIC 3205
www.affirmpress.com.au
10 9 8 7 6 5 4 3 2 1

Text and copyright © Sarah Brooker 2020
All rights reserved. No part of this publication may be reproduced without prior permission of the publisher.

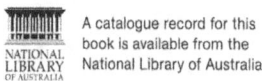 A catalogue record for this book is available from the National Library of Australia

Title: My Lucky Stroke / Sarah Brooker, author.

Cover design by Design by Committee
Typeset in Garamond 12.5/17.5 by J&M Typesetting
Proudly printed in Australia by Griffin Press

The paper this book is printed on is certified against the Forest Stewardship Council® Standards. Griffin Press holds FSC chain of custody certification SGS-COC-005088. FSC promotes environmentally responsible, socially beneficial and economically viable management of the world's forests.

Author image credit: ABC Conversations

TABLE OF CONTENTS

Prologue: A letter to Richard Fidler	iv
Part One	1
Chapter One: Once There Was a Girl	2
Chapter Two: The Bachelorette of Behavioural Neuroscience	26
Chapter Three: Nine Simple Words	53
Chapter Four: Breathe	76
Part Two	104
Chapter Five: Wake Up	105
Chapter Six: A lesson in memory	129
Chapter Seven: Mind of a Child, Body of an Adult	158
Chapter Eight: Leaps and Crashes	184
Chapter Nine: Small Steps	209
Part Three	235
Chapter Ten: Brave New World	236
Chapter Eleven: Sarah is a Little Bit Different	262
Chapter Twelve: Honourable Mentions	290
Chapter Thirteen: What Are You, If You Aren't a Neuroscientist?	314
Part Four	340
Chapter Fourteen: Independence	341
Chapter Fifteen: Alan – A Different Kind of Person	366
Chapter Sixteen: When One Door Closes...	391
Chapter Seventeen: Teacher	421
Chapter Eighteen: Student	443
Chapter Nineteen: It's Not a Wedding, It's a Barbecue	465
Now You Have Read My Story, You can Decide	477
Acknowledgements	486
Back Cover Material	492

On New Year's Eve 2002, Melbourne-born Sarah Brooker was studying to become a neuroscientist when a freak accident put her in a coma for weeks. When she woke up, she had no recollection of her old life.

Since the accident, Sarah has achieved Honours and a PhD, and worked as a rehabilitation consultant, counsellor, waitress, tutor, behavioural neuroscientist, student support officer, and high school teacher. She lives near Adelaide, where she works as a relief teacher in high schools and disability units, and lives on a farm with her husband, Alan.

*In this world, you must be oh so smart,
or oh so pleasant.
For years, I was smart.
I recommend pleasant.*
– JAMES STEWART, *HARVEY*, 1950

Dedicated to anyone who is a little bit different, and who, at some stage, has felt a little unsure or misunderstood. Hopefully, this will help you feel a little less alone.

Prologue

A letter to Richard Fidler

March, 2016

Dear Richard,

I am disabled – broken.

My eyes don't move in sync, I am deaf in one ear, I have no sense of smell, my body won't make hormones anymore and I have little control over my emotions owing to an acquired brain injury that has left me without the middle third of my frontal lobe, a rare condition called orbitofrontal disorder (or syndrome or something else appropriate to mean 'broken bit').

I wasn't always like this.

I was in a coma. Then I woke up.

I couldn't comprehend where I was, and didn't know who I was. I looked at the face of my identical twin sister – and didn't know who she was. I was twenty years old and I had a stroke. That would have been a bad thing on its own, but I happened to be driving my car at the same time. That would also have been a bad thing, but then I hit a pole. The benefit of all these things is this: had I been alone, at home for example, the stroke would have killed me. Had I been conscious when the car skidded and hit the pole, my reflexes would have been to turn the steering wheel, and I would have been the centre of impact, and I would have died. Two negatives really do make a positive.

The other lucky part is that this happened one kilometre from the hospital. I received attention fast, within the critical time required to result in optimal recovery of the brain. But sometimes I think that part – my recovery – is the unlucky part of the story.

My disability is invisible. Had it not been for the hard work of countless surgeons, neurosurgeons, neurologists, psychologists, physiologists, occupational therapists, ear-nose-throat specialists, speech pathologists and hospital staff, I would not have recovered as well as I did. Had it not been for the patience of my honours supervisor, or support of my family, or my own stubborn determination, I would not have achieved all the things I have. And then you might believe me.

I am tired of people who promise to be discreet when I tell them about my disability. Why? Do I have something to be ashamed of? By staying quiet about my disability, my hidden brokenness, I perpetuate your ignorance. You fail to understand when I misinterpret your body language, or when I make social blunders, or behave oddly in some other fashion. You fail to recognise that my world is not worse because I can't smell, just different (in many respects, I would be inclined to say I am better off for that).

You fail to understand how incredibly important it is that I take my medication – and even if you count the ten tablets I take every day, you won't ever know how hard it was to find the balance of hormones and anti-seizure medication to keep me as close to 'normal' as I am now. You can't possibly ever understand how liberating it is for me, for the first time in my life, to not have a neurologist. You certainly won't get that. And you won't understand how painful it is to not see the world as sharply as I did before. Because I still have an IQ that is in the high-functioning range.

I sometimes wish I was wheelchair bound, or lost my ability to talk, or was completely blind or deaf, or that the hair never grew back over the hole in my head – then you could see it. You would see the disability – and there would be no need for me to patiently try to explain exactly what is wrong with me. I wouldn't feel the need to justify my brokenness or feel like a fraud.

So that's why I am writing this. To promote awareness. But also to tell you – apart from my frustration at people's fear of disclosure leading to ignorance – that the car accident in 2002 was probably one of the luckiest events in my life.

If you would like to give me the opportunity to tell my story to you on air, please contact me.
Regards,
Sarah Brooker

Part One

**Pre-accident Sarah
(1982–2002)**

Chapter One

Once There Was a Girl

Once upon a time, there was a girl. She looked like me, had a twin sister, like me, and to the best of everyone's knowledge, she was me. But she wasn't me. The Sarah Brooker who existed before 31 December 2002 was a girl so wholly different to myself that I barely identify with her.

All I know of her are facts. The little stories and family legends about the things she did and her responses to the world. I don't know if I would have ever acted the way that she did, and I struggle to imagine whether she would act like me.

But I'll let you decide.

Let me introduce Sarah.

Sarah and her identical twin sister, Abi, were the youngest of four children.

It was nearly impossible to tell the two young girls apart. Both had hazel eyes, crooked teeth and dimples. They had straight dark hair with messy fringes, testament to their mother's hairdressing attempts each summer.

The twins grew up on a small farm in a tiny country town that was barely large enough to make it onto a map. From the moment they could walk, they were enthusiastically playing among the bracken with bare knees and gumboots, exploring the paddocks, dams and bushland with the type of vivid imaginations that only young children can understand. Their exaggerated sense of bravado was enhanced well beyond that of other preschoolers, simply by the fact that they always had each other. No matter how great the mischief, they would always be there to watch the other's back.

Abi had Sarah. Sarah had Abi. Nothing could go wrong.

Sarah was in Grade One when the seizures began.

Friday afternoons were reserved for story time. Abi and Sarah loved story time. They would eagerly race to the carpet and sit cross-legged in the front row to get the best view of the pictures.

Abi was one of the smallest and fastest students in the class, and often reached the carpet first, spreading her arms and legs as far as she could to save a place for Sarah. In return, Sarah saw it as her duty to quieten the class so that she and Abi could hear the story. After joining Abi on the carpet, she would immediately start shooshing the nearest students, frowning at anyone who dared to speak and dobbing on those that did.

This particular Friday afternoon, their teacher had selected one of Sarah's favourite stories: *The Magic Pudding.* The teacher had barely made it through the third page when there was a confused cry from one of her students. She looked up to see that Sarah had fallen backwards. The teacher looked on in horror as Sarah's tiny body jerked around the mat, convulsing to the rhythm of her choking and gurgling.

Then, just as quickly as the seizure started, it stopped. The little body lay motionless on the mat.

Abi watched with the same silent curiosity as the other children. She had never seen a seizure before. It didn't look scary; it just looked like Sarah was kicking around on the floor. Then she fell asleep. She'd wake up soon. She had to. She was Sarah.

Sarah, of course, had no idea what had happened. One minute, she had been listening to the adventures of Bunyip Bluegum and his friends, and the next she was lying on a small, firm bed in the silence of the school sick bay.

Sarah raised her head off the pillow, sleepy and disorientated. She looked across the room to see Abi sitting on a plastic chair. Abi had her head down, deep in concentration, folding an elastic around her fingers.

Sarah lay in silence and watched her sister for a while. It slowly dawned on Sarah that she didn't really know why she was in the sick bay. With increasing concern, she realised that both she and Abi were missing story time.

'What happened to *The Magic Pudding?*' she asked.

Abi smiled when she heard her sister's voice and looked up from her hands.

'Ms Williams stopped it when we brought you over here. I dunno if she kept reading it. You've been asleep for ages ... like, hours!' Abi told her emphatically.

They heard a commotion start on the other side of the wall. Their mother, Donna, had arrived, and it sounded like she had taken the news about Sarah's seizure in the way that any young mother would do. It sounded like she was panicking.

'Where is she? Is she okay? Will there be any repercussions? What's wrong with her?' Abi and Sarah looked at each other quietly. They weren't sure what their mother was worried about. After all, all that had happened was that Sarah had fallen asleep during story time.

Lots of people fell asleep.

It was three weeks, and five seizures, before Donna could get an appointment for Sarah to see her local doctor. The doctor referred them for an electroencephalogram (EEG) at the Royal Children's Hospital in Melbourne, four hours away from their little country town in Gippsland.

Donna told Sarah that if she was brave during the EEG, she would get a Barbie doll. Sarah had no real use for a Barbie doll, but went along with it anyway. She and Abi would be able to use the doll for *something*.

The Royal Children's Hospital in Melbourne wasn't like anything the small country girl had ever seen. Doctors, nurses, receptionists, and patients scurried across the foyer floor to mysterious, unknown locations in the hospital. Sarah could have watched them all day, and maybe followed someone to see where they went. But she never got the opportunity. Her mother took her hand and hurried her through the bustle to the neurologist's rooms.

The calm silence of the neurologist's waiting room was a stark contrast to the exciting bustle of the hospital foyer. Bland classical music played softly from speakers on the receptionist's desk. Adults sat in chairs that lined the walls, while some children quietly played at a toy box in the corner of the room.

Sarah wished she'd thought to bring a colouring-in book. She didn't fancy approaching the toys in the corner without Abi beside her. She sat on one of the scratchy plastic chairs that lined the waiting room. Holding onto the armrests, she crossed her ankles and watched them swing.

Forwards. Back. Forwards. Back.

Hospital was boring.

She wished Abi was with her.

Eventually, a technician entered the waiting room and called Sarah for her test. She was taken to a room full of strange looking machines and computers. Her boredom was instantly forgotten and replaced by curiosity.

The technician sat her in a large leather reclining chair. Sarah couldn't wait to see how far she could extend her tiny legs. She looked around for the lever to pull, and found a remote control covered with lots of colourful buttons. Sarah longed to push them all and discover what they did. She privately fantasised about all the fun that she would have playing with the chair as soon as the adults left the room.

But the adults didn't leave the room. Instead, they fussed over Sarah and the machines that surrounded her.

She was intrigued by the wires and glue that the technician started to attach to her head. She fancied that they may stay on there forever, and imagined what it would be like having wire for hair. Sarah told the technician all about a doll that she and Abi had made that had wire hair.

'We got in trouble for that, because it was our big sister Greer's favourite doll. Mum made us take off all the wire. We had to use a whole bottle of nail polish remover to get rid of the glue.'

Then a thought struck Sarah.

'Am I gonna be like Greer's doll? Are you sure that you have enough nail polish remover to take off all these wires?'

The technician laughed and promised that the wires would come off easily, and that the glue would wash out with a bit of shampoo. Once he had placed the last wire on her head, he stepped back to admire his work and then turned on the EEG machine.

'You won't feel a thing. Just relax.'

But Sarah couldn't relax. She had forgotten all about the trauma of washing the glue out of her hair. She had even forgotten about the remote control that lay beside her, which was still waiting to be played with. She was completely distracted by what she saw coming out of the printer on the other side of the room. It was an endless sheet of paper. Longer than anything that she, or Abi, had ever seen before. It was covered with millions of lines with peaks and troughs that were printed on it as it fed through a large machine.

Tick, tick, buzz. Tick, tick, buzz.

Hospital was exciting.

Sarah had so many questions about the mysterious paper. 'Why does that line go higher than the others? What does the flat line mean? Can you see what's happening in my brain?'

The technician shook his head and smiled at the curious little girl. 'Reading all these lines is the job of the *neurologist.*'

Once the EEG finished, the technician said Sarah had been so brave that she could take some of the paper home. Sarah thought that paper was a gold mine. Paper was far more useful than any Barbie doll that Mum could buy! She couldn't wait to show Abi.

But, for all the hours of entertainment that the treasured reams of paper would bring, a much more important seed was planted that day.

Somewhere in the world there was a person called a *neurologist.* They were smart enough to understand the sheets of paper that came out of the EEG, and they understood what happened in the brain!

Sarah wanted to be that smart. She wanted to be a *neurologist.*

Sarah's neurologist *was* the smartest man in the world. Not only was Dr Thorpe able to answer all her questions about the brain, but he was also able to tell the young girl why she was having seizures. *And* he gave her more paper.

The tall, wise man smiled across his desk at Sarah, Abi and Donna. In a calm but serious voice he explained that, although the EEG had not captured what was causing Sarah's generalised seizures, the tests *had* captured something else; during the EEG, Sarah had had multiple absence seizures.

'But you didn't notice those, did you?' he asked the small, dark-haired girl. She nodded to confirm his news. She *hadn't* noticed. He *was* clever.

He explained that these seizures were a result of overactivity in specific regions of Sarah's brain. She had a condition that meant she would need to take anticonvulsant tablets every morning and keep a journal of any little absences or seizures that she (or Abi) noticed.

It had a name. *Temporal lobe epilepsy.* Sarah liked the way it sounded. It had the kind of name that sounded very important. The kind of name that only someone who was very smart would understand.

At school the next morning, Sarah was very proud to present the pictures of her brain for show and tell.

Sarah waited eagerly, cross-legged on the carpet, patiently sitting through stories that the other children had. Even though Sarah *knew* that her show and tell was far more interesting than any of the other students', she politely listened to Michelle's story about her new horse, and David's story about his new toy trucks. She watched the clock, counting down the seconds of their stories, praying that neither of them went over their allocated three minutes.

Finally, it was her turn.

She reached into the box she had brought home from the hospital and pulled out one of the reams of paper.

'This is what the doctor gave me when I went into the city,' she said, waiting for the class to make the appropriate *Ooooh* that was always given at the start of a *good* show and tell.

Michelle put up her hand.

'Yes, Michelle?' asked Sarah, feeling very important.

'Why did the doctor give you paper?'

'Because *that* is how he could tell what was wrong. I have something called temporal lobe epilepsy, and you can see it on this sheet of paper.'

'*Ooooh,*' said the class in unison.

Sarah was excited that her classmates appeared as interested in the brain as she was. She went on to explain that the brain used electricity to work '...just like a TV', and that sometimes that electricity blacked out or had a surge '...just like what happens in a storm'.

David, who had lost interest after learning that Sarah didn't have any colouring pages, started to play with his toy trucks on the floor.

Sarah unfolded the sheet of paper, revealing the horizontal lines that appeared to zig and zag in tandem.

'And so, when I have a fit, which is actually called a seizure, *this* part of my brain is overactive and this part shuts down.' Sarah pointed to two different lines on the EEG. She wasn't sure if that was entirely true, but she imagined that was what it would have looked like.

One by one, David's friends lost interest, and turned to join in with his silent truck rally at the back of the classroom.

Oblivious to their disinterest, Sarah continued her lecture, providing analogies and images about the way that the brain worked. But she was well over time and nearly every classmate before her was bleary-eyed and restless.

The more polite students attempted to stay awake by playing with their shoelaces or bits of paper on the carpet. Other classmates rested their heads in their hands and stared out the window or lay down on the carpet and closed their eyes. They simply could not follow the confusing stories that Sarah was telling.

Only one pair of eyes, and one little brain, stayed alert for the whole lecture.

Abi sat in the front row, proud as punch of her twin sister.

Abi and Sarah were in Grade Two when their parents separated. It wasn't a nasty break-up. Their parents were very good friends, but their mother was a city girl and their father was a country boy, and neither lifestyle is compatible with the other. Abi and Sarah, and their brother and sister moved with Donna to the suburbs of the Mornington Peninsula.

The twins didn't understand their new suburban classmates. No one climbed trees or played 'schools' or 'sums'. The local girls played netball and collected dresses and Barbie dolls. They wore their hair in tidy ponytails and dressed in skirts and white socks that never seemed to get dirty. At recess, they sat at tables gossiping about boys, Hollywood celebrities, TV shows and popstars.

Abi and Sarah didn't do any of that. Abi faced the challenge of trying to fit in. She played school sports and joined all of the school clubs that she could. Abi learned that participation and support could go a long way, and it was through this pleasantness that Abi found friends.

Sarah, on the other hand, saw no use for the other girls and did not seek their approval. She was committed to becoming smart, like a neurologist. She embarked on a quest to learn all the facts that she imagined a neurologist needed to know. Neurologists didn't need to know how to colour within the lines, or the lyrics to Nirvana's 'Smells Like Teen Spirit' – why did she have to?

Throughout their high school years, Abi continued her mission of participation and acceptance, while Sarah continued to ignore her peers and maintained her quest to be smart enough to become a neurologist.

As the twins grew up, there was only one area of Sarah's life that could take her attention away from science: music.

Music had always been present in Sarah's world. Throughout their teens, the long car rides to visit their dad were spent singing everything from Frente! to Dr Hook. Many hot summer afternoons would see the girls in traffic, windows down, happily singing, 'I got stoned and I missed it...' They were blissfully unaware of the meaning of the words and the looks from passengers in nearby cars.

Then Sarah found guitar.

It started with a few simple chords – simple progressions that Abi played her clarinet to. Then one of Greer's friends offered Sarah guitar lessons.

Tim was an excellent guitarist in his own right. Hours alone in his room were spent practising scales and chords. He didn't simply *learn* chord progressions and compositions; he studied the guitar with the same passion and enthusiasm that Sarah had for neurology. Tim dreamed of someday becoming a professional musician – a dream that would come true many years later, on the other side of the world.

'Just a few lessons' was the initial agreement. 'Just until you know how to play more chords.'

Tim stayed in Sarah's life for more than a couple of lessons. He would become one of Sarah's best friends and her high-school sweetheart. To outsiders, they were an oddly matched couple. Sarah was, for all intents and purposes, serious and rather aloof. Tim was extremely social, and friends with everyone in the school. But they brought out things in each other that the rest of the world could never have seen.

'You're just not like other girls ... or other people for that matter,' he once told her, as they walked along their favourite local beach. 'You don't judge, or gossip, or try to impress people. You're just *you,* you know?' Sarah smiled. *How could she be anyone else?*

For her part, Sarah loved Tim's creativity. He was forever pointing out funny-shaped clouds, silly-sounding words, or trees that looked like things. It reminded her of the creativity and freedom that she and Abi had as small children. A creativity and freedom that she would have lost, had it not been for Tim.

But it was through guitar that Sarah found the most freedom. With Tim's instructions, Sarah wrote more than seventy songs. Music was probably the only thing in her life that came close to challenging her love for science. And it did come very close.

In Year 10, Sarah did her work experience within the neurology department at Monash Medical Centre, assisting technicians to conduct EEGs.

Sarah felt superior and important when she met her first patient. She studied the man with distaste, as he stooped through the door and walked into the examination room.

His flannel shirt and denim overalls were covered in dirt patches and the occasional straw of hay, as though he had stepped directly off his tractor and into the hospital. Sarah privately thought that he should have given the occasion more respect than that.

Oblivious to Sarah's snobbery, he smiled a warm greeting.

'G'day. What's this then?'

'My name is Sarah Brooker. I will be helping conduct your EEG today,' she informed him, in as professional a tone as she could manage.

The supervising technician approached the man. 'Sarah is a work-placement student from the Mornington Peninsula,' she explained, giving an apologetic smile that was conspicuously warmer than Sarah's greeting had been.

'Oh, work experience, eh? Good for you! How old are you?' The farmer settled into the chair that the technician had motioned to and waited for her to prepare the wires that would be attached to his head.

'Fifteen,' Sarah said defensively. 'I'm going to be a neurologist.'

'Is that right?' The man chuckled and shifted his weight, trying to find a position that would accommodate his size for the duration of the EEG. 'That's a huge commitment. There's years of study in that, isn't there?'

'It's a minimum seven-year university degree – double that if you are serious about your career,' Sarah replied. She picked up a clipboard on a shelf next to her, pretending that she had some sort of role while the technician prepared the EEG. 'But it's important to study that long,' she continued, pretending to read the papers on the clipboard. 'There's a lot to learn when you study the brain; it's not as though someone could knock it over in three years.'

She looked up at the farmer to emphasise her next point.

'And seven years is nothing at all, given that I'll be working until I am at least sixty-five.' Sarah had thought this last part was particularly clever, because it proved that she thought about her actual career, not just the pathway she'd take to get there.

The farmer let out a whistle. 'You sound like you know what you want. Well, good for you!' He smiled at her again and scratched his chin. 'So ... you're here to learn about it now, are you? Are you nervous?'

Sarah gave the farmer a quizzical look. *What was there to be nervous about?*

'No. Not at all.'

The second patient that Sarah met was almost the opposite of everything the farmer had represented. She was a professional-looking woman, who exuded a self-imposed authority over the technicians as they worked around her to set up the EEG.

Sarah expected that, as the woman acted so important, she would appreciate Sarah's drive and initiative in undertaking work experience at a hospital when she was only in Year 10. However, Sarah was not even partway through saying as much when the woman cut her off.

'What?' she asked, directing her outrage to one of the technicians. 'What sort of a place is this? Some kid, who isn't even sixteen, is allowed to sit in? What am I, some sort of freak show?'

Sarah thought this was rather naive of the woman. Monash Medical Centre was a teaching hospital. What *had* she expected? Nonetheless, the patient's rights to privacy were valid and Sarah was taken to another room to read until the test was over.

It didn't concern Sarah in the least that the patient had been so upset. What she learned in the waiting room was far more important than that.

It was filled with hundreds of journals that documented research on the brain. There were stories about neurological disorders: epilepsy, autism, motor neuron disease, Alzheimer's disease and Parkinson's disease. There were pictures of the brain from all different angles that accompanied stories about new drug therapies and treatments for neurological diseases. She didn't understand what the articles were saying, but she imagined that the neurologists must have known.

The discovery of the journal articles brought with it another amazing revelation: there were people who knew about the brain before neurologists did. This meant that they maybe knew more about the brain than neurologists. These people were called *neuroscientists.* Sarah's career path changed that instant. She gave up thoughts of be a neurologist, and set her sights on becoming a neuroscientist.

As Abi and Sarah reached the end of high school, they started to think about university. Sarah knew she wanted to be a neuroscientist, but she could not find a course or university that could get her there. Abi had no idea what she wanted to be and could not find a course or university that inspired her to make a decision. Together, they scrutinised potential universities and degrees, trying to anticipate where the rest of their lives would take them, unsure of the paths they would take.

The twins' university degrees turned out to be remarkably similar. Abi was accepted into Swinburne University to study an applied science degree with two majors: psychology and psychophysiology. Sarah was accepted into the Bachelor of Behavioural Neuroscience, a new degree at Monash University. The main difference between the two degrees was that Abi's had a stronger emphasis on people, while Sarah's had a stronger emphasis on the brain.

Once they started university, the twins found themselves in the same situation they had been in when they changed primary school, all those years ago. They were both in strange new worlds, separated from each other, and unsure what was expected. Each girl was privately comforted by the fact that somewhere in another lecture hall, on the other side of the city, her twin sister was learning the same thing. They would survive university together.

Abi had Sarah. Sarah had Abi. Nothing could go wrong.

Chapter Two

The Bachelorette of Behavioural Neuroscience

It wasn't yet 7:30a.m. and the university was still asleep. Over the next few hours, the lawns would fill with the typical assortment of campus characters: students carrying tote bags, laptops or skateboards, deep in conversation about the day's classes or the weekend's adventures; professors carrying books and notes in preparation for their next lecture; and groundskeepers on quad bikes, towing trailers full of shovels, leaf blowers and bins. They would pass each other, adding to the noise and bustle of university life, oblivious to the others' existence.

But that was yet to come.

On early winter mornings, Monash University wrapped itself in a blanket of Melbourne fog and slept through the cold drizzle.

That morning, Sarah sat alone on the cold cement walkway outside the lecture theatre. The doors would not open for another fifteen minutes. Armed with two highlighters and a ballpoint pen, she was studying the morning's lecture notes. More than *studying.* Sarah was *hunting.* She was searching for tiny gaps in the information, things that the lecturer may have left out, so that she might ask a question and learn something new. It was Sarah's first year of university. She loved these early morning study sessions where she could sit alone in silence and immerse herself in the strange and exciting things hidden in her lecture notes.

This morning's lecture was on DNA replication. They had covered the basics earlier in the year and Sarah remembered thinking at the time that the process sounded simple enough. But, then again, *nothing* in biology is simple. She seemed to be forever learning about proteins and enzymes that folded around each other in beautifully complex dances in order to keep body systems in check. Sarah hoped DNA replication would be the same.

The wind blew again, this time bringing with it a chill that passed straight through Sarah's coat.

Her watch ticked over to 7:45a.m. and the lecture hall doors unlocked. Sarah stood up off the cement, straightened her jacket, heaved her bag up onto her shoulder and entered the lecture theatre.

This was what she lived for.

While Sarah immersed herself in the wonders of her degree, Tim fully immersed himself in music on the other side of the university. Even though they lived together in Mount Eliza and went to the same university, they were worlds apart during the day. Sarah worked on the weekend, and Tim played in a band on Friday and Saturday nights. The rare days that they both had off were a magic relief where they could both break from the intense worlds they were building at university and simply *exist* in each other's company.

They spent hours walking together along the Mornington Peninsula, exploring rock pools and building sand castles while they chatted freely about people they knew and stories they had heard.

After scrambling across the rocks one day, they came across a small white beach. They walked towards the water's edge, listening to the waves gently lapping on the shore.

'This is a nice spot,' Tim said, as he sat down on the sand and pulled his knees up to his chin. Sarah lowered herself next to him, took off her sneakers and pushed her feet into the sand.

'Do you think that staring at the ocean actually changes our brain waves?' Sarah asked quietly. 'Just sitting here, looking ... it's hypnotic. I wonder why.'

Tim picked up a twig and started to sketch a picture in the sand between them. Sarah silently watched the cartoon between them evolve. She loved his drawings.

'What are you drawing?' she asked, as she began to recognise faces and shapes form in the sand.

'Don't really know yet,' Tim said absentmindedly.

'Hmmm,' was all that Sarah could reply.

They sat in a comfortable silence for a short while – Tim busily sketching in the sand, Sarah watching waves, trying to calculate their speed.

'Ah-ha!' Tim called triumphantly, satisfied that his cartoon was complete.

Sarah looked between them. What had once been a smooth surface of sand had been transformed into a scene of chaos. A policeman with enormously long legs was chasing a buggy down the street, leaving a trail of mayhem behind them.

'Look, I even added you!' Tim laughed, pointing to a young girl with pigtails who was clutching a case of some sort to her chest.

'That looks more like Penny from Inspector Gadget!'

'No. It's you, and you have a laptop because you're a nerd!' Tim teased, proud of the masterpiece he had made in the sand.

'Da-da-da-da-da, Inspector Gadget!' he started to sing.

He gave up singing and started to whistle. When he got sick of that, he tapped his cheeks, attempting to make the melody as he went. After a while, Sarah could even make out most of the theme song. As Tim tapped his cheeks and contorted his face to play Inspector Gadget, Sarah laughed along. She was silently proud to be a part of this moment. She loved how creative Tim was, and in that instant, she was a part of his creativity.

They sat on the beach for another half-hour before putting their shoes back on and making their way back along the shoreline. A near perfect day. Although Sarah loved university and would not have traded her life there for anything, she felt sad at the end of days like this one. Even though she knew she'd see Tim each night when she came home, it would be at least another week before they got to spend *time* together.

Towards the end of second year, Sarah got her first exposure to surgical procedures.

The medical students had been allowed to dissect real cadavers since the beginning of the year. Sarah heard them relay horror stories about the bodies that lay motionless in the freezers of the cold physiology labs, and listened to them complain about the stench of formaldehyde.

They don't know how lucky they are.

The closest the neuroscience students got to human tissues were the plasticised brains that sat neatly in a cardboard box at the back of the laboratory. The old brains could be taken apart and put together like three-dimensional puzzles. They had been useful in first year, when students were familiarising themselves with different structures, but by second year they had lost their novelty.

The neuroscience students agreed that in *real life* the brain was far more exciting than any other organ of the body. But as they sat in the physiology labs, faced with plastic puzzle pieces, the neuroscience students eyed the mysterious tissue samples in the jars that lined the walls, wishing that they studied other organs and handled real tissue samples.

Today, they may get their chance.

Today, the plasticised brains were nowhere in sight. In their place, on the demonstrator's bench at the front of the room was a mysterious ice bucket, a white surgical board and a series of scalpels. *This could only mean one thing...*

The demonstrator stood smiling at his students from behind his blue surgical mask, gloved hands resting in his lab coat pocket.

'Well, don't be shy. Come on up and take a look. You won't see anything from back there!' he teased, still smiling at the expense of the nervous second year students.

Sarah was among the first to reach the front of the lab. She found herself a prime position, standing immediately beside the jovial demonstrator. Others were not so lucky, and had to stand on the other side of the bench.

I may get to touch it!

The demonstrator lowered his hands into the ice bucket, and carefully lifted out a wet, bloody mass that was no bigger than a child's football. Cradling the soft brain in his hands, he held it up for the students to see.

Sarah studied the unremarkable glob in front of her. It didn't look much like the plasticised brains. It was much smaller for a start.

'What sort of brain is this?' she asked.

'Cow's brain,' the demonstrator replied, as he gently placed the brain onto the white surgical board.

'Oh.' Sarah could not hide her disappointment. 'How different is it from a human brain?'

A tutor who had been standing quietly behind them suddenly came to life.

'It isn't too different,' she said. 'Except for the forebrain. If you look up at the screen here...'

The students on the other side of the bench turned their attention to the tutor as she explained the differences between bovine and human brains. But Sarah was too distracted by the demonstrator and the cow's brain in front of her. She had other questions that needed answering.

'How fresh is it?' Sarah asked.

The demonstrator chuckled beneath his mask. 'It was only killed this week and we picked it up this morning. It's relatively fresh.'

Sarah was conscious that the tutor would soon finish distracting the other students. They would turn their attention back to the demonstrator, and she would run out of time to get this extra information.

'How is it stored?'

'It's frozen,' the demonstrator replied as he sorted through the tools on his bench. 'It's safe to freeze brain tissue. It isn't ideal for some things, but it won't change too much – not for today's purposes.' He paused for a moment, and then looked up from his tools. 'It's good to see you question these sorts of things.' He noticed the tutor wrapping up her talk. 'But now we really must get on.' He started to motion towards the other students.

Alas, Sarah's interrogation wasn't quite over.

'Where has it come from?'

A heavy-set girl further up the bench rolled her eyes, and her two smaller companions giggled. Sarah gave them a disapproving glance and wondered whether they valued their education. The demonstrator didn't notice the girls' laughter and continued to answer Sarah's questions. 'The local butcher,' he replied.

Sarah gasped. She had imagined, being something as precious as a brain, that they would be stored in a special facility, frozen and isolated from the world.

'They are that easy to get? Just like that? Just from the butcher?' she stammered.

'Well, yes, of course. People eat brain. I mean, I don't, but people do.' He chuckled, clearly entertained by Sarah's response to the gruesome news. 'In fact, it's eaten all over the world.'

Sarah could not believe what she was learning. She knew that some people ate crumbed brains, but she never imagined cooking it at home. Not something as precious as the *brain.*

'How much are they?' Sarah asked, trying to regain her composure.

There were sniggers among the students on the other side of the counter.

'Gonna cook some up, Brooker?' a boy asked.

Sarah scowled at the ridiculous notion, but she didn't reply. She had learned from Abi that it was important to get along with her peers. *Not* pointing out the stupidity of his statement was as friendly as Sarah was going to get.

'Right, people!' the demonstrator called, 'We must get on. Once it reaches room temperature, the brain will get sticky ... then what sort of a demonstration would this be?' he smiled at his joke.

Once again, the students gathered around his workbench.

He picked up the brain gently and nursed it in his hands, giving the impression that the whole structure would unravel if he didn't hold it properly. One by one, he started to point out regions of the brain, or folds that were worthy of note, and told the students stories about their function or discovery. This went on for the next hour – the demonstrator gracefully slicing through the brain to reveal the structures deep inside, telling the students stories as he went. He handled the brain with an elegance and skill that Sarah longed to develop herself.

As the dissection came to an end, she couldn't help but think of the incongruent nature of the brain's structure and its function. All the other parts of the body had a structure that *somehow* hinted at their purpose. Bones were strong, for support. Muscles were flexible, to contract and expand. Blood vessels were tubes for blood to flow through them. *How could this mushy, fragile mess of goo be responsible for our thoughts, feelings and actions?* This incongruence made the brain even more mysterious, and Sarah couldn't wait to solve the puzzle.

At the beginning of their third year at university, Sarah and Tim broke up. It was a peaceful separation, and they remained very good friends, but live gigs and recording studios were just not compatible with textbooks about brains. So, Sarah and Tim went their separate ways.

Sarah moved with Abi into a small apartment in Clayton.

The industrial suburb was relatively quiet with wide roads. Freight trucks dripped oil as they lumbered their way between the houses and into the truck depot behind the twins' apartment. As a result, the neighbourhood roads had a continual dark sheen.

The twins felt the freedom that all young adults feel when they first move away from home. They were *real* grown-ups now. They'd playfully argue over whose route was the fastest to the shopping centre, and race each other there. The race rules were simple: they had to drive 'normally'. However, 'normally' had a different meaning for each of the girls. Abi tore around the streets in an old Torana, while Sarah meticulously negotiated traffic in an aged Datsun Bluebird.

Sarah loved her car. It was a family heirloom – it had been her grandmother's, then her father's, and now it was *hers.* Over the years, the car had developed a personality of its own, and puttered around the streets like a content little old lady who had all the time in the world. Sarah had even given the car a name – BAJ – inspired by the licence plate.

Abi was adamant that *her* route to the shops was ten minutes faster.

'That's only because of the way you drive,' Sarah pointed out.

'What do you mean?'

'Abi, no one drives as recklessly as you, and you know it.'

Like most P-platers, Abi drove as though she was invincible. She did not keep to the speed limit, and quite often cut people off rather than waiting her turn to enter the traffic. She manoeuvred her Torana quickly through the back streets, avoiding traffic lights and darting around corners. Sarah thought it was amazing the way her twin could get the old beast to move.

Deadly, but amazing.

'You do understand that you are driving a one-tonne weapon,' Sarah lectured. 'Driving is a privilege, not a right, and you should treat it that way. You're a potential murderer sometimes.'

Abi had heard this lecture before. They had gone through this ever since she had first got her P-plates. Sarah was the more sensible driver. They both knew it. Sarah was more cautious and respected the roads much more. Rules were created to be followed. And Sarah, it seemed, was created to follow rules.

The result of this ongoing joke was that if they went somewhere together, Sarah drove.

Living as grown-ups in their apartment in Clayton, the girls fell into a simple routine. Abi spent most of her time in the city, either with her friends, at work or at university. Sarah spent most of her time at Monash. The two girls came and went when they wanted, trusting that the other was safe.

Abi had Sarah. Sarah had Abi. Nothing could go wrong.

Wednesday afternoon tutorials were dreaded by most of Sarah's classmates. Not because they were boring – far from it. It was widely accepted that neuroanatomy was one of the more exciting classes that they studied. But every Wednesday afternoon the students competed with each other to demonstrate their knowledge of the brain.

The neuroscience students were high achievers. They were competitive and smart. But there could only be one person at the top of the class, and more often than not, most students found themselves in the bottom twenty-four.

Though Sarah never admitted it, she was just as competitive as the rest of her peers. While Sarah was not always the top student, she was certainly among the top half. The weeks that she did not get top grade, she chastened herself severely. Second place was not good enough. Second place was merely the first of the losers. Many of her peers shared this mentality. Which is why they hated Wednesday afternoons.

This particular Wednesday was no different to any other. The twenty-five neuroscience students crammed into a small tutorial room in the top of the anatomy building, uncertain of their weekly fate. They knew the drill. One by one, images of brain sections would appear on the screens before them. They would be asked to record details of each section that appeared. Sometimes they were trick questions, but mostly not: 'What region is this?' or perhaps 'What pathways could be here?' or 'What disorders may be associated with malfunction in this part of the brain?'

Sarah quietly entered the tutorial room with the rest of the neuroscience students. She took her place at the front, removed a pencil from her black leather pencil case, and waited for the test to start. Once it began, a traumatised hush fell across the room. The first MRI appeared on the screen.

Sarah gave a sigh of relief. It was clearly forebrain. She could see the skull and the beginnings of the facial bones. There would not be too many structures here that she would need to link together. *He'll probably ask about Phineas Gage...*

They had been taught about Phineas Gage in first year psychology, and heard the story again in second year. Sarah was in no doubt that they would probably hear all about him throughout third year too. And why shouldn't they? It was an interesting story. To Sarah's understanding, it was the first *real* evidence that the brain controls personality.

Phineas Gage was a twenty-five-year-old male. He was a muscular man of average height and exceptional health. His bosses loved him. Men wanted to be him. Women wanted to marry him. He was a hard worker, and (despite never having gone to school) a shrewd businessman.

And he loved his job.

Phineas directed a railroad construction gang, whose job it was to prepare the rocky terrain so that they could lay train tracks. To do this, they bored deep holes into the rocks, and packed the base of these holes with blasting powder and a fuse using a long iron tamping bar. The fuse was then lit, the powder exploded, and rock turned to rubble.

When Phineas became a foreman, he had his own tamping bar custom made. Unlike the usual tamping bars, which had a solid head for striking, Phineas's was long and javelin shaped. It was 1.1 metres long, 3.2 centimetres in diameter, and weighed 6 kilograms.

These seemingly insignificant details probably saved his life.

In autumn 1948, Phineas was leading a crew for the construction of the Hudson River Railway Line. It was late in the afternoon. Phineas was momentarily distracted by the men working behind him. He turned his head over his right shoulder and opened his mouth to say something to them.

At that exact moment, his beloved tamping iron accidentally set off the explosive in the hole that he was working on. The tamping iron shot up into the air and landed on the ground 25 metres away.

But first, the bar passed through his skull. It entered the left side of his face, passing behind the left eye, through the left side of his brain, and out the other side of his skull, through his frontal bone.

Had he been using the traditional tamping irons, the force of this would probably have smashed his face, shattered his skull and killed him. As it was, the smooth iron simply passed through his head and fired straight into the air, taking the front third of Phineas's brain with it.

Amazingly, Phineas did not die. He actually walked away from the accident. There are reports from his doctor that Phineas was able to relay the whole incident quite coherently.

But he deteriorated from there.

His bosses reported that he became the exact opposite to everything that he had been. He showed no respect for his co-workers and used profane language. He did not take advice, and often got into fights. He made inappropriate advances on women. He made plans for the future, but quickly became distracted and abandoned them for more appealing projects. He was a child in his mental capacity, but had the body (and the passions) of a strong man. He was so radically changed that his friends and acquaintances agreed that he was 'no longer Gage'.

Sarah longed for her tutor to ask the class about disorders associated with malfunction in the forebrain. She knew the story of Phineas Gage well – as did everyone else there. It would be an easy start to the test.

But he didn't ask that.

He pointed to a dark structure that was nestled between the brain tissue in the middle of the image.

'Name this artery, and describe the areas of the brain that it feeds.'

Sarah knew this. *Anterior cerebral artery. It supplies blood to the anterior frontal lobe and medial parietal lobe.* It wasn't half as exciting as Phineas, but at least she knew that some of her classmates may get it wrong. There was a chance that she may finish on top this week...

A new topic of conversation emerged towards the end of third year, and it caused some discomfort among the more competitive students: *honours.*

There were very few positions – not nearly enough for every neuroscience student. Only the very best would be offered a place. Sarah knew of girls who silently celebrated their friends' downfalls, privately hoping that it would open a space for *them* in a professor's lab. Sarah even wondered if she detected sabotage in a few cases.

In Sarah's mind, there was no question that *she* would get into honours. As far as Sarah was concerned, she was *always* going to be a neuroscientist. The only thing that she had to do was choose the right supervisor.

Sarah found that supervisor in the medical faculty, in the pharmacology building. Dr Richard Loiacono was the head of the neuropharmacology laboratory. His lab studied the roles of different receptors in neurological disorders. He had given the neuroscience students a series of lectures on the role of dopamine at the beginning of the year. Later in the year, Sarah met him in another subject, when he taught neuropharmacology.

Richard was a natural teacher. He was not afraid of personalising lecture material so that students understood it better. More than once, his pet Dalmatians appeared to help students remember one neurotransmitter or another.

Richard was one of the few lecturers who stayed back after lectures to answer Sarah's questions. Sometimes he was prepared for her, other times not. On more than one occasion, he seemed surprised by how she scrutinised the lecture material, and how she questioned the minutiae of a pathway that he had just taught.

As Sarah got to know Richard better, she visited his office to ask even more questions. Late in the afternoon, she would knock on his door, to be greeted with 'Sez! Hi. Come on in. What can I help you with today?'

Sarah would dump her bag and take a seat in Richard's office, before launching into her barrage of questions about topics they had covered that week.

During Sarah's visits, Richard showed her through his lab and introduced her to his two PhD students. Sarah noted that the two girls were working on their own projects investigating schizophrenia and Alzheimer's disease. There was plenty of room for a third student, with a third neurological disorder to study...

Richard had told Sarah about his interests in Parkinson's disease, and how he planned to take on an honours student the next year. They probably both had it in their minds very early on that Sarah would be the new student to come study in his lab. By the time Sarah was formally offered a role in the honours program, she and Richard had already planned most of her project. Sarah was set to start her honours degree in 2003. She was going to study nicotinic protection in a mouse model of Parkinson's disease under the supervision of Dr Richard Loiacono.

Sarah reflected on how long it had taken her to get there. Fourteen years ago, her eight-year-old self had stood in front of a classroom of twenty-eight bored pairs of eyes, and enthusiastically attempted to explain the beautiful complexities of the brain. Though she had barely understood it herself, the eight-year-old girl had felt so *wise* as she described the brain's electric signals, and what happens when they don't work properly.

Sarah recalled being scorned by a patient when she was on work experience at fifteen. Now, she privately thanked the woman for having her sent out of the examination room. Had that not happened, Sarah would never have discovered those beautiful articles that were written by *neuroscientists.* She would never have been inspired to follow in their footsteps. She would never have learned about DNA replication or about Phineas Gage or any of the other amazing things that she had seen so far at Monash University.

Now, Sarah was finally ready. She had found herself a supervisor who she could respect and who was as passionate as she was. She would complete her honours, go straight into a PhD and then do her post-doc. She had fallen in love with the idea of studying neurodegenerative diseases. In her most private aspirations, she imagined what it would be like to have her own laboratory in the university, with her own honours and PhD students.

And it was all about to start in 2003, when she started her honours.

Sarah was finally going to become a real neuroscientist.

Chapter Three

Nine Simple Words

Sergeant Adrian Brooker watched the storm roll across the city on the great computer screens above his desk. As the rains flooded the suburban streets, emergency calls flooded into the police communications centre. *It's going to be a busy night,* he thought. Night shift on New Year's Eve was always chaotic, but the heavy rain was dangerous, especially after the dry spell they'd had. Heavy rain and oily roads were never a good mix.

He leaned back in his seat and stretched, catching a glimpse of the gift bag tucked under his desk: a birthday present that his daughters had given him earlier, over lunch. Abi, Sarah and Greer had bought him a navigation system and it was exactly what he wanted. He smiled as he recalled their pride at having found the right one. It had been a lovely lunch, traipsing up and down Southbank and talking about resolutions for the New Year. He was lucky to have such wonderful girls.

He was still thinking about their afternoon together when a Senior Sergeant entered the room. Adrian nodded a greeting, but the Senior Sergeant's face was hard to read as he picked his way through the communications centre. He was holding a phone in one hand. *Is he coming to see me? Why?* Adrian raised a questioning eyebrow as the Senior Sergeant reached his desk, but the Senior Sergeant just put his hand on Adrian's shoulder and held the phone out for him to take.

He only had to hear nine words to know his life had changed.

'Car accident. McNaughton Road. Three women. One possible fatality.'

On the morning of New Year's Eve 2002, Abi and Sarah sat on either side of the old wooden desk in the lounge room of their apartment. Sweating under a tiny motorised hand-fan, Sarah studied a rental application form. 'How many applications have we made?' she asked.

Their lease was expiring in January and they needed to find somewhere new.

'Only three,' Abi replied. 'We should drop off the rest today.'

'Okay, bring them with us then,' Sarah said. 'Come on, we'd better get ready.'

Abi and Sarah had planned to have lunch with their dad and older sister Greer at Southbank to celebrate his birthday. It was New Year's Eve, so Southbank was bound to be busy and Sarah wanted to arrive early to get a park.

'Are you sure you don't want me to drive today?' Abi asked. She smiled as she threatened to pick up her car keys. 'My Christmas gift to you!'

Sarah laughed. 'New Year's Eve traffic? Nope. I am definitely driving.' Sarah picked up her own car keys and walked towards the door. 'BAJ wants to come anyway.'

Abi played along. 'Won't she want to play with the other cars in the car park?'

'Nope. She doesn't like them. Anyway, she'll want to see Dad on his birthday and reminisce about the old times...' Both girls were still laughing and bickering about who was more responsible as they got into Sarah's car, pulled out of the driveway, and drove up to the city to see their father.

Despite the crowd and bustle of Southbank, the birthday lunch was a very relaxed affair. Greer was the first to spot a table in the middle of the bustling Crown Casino food court. 'Table, ahoy!' she called excitedly. Abi saw where she was pointing and immediately dashed to the table, spreading her arms across it in feigned protection against other diners.

'Good timing, lassie!' Greer exclaimed in a fake Scottish accent. 'You've done an outstanding job!'

Abi and Sarah exchanged an excited look. Greer was in fine form today and was bound to have them all in stitches as she reeled off impersonations of Shrek, The Mask or Hugh Grant. If they were in luck, there may be monologues that would contain all three at once!

While they ate, their conversation was light-hearted. True to form, Greer kept everyone laughing at her impersonations. Abi and Sarah shared stories about things that had been happening around the universities over the Christmas break. Their father laughed along with the merriment.

They eventually got around to discussing their New Year's Eve plans. Greer, Abi and Sarah would be driving back to Clayton together, but they were planning to separate, and spend New Year's with each of their friends. Adrian had to work night shift in communications at Victoria Police. It was a busy time of year and tended to be all hands on deck, birthday or not.

After lunch, they took their time walking through Crown Casino and down to the police station. Entertained by buskers and the antics of post-Christmas shoppers and New Year's Eve revellers, they were blissfully unaware of what the next twenty-four hours would bring.

As they neared the police station, the girls kissed their dad goodbye, then made their way back to Sarah's car. Greer called shotgun and skipped around to the front passenger seat while Abi wrestled with the back passenger door and slid in behind Sarah.

The Princes Highway was probably not the best route that Sarah could have chosen. The New Year's Eve traffic made it a very slow journey, but the girls barely noticed.

They were too busy singing their way through the soundtrack of *The Little Mermaid.*

They were passing Sarah's beloved Monash University when the sky opened up. All the rain that had been held back through the summer fell at once. The hot, dry suburbs breathed a sigh of relief as several months' worth of heat, dust and oil washed away.

'Someone's plans are going to be ruined tonight,' Abi said, looking out at the rain.

'*Darling, it's better, here where it's wetter. Take it from me!*' Greer sang, mimicking one of the *Little Mermaid* characters perfectly.

The girls laughed. Greer was right. *How could rain be bad?*

'Sarah, we forgot to hand in the forms!' Abi said, turning serious.

It was easy enough to turn back. Even in the sudden rain, the real estate offices couldn't be more than fifteen minutes out of their way. Sarah nodded in the rear-view mirror at her twin. 'No problem, we'll head there now.'

Abi spent the next twenty minutes jumping in and out of Sarah's car, racing through the rain, dropping applications through mail slots of each real estate agent and then racing back through the rain to jump into whichever car door was closest.

After dropping off the last application, Abi slid into the back seat behind Greer.

'I heard that Alanis Morissette song the other day,' she said, as she shook the water from her arms. '"Uninvited" – remember it?'

It was the only cue they needed. The girls broke into song, harmonising the melancholy lyrics of 'Uninvited', trying to hit the same notes that Alanis Morissette created in the chorus. They weaved their way slowly through the rain towards Abi and Sarah's Clayton apartment, singing the sad melody as they went.

'*Ugh.* This one is too depressing. It's New Year's Eve. Let's do something happier?' Greer suggested.

'Like what?' Abi asked, leaning towards her sister.

'"Shameless"!' Sarah said, big smile on her face.

'Which one is that?' Abi wasn't as great an Ani DiFranco fan as Sarah and Greer were. While she knew how every song went, she didn't know their names.

'*Baahh na-na-naa-naa,*' Greer started grunting the first few notes of the song. All three girls laughed, and the twins immediately joined in. They were still laughing and singing as they pulled off the Princes Highway onto McNaughton Road.

Only 500 metres and they'd be home.

Abi

The accident is hard to write about. Not because it was particularly difficult – it wasn't. Accidents tend to be easy; that's why they're accidents. But the recall of the accident is something else. We all remember it differently. Greer and I remember it differently, Dad remembers other details, Mum remembers other details.

Science tells us that memory is fallible. Memory is particularly poor if the person wasn't paying attention at the time. And to be candid, I don't think any of us were paying attention. It was a routine drive in our local neighbourhood. Sarah was driving. What was there to pay attention to?

So, keep that in mind. Memory is fallible. But with that, here is what I remember. Some of it is broad contextual memory, some of it is finer detail that had significance in the days that followed. Most of it has been shaped by the telling and retelling of events over the years following the accident.

First, it was New Year's Eve. I know I had plans for the night; I couldn't tell you now what they were. At the time they were important. I had a shift the next day at the café where I worked. I was a terrible, clumsy waitress. My boss resented me, but I was the only one who would agree to work on New Year's Day. So, it would be her and me, at 6:00a.m., serving breakfast to the drunk, hungover and high people of Port Melbourne. Happy new year to us!

Second, it was Dad's birthday. We three girls had met him in the city (so adult of us!) and had lunch on Southbank with him before he went in to work.

Sarah had a baked potato for lunch. I know that, because for the next few weeks we would wonder to each other whether a baked potato would be Sarah's last meal. I also could not eat baked potatoes for the next few years without wondering if that was going to be *my* last meal.

After Dad went to work, us three girls went shopping at the casino. I bought something – a hat, I think – that I would wear every day for the next few months. I had bought it with Sah, so I didn't want to separate from it. I lost it at some point, and now I can't even remember what it was.

So, we were driving back from the city. Sah was driving. Greer was in the front passenger seat. I was in the back. The weather had been sunny and was now starting to rain. The roads were slippery. Sah pulled away from the light and drove down McNaughton Road.

As the car took a left-hand bend, it started to slide. I think I remember Sah grunting. The car slid across the road. I saw the pole that we were headed towards. I grabbed my seatbelt and the handgrip at the top of the door and braced myself. There was a loud crash, the sound of breaking glass, and I swung forward. I remember being surprised at how little I had moved. Surprised at how well the seatbelt and the hand grip had kept me steady.

A second or two of silence. Greer called out, 'Is everyone okay?' I called back, like a roll call. I'm okay. Greer's okay. Sah? No reply from Sah. From where I was sitting, she looked like she was staring at the steering wheel, but not responding to us. Greer was calling out to her.

I don't know how I got out of the car. It wasn't through the door. Some family members tell me I kicked out the back window, but I don't remember. I ran around to the driver's side. The driver's side of the car was wedged up against the pole, and the seat behind the driver was completely crushed. I could see Sah and Greer more clearly. Greer was still in her seat, crying, saying that she couldn't make Sah's bleeding stop. Sah was gasping. There was blood on her head, on her throat, and in her mouth. Greer was trying to apply pressure, but not sure where or how without cutting off Sah's breathing. She was a nurse, but nothing in her training had prepared her for this. No one had taught her how to correctly hold her sister's head in place while she attempted to stop the bleeding after colliding with a pole.

I heard sirens. I don't know who called them so quickly, but I was so glad that they did. I remember seeing a young man and woman standing nearby. I didn't know what to do so I started talking to Sah.

'You'll be okay. Help is on the way. Can you hear the sirens? They're

> coming for you. They'll help you. You'll be okay. It's okay.'

Sarah leaned over the steering wheel, staring through the blood. She couldn't understand why there was so much blood or where it had come from.

She could hear Greer screaming. It was a frantic, high-pitched wail of panic, but Sarah couldn't make out the words. *What is Greer panicking about?* Sarah looked around in search of her older sister but couldn't see through the blood that was filling up her view. Sarah blinked desperately and tried to focus on *something,* anything to distract her from the screams and the blood, so that she could figure out what was happening.

She eventually found the steering wheel. She could make out two crooked and bony hands that seemed to be crushed and folded around the steering column. Sarah was confused to discover that they were *her* hands. She had never noticed that they bent in so many awkward directions before. In fact, she had never even noticed that her arm had as many bends or bones poking out of it. It appeared that her right arm actually had three elbows. The highest one poked through her skin. Why hadn't she known this until now?

Sarah's confusion was pulled away from her arms by a new bout of screaming from Greer. She could hear Abi's voice too. Though she did not sound as hysterical as Greer, the wobble in her tone confirmed that *something* was wrong. If only Sarah could make out the words...

She tried to concentrate.

'You'll be okay. Help is on the way. Can you hear the sirens? They're coming for you. They'll help you. You'll be okay. It's okay.'

Sarah couldn't understand who Abi was talking to. *Who is going to be okay? Okay from what?*

Sarah wished she could understand Abi. She wished she could see Abi and Greer. She cursed the blood for blocking her view. Sarah didn't like the blood. It was confusing and disturbing.

Sarah listened harder. Just as Abi had promised, the wail and scream of ambulance sirens appeared in the distance. They were coming.

Sarah listened harder for her sisters. Abi's voice was gone, and Greer's screaming stopped ... No, not stopped. Just distant ... further away.

Sarah could hear men's voices now. Confident, authoritative voices.

'No, sir, we can't get her out from that side. We'll have to cut her out.'

Cut who out? Out of what?

Sarah realised with horror that it was *her* that the male voices wanted out. They wanted to cut through BAJ to get her out of the driver's seat. *Why don't they just open the door?* She couldn't understand.

Sarah cursed to herself, making an inventory of the rest of her body. She wished her legs would move, but then again, they probably would not be any use to her – they were in too many pieces. *Why are they in so many pieces?*

Sarah was determined not to let the strange men hurt BAJ. She didn't care how broken she was, they would *NOT* break BAJ! She needed to find a way out. The driver's door seemed to be stuck against a telephone pole, but the front passenger door was open. She had to get over there. Sarah decided that the left side of her body was more 'together' than her right. That was the side that she would try to move. She picked what she could of herself up and rolled across the car seats.

Sarah tumbled out of the front passenger seat and landed hard against the road. She stood up on her shattered legs, held her left eye in her socket with the hand that had the fewest bones poking out, and ran towards the authoritative voices. If they would only just see that she was out, they would not hurt her precious BAJ.

Three more steps and they'll see me.

Darkness.

Abi

Over the next few days, we would discover a multitude of details about what had occurred that are so ludicrous when pieced together that they sound like they are fiction. But they weren't. Some were literally life-saving bizarre anomalies, some were heart-breaking coincidences. Any other family would have said that they were divine interventions. But we didn't believe in divinity. Sah didn't believe in divinity. She believed in science. So instead, they are a series of improbable but not impossible events.

Can I tell you what they were? I think I'll tell you here, but I don't tell it as well as Sah, because I was high on a green pen (and later, Panadeine Forte) when I was learning all these details.

First, the aneurysm. Sah had an aneurysm at the exact moment that the car started to skid. That aneurysm could have and would have killed her. Except that when the car crashed into the pole, she had smacked her head and broken her skull, and the pressure from the aneurysm had been released. So the car crash saved her life from the aneurysm.

Next, the pole itself. The pole was a heavy, metallic thing with spikes sticking out all the way around – I think these are supposed to be for workmen to climb; I'm not sure. The angle at which the car hit the pole meant that Sarah's head had collided precisely between two spikes. Any more or less spin and things could have been a lot worse.

Next, the hospital. I'm still vague on this, but I think we were told (I was on the green pen at this point, so my memory is definitely skewed) that Sarah would be taken to the Monash hospital because she needed the most urgent treatment. In doing that, the hospital would not have the resources to treat Greer or me quickly. We were taken to Dandenong Hospital instead. The doctors on staff at Monash who would treat Sarah that night were among the leading doctors and neurosurgeons in Australia, several of whom would remain Sah's doctors throughout her recovery (Dr Danks? Dr Right? Dr Chen? I wish I could remember their names).

Next, the rear passenger seat. Okay, this one isn't about Sarah, it's about me. I had been jumping from left seat to right seat, on that trip home. Had I jumped back into the right-hand side of the car last, there is a high chance that I would have been crushed in that accident.

I don't like thinking about what *might* have happened. There's not much point thinking about what *might* have happened, because that's not what happened. I'm just very glad that I was on the left-hand side.

Next, Dad. Dad worked at D-24, monitoring and managing all the 000 calls across the state. From the start of his shift, he had been watching that rain, that terrible storm, travel across the country. As it moved further west, so did the calls about traffic accidents. Eventually the storm reached and passed over Clayton.

Car accident. McNaughton Road. Three women, one possible fatality.

***

Adrian

When I first learned about the accident, I wasn't sure just what I was going to see. My first thought was that they might have grazed the gatepost as they drove into their home. But when I spoke to Greer on the phone, I noticed that she was not answering my questions. She put Abi on the phone and Abi told me straight away that they had slid sideways into a pole and Sarah was not okay. I obtained the location of the accident and went to tell my own superior what had happened. He told me to take the company car and let him know what happened.

Any parent would feel a sense of panic at this stage, but I tried to remain calm as I approached the accident. Sarah's car was hard up against a power pole, indicating that the point of impact was at the driver's door. There was an ambulance and police car already there. I told them that I was not there as a supervisor, but as the father of the three girls involved. Normally, when a police divisional van attended any scene and a Sergeant arrives they report straight to him and he takes control. But not this time.

Luckily, at the time of the accident there was an ambulance passing and they stopped to assist. After assessing the situation, they called a second ambulance to the scene because Sarah would take all their resources, and the other two girls would need the second ambulance. Sarah was taken straight to the Monash hospital, which was just a few streets away, and Greer and Abi were conveyed to Dandenong Hospital.

Sarah shut down the emergency department at Monash Medical Centre, but apparently she was lucky there in a way also. When she arrived, there were two of everyone that was needed to treat her, due to the shift change. They were doing their change over when she arrived.

Their mother, Donna, and I knew that Greer and Abi were relatively okay, physically, but we were not able to speak to Sarah because she was rushed away in an ambulance. Greer's boyfriend picked the two girls up from the Dandenong Hospital after they had been checked and treated, and brought them to Monash to join us.

That was the longest night of my life. We had not seen Sarah at all since the accident and were waiting for updates from the doctors from time to time. Sarah was lucky again because there were two neurosurgeons present to operate on her. We were getting different reports from different specialists and none of them were very good.

Finally, we were told that we could see her briefly but she was not responding due to induced coma, so although we could speak to her she could not reply. She had been admitted into ICU and had tubes and wires connecting her to machines that made all different kinds of noises as they kept her alive. Her head had been shaved and was bandaged. She was alive, for now, but she was barely Sarah. We were completely unprepared for the wires, tubes, and bandages that wound around the body

> of our daughter. She seemed a completely foreign sight to all of us.

Sarah's parents were awake all night on New Year's Eve 2002, keeping vigil beside a bed that contained a shaved and bandaged broken bruise of a girl. Silently, Sarah's father prayed to a God that she never believed in to let her live. Sarah's mother listened to the machines and hoped that Sarah's beloved science would prove its worth and keep her alive.

Sarah Brooker may or may not have died that night. It is all a matter of perspective. If you place your faith in the God that Sarah never believed in, then she died. The *soul* of Sarah Brooker disappeared.

If you place your faith in the science that Sarah loved, then she lived. The *body* of Sarah Brooker survived.

She certainly ceased to exist, and I woke up in her place.

Chapter Four

Breathe

I didn't die. I was broken, but I didn't die.

The car accident left me more than a little battered. I had fractures to the face and skull, and had cracked the top vertebrae of my spine. My left eye had come out of its socket and my right femur had broken in two. I had dislocated my pelvis and cracked my hips. My lungs were bruised and full of blood.

But had I not been that broken, I would have died.

The doctors later explained to my family that an aneurysm that had formed on one of the major arteries at the base of my brain had burst, causing a subarachnoid haemorrhage (SAH) moments before my car hit the pole. My sister Greer translated this for Mum and Dad. She explained that a 'balloon' had grown on one of the major arteries in my brain, and it had been filling with blood. As my car skidded across the road, the balloon burst, filling the space between my brain and my skull with blood. This not only meant that blood couldn't get to my brain, but it also meant that my brain was being squashed by the pressure of blood filling my skull.

If I had been home alone when this happened, I would have died. But I wasn't at home, or alone; I was behind the wheel of a car that was about to collide with a telephone pole. I would hit my head, crack my skull, and release the pressure. In seven minutes' time, an ambulance would arrive to take me to Monash Medical Centre. In an attempt to save me from my 'brokenness', they would discover the SAH, and it would be treated in time to save my life.

Had the accident not happened, the SAH would have killed me.

If I had been conscious in the moments before the car collided with the telephone pole, I would have attempted to brake. With wheels locked, the car would have glided with greater ease across the road, and the driver's seat would have been the centre of impact. But I wasn't conscious – not until *after* I hit the pole.

Had the SAH *not* happened, the car accident would have killed me.

Combined, the car accident and the SAH saved my life.

The official medical reports state that when the ambulance arrived, I was *conscious, confused and angry.*

But I don't remember that.

I don't remember any of it: holding fast to doors and seatbelts, watching the pole get closer and bracing for the collision, confirming that everyone is still alive, and then learning that someone might not be...

I won't ever remember those things.

Abi and Greer do.

I think that makes *me* the lucky one.

I was lucky at the hospital too. At the exact moment that I arrived at Monash, handover was happening between the evening and night shift staff. This means that there were twice as many surgical staff at the hospital as there ordinarily were. I needed them all, and more. I put the entire emergency unit into shut down.

I went straight into theatre. The aneurysm was blocked with a coil, and the blood was drained from around my brain to release the pressure. My lungs were also drained. Damage that was *relatively* less urgent was treated the following day.

Relatively.

It's funny how everything is relative isn't it? 'Less urgent' treatment included inserting a steel rod through my thigh. I suppose, in other situations, a steel rod would be urgent. It just shows how 'broken' I was. I was admitted to intensive care, where I stayed for a very long time.

The intensive care unit is not like any other place in a hospital. It is not a ward where people are treated for illness. ICU is not a place of healing. ICU is a place of survival.

Twenty-three beds, each surrounded by their own battalion of heavy machinery, fill the ICU. Each battalion *slurps, sucks* and *whooshes* to its own rhythm. Most of the noise comes from the ventilator, which is no taller than the bed. It *slurps* and *whooshes* continuously, as it breathes for the patient. Syringe pumps stand tall at the head of the bed. They calmly deliver medications and fluids down clear tubes into the patient's body. The ICU bed monitors, a pair of screens that are filled with numbers and charts, keep track of the patient's vital signs: blood circulation, oxygen levels, body temperature, cardiac output, intracranial pressure ... if you can put a number to it, it is measured.

The continual *slurp, suck, whoosh* is disconcerting at first. But the doctors and nurses who work here know and depend on that rhythm. It means everyone is safe. When a machine screams out of synchronisation with its team, they know that *something* is not as it should be.

The patients themselves lie still, tangled in endless tubes and hoses that connect them to the machines: large opaque hoses connect mouths to ventilators; thin clear tubes connect the syringe pumps to the body; nasogastric tubes run from the nose and stomach to drain bile. Blood pressure cuffs are wrapped around arms, and thumbs are covered by clips that measure oxygen.

Weighed down by all these tubes, patients remain motionless. This is just as well – movement in any direction is hazardous.

Among the machines, beside each bed, sit the family members. In quiet pairs they hold vigil: praying, whispering, crying ... anything to reach the lifeless suspended form of their son, daughter, husband or wife. They carry phones, sunglasses and wallets – all relics of the 'outside' world that are useless in here.

This is a place of survival, not treatment.

While the quiet chaos of the machines stays locked inside the ICU, an emotional silence flows through the locked doors and into the waiting room. Families gather here in silence. These are the unlucky ones. Not because they have received bad news – 'unlucky' because they have not been chosen to enter the ICU.

The *waiting* is the torture. *Waiting* for news. *Waiting* to be allowed in. *Waiting* for their turn to take vigil by the bed of a lifeless body.

And it was here, on the plastic chairs of the ICU waiting room that Dad sat on New Year's Eve, his birthday, numb and confused. He was supported on either side by two men who had driven him to the hospital. Dad is a policeman. After receiving the call that his three daughters had been in an accident, he was put into a police car and taken to the accident scene, bells and sirens wailing. After seeing the crash site for himself, Dad followed my ambulance to Monash Medical Centre in the police car. There was not enough room for him in the ambulance.

Mum arrived at the hospital after Dad.

As she stepped out of the lift, four men pushing a stretcher hurried past her calling statistics and terms to each other, presumably about their cargo. It was a long lifeless body of a female. She should have been a body, but she wasn't. She was a puzzle of body parts that were held together by bolts and braces, and bound in tubes, gauze and bandages.

Her face was blue and badly smashed: her left eye was covered with a blood-soaked bandage, and the right one was closed. Her head, a swollen and bruised mass, rested on a mess of blooded hair and seemed to be attached to her body by a neck brace. Arms and legs were limp blue extensions that were falling out of a hospital gown that had once been white but was now soaked in the girl's blood. Her right leg, now in two pieces, was held together by a large steel frame.

Mum watched in horror as the orderlies raced passed her.

What is going on? What is happening to that girl?

As they pushed the trolley through the doors to the ICU, Mum realised what had just passed.

Was that Sarah?

It had been a long night. Mum and Dad had an unspoken agreement to stay awake if the other fell asleep. At least one of them *must* be awake to hear any news. At some stage during the night, Mum had fallen asleep. Someone had placed Dad's blue police coat over her. As she slowly drifted back into consciousness, she heard a doctor addressing Dad.

'Mr Brooker?'

The doctor looked exhausted – it had been a busy New Year's Eve, and his shift had been extended by another few hours. Even though he remained composed, Mum got the sense that he was uncertain about something.

Dad nodded a response. 'Yes?'

'I'm Dr Danks. I am one of Sarah's neurosurgeons. Is your wife here too?'

One of? Why does she need more than one neurosurgeon?

'No. I'm not his wife. I'm Sarah's mother, Dee,' Mum said, rising from the seats. She was impatient for any news that the neurosurgeon had. 'Tell us what has happened.'

Dr Danks told my parents that I had a subarachnoid haemorrhage. He explained that this meant that the balloon that had formed on one of the arteries at the base of my brain had exploded. The blood from the artery was increasing the pressure around my brain, which was likely to have done a lot of damage had it not been for the severe fractures to my face and skull.

'We can reduce the pressure by drilling a burr hole, but we need to stop the bleeding, and we need to decide how to do that, quickly.'

My parents looked at him, blank faced and terrified.

'We can do one of two things to try and stop it,' he continued. 'We could place a "clip" at the base of the balloon, and give the artery time to heal itself. But this is invasive. Our other option is to "coil" it. We won't have to go through brain tissue. We'll insert the coil through her arteries. The coil will block the hole and will have a smaller chance of re-bleeding. However, this is a *very* new technique. We can't guarantee that it will work. But, if it does work, it has a lower risk of making any brain damage *worse.*'

Mum and Dad tried to follow what he was telling them. I am not sure that they understood fully until Greer explained later on. What they understood was that *clip equals brain damage and coil probably doesn't.*

They nodded their heads in agreement.

Go ahead with the coil.

Dr Danks looked into my parents' eyes. 'I need you to know one thing.

Neither procedure is safe, and she is very badly injured. We are trying our best to save her...' He hesitated, there was more to say. '...I am sorry to say that it is highly probable that you will lose your daughter tonight.'

Dad felt his legs give way, as the grief swept through him. The two policemen that had accompanied him to the hospital rushed to his side to hold him up.

Mum turned to the chairs and lowered herself down. As she put her head in her hands, she saw an image that she would hold onto for the months to come. She thought of me, not as a broken body but as the tall proud girl I had always been. In her head, I smiled and gave the thumbs up. 'It's all good Ma. I'm fine. It's all good.'

Slurp. Suck. Whoosh.

One day passes. Then two. Then three.

I had survived the coil surgery only to join the suspended lifeforms in ICU, where I remained unconscious and in a coma. The ventilator and bedside monitors kept synchronised rhythm beside me. They were the only testament to my survival.

Abi, Greer, Mum and Dad took turns holding vigil by my bed. My older brother, Adam, couldn't be there because he had his own young family to support in Cairns, some 3000 kilometres away. He had agreed with Dad that flying down to Victoria wouldn't solve anything. He was better off staying where he *could* do something.

In ICU, all that Dad, Mum, Greer or Abi could do was hold my hand and talk. Doctors suggest that family members do that – talk. The say that a patient in a coma can hear family members' voices. I can neither confirm nor deny that they are correct. I don't know if I heard Mum, Dad, Abi or Greer talking to me. But I think talking helps family members deal with grief – so what's the harm?

Abi

I remember the first time I saw Sah in ICU. She was long (so long!).

Her eyes were closed and non-responsive. They wouldn't flicker like her eyes used to when she slept. They were still. We were advised to talk to her. We were told that often, people in comas can hear you when you speak. '...So talk to her, tell her about your day.'

I told her where she was. I told her everything I wanted to hear and everything I thought she would say to me: that she was okay, that she was in safe hands, that the doctors said there was some chance of recovery. I didn't tell her how little a chance.

They told us we could hold her hand. They told us to try and get her to respond by squeezing: once for 'yes', twice for 'no'.

Her skin was cold and dry. It didn't feel like Sarah. It didn't feel like anyone I knew.

Her hand didn't respond when I held it. There was no pressure or muscle responding to my touch. No 'yes' squeeze. No 'no' squeeze. No

> squeeze at all. She wasn't going to respond for a long time.
>
> It didn't matter. Touching her hand; feeling that cold, dry arm; whispering to her that she was in ICU and everything was going to be okay – all of that was comforting for us.

Slurp. Suck. Whoosh.

Five days pass.

Mum and Dad sat by my bed, listening to the rhythms of the machines and watching for any signs that I would wake up.

The *slurp, suck,* and *whoosh* of the machines drowned out their uncertainty, and they found themselves silently watching a cloudy yellow fluid fill a bag that was attached to my lungs.

A young doctor entered the cubicle.

'Should that be doing that?' Mum asked her, gesturing to the bag.

The young doctor tucked her dark curly hair behind her ears, pushed her glasses back on her nose, and calmly approached my bed to examine the offending fluid. She gave my parents a reassuring smile.

'Sarah has developed pneumonia,' she said, reaching for the clipboard at the end of my bed to record data from the monitor. 'It has caused fluid to build up around her lungs, which needs to be drained.'

'But can't they just drain it in surgery or something?' Mum asked. The doctor held the clipboard to her chest, adjusted her glasses on her nose. 'Pneumonia is common among patients like Sarah who require mechanical ventilation.' The ventilator *whooshed* as if to confirm its own purpose.

'We need Sarah to expel the fluid at her own pace. When it slows down, we'll know she is doing that.' The doctor placed the clipboard back on the end of my bed and gave another reassuring smile before leaving the cubicle.

My parents sat in silence among the beeping machines. Their heads filled with images of bags constantly filling with fluid from the lungs of their broken daughter.

Sarah had pneumonia.

The ventilator *whooshed* next to them, as it went about its job breathing for me.

The ventilator can breathe for Sarah for now ... Will she ever breathe for herself?

Slurp. Suck. Whoosh.

> ### Abi
>
> I remember early on a doctor in ICU running the family through numbers.
>
> Percentages, odds on the chances of Sarah's recovery. Twenty-five per cent? Ten per cent? Some small chance that her organs would all recover to full strength. A smaller chance again that she would wake up. A smaller chance that she would walk. A smaller chance again that she would talk. What about her cognition? Someone asked. It was impossible to tell. All these proportions, and there was an improbably small and nonestimable chance that she would wake with her wit, her knowledge, herself.

I don't know if someone said it, or if I realised it, but it dawned on us that the chances of her full cognitive recovery were so small that they might as well be zero. So – take that logical, reasonable, sensible part of yourself, and just throw it away. Don't replace it. Don't hope on it. It's gone. And no matter what you are doing at any time of the day: sleeping, waiting to sleep, making breakfast, watching television, getting dressed, everything that you do, that part is still gone.

Relentless grief.

But at the same time, there was this shadow to the grief, there was a gratefulness.

There was still a person in that bed. Sarah was strong, she was tough, she didn't take bullshit. This mess around her, these broken bones, this loss of blood. It wasn't enough to stop her.

Be grateful.

Once, I saw another family talking with a doctor about organs. I heard the doctor say gently 'think about it' and I heard the family mutter 'Which organs...' Someone explained later that they were talking about donating their loved one's organs. Their loved one was going to die, and they had the decision of whether or not to donate the heart, lungs, eyes, to help others live. What a choice. What a time to be making that choice. We never had that conversation with our doctors. I remember thinking it hadn't hit the point where we were talking about organs. So – grateful. She was tough. For everything else that she was going through, we weren't talking to doctors about organs.

So – grateful.

There were smaller things too, outside the ICU that held this tension between grief and gratefulness.

A few days after the accident, mum made Greer and I an appointment with our hairdresser. I think the idea was simply to wash our hair, to help us remove the glass from the accident. I couldn't wash my hair with my broken finger, so it was a relief. There was the gratefulness.

> Such a nice gesture. But it wasn't something I could enjoy or justify in my mind. Sah was lying in ICU and here we were getting our hair washed. So, there was the grief.
>
> After the appointment, Greer found another piece of glass in her hair and quietly threw it away.

Slurp. Suck. Woosh.

Seven days pass.

Mum sat beside my bed, holding my hand and talking.

'*They* can sing for you for now, darling. So long as *they* keep singing, I know you'll come back,' she said, referring to the noises of the machines that surrounded my bed. 'But will we ever hear you sing again?'

She fought to hold back tears. *Sarah doesn't 'do' emotion.* But Mum knew she'd have to let it all come out eventually.

Mum gently stroked the scabs that were now forming on the back of my hand. 'It's bruised, darling, but they say it's not broken.'

She cast her eyes over the rest of my body. My leg was still held together by a large, steel brace; there were tubes coming out of my lungs, arms and torso; my left eye and newly shaved head were still covered in bandages; and my face was bruised and swollen. 'At least your hand isn't broken, darling. Now all you have to do is wake up.'

She was beyond exhausted. Mum's time was spent running between two different hospitals. In one hospital, she watched her daughter dying. In the other, she watched her mother do the same.

How many people can I lose at once?

She hung her head, at a loss for words, trying not to let the tears fall. Minutes went by. They turned into hours.

Slurp. Suck. Whoosh.

Ten days pass.

Tim had been the only one who had not been allowed to visit me in ICU.

'He's not immediate family,' the doctors said. 'Just wait.'

So, he waited.

After ten days of waiting, Tim was finally given permission to enter.

'Dee, I don't think I can do this,' he told Mum. 'I'm not sure I can ... What does a coma *look like?* What if it's a *bad day?*'

'Be brave, honey.' She gave his hand a gentle squeeze, 'I'll come with you.'

The doors clicked open.

As Mum led Tim through the ICU, she struggled to think of how she could best prepare him for what he was about to see.

'You mustn't cry, Timmy. Just talk to her. She can hear you. Say things that she will recognise.'

They walked through the beeping machines and stopped at the foot of a bed.

Tim's grip on Mum's hand tightened and his face went white.

'She's not Sarah.' He stammered as he stared at the unconscious body before him. 'Well ... she's ... a blue body. A Blue Girl.'

His simple phrase was right. I didn't look like *Sarah*.

My head was shaved, one eye was swollen and closed and the other was bandaged. A giant steel frame supported one of my legs, and all remaining limbs were bound by tubes carrying fluid to and from the machines surrounding the bed. But, to Tim, the most horrifying thing was the giant swollen blue face that hid behind a respirator mask.

A Blue Girl.

Scared and trying to accept the reality of my bruised existence, Tim froze.

'If I don't recognise her, how will she recognise me?' he whispered.

He stepped past Mum and sat down on the chair beside my bed. Then, without a word, he opened his mouth and started tapping his cheeks.

Playing 'Inspector Gadget' was something that *only* Tim did. That innocent party trick that he had mastered years ago sitting on the beach with me was the *only* way he could connect.

Sitting among the machines as they buzzed and whirred around him, nurses looking on, Mum crying at the memory, Tim tapped 'Inspector Gadget' on his cheeks, praying that somewhere, I would hear him.

I remained asleep.

Slurp. Suck. Whoosh.

Two weeks pass.

Mum sat down at the dining room table in her Mount Eliza home. It was quiet here. Strangely quiet.

How long was it now? Two weeks? Is that all? Is that long?

She looked at the clock. It was only 11:00a.m.. Exhausted, Mum rested her head in her hands and closed her eyes for a moment.

Instantly, her head filled with horrifying images. The calm *slurp, suck* and *whoosh* of ICU had been replaced by mayhem. I struggled in my hospital bed, choking, gagging, and crying for help. I could not breathe and the ventilator was not working.

Mum felt the panic rise in her chest. This was not just the sort of anxiety that a mother feels when she is away from a sick child. The image that she had was far too real for that. Mum knew that I was genuinely in danger. She had to tell the hospital.

'It's urgent,' she told the nurse when she was finally put through to ICU. 'Sarah's in trouble.'

'Sarah is in surgery now with the doctors.' *She's in surgery? Why is she in surgery again?* Mum wanted to ask, but there wasn't time.

'She's in trouble. You need to tell the surgeons. She can't breathe. Something is wrong.'

Mum heard the nurse sigh. 'I can go and check for you, but she's with the surgeons. She's in good care.'

It sounded like a brush-off. But Mum didn't say that. Fighting with this woman would only waste time. Mum needed to get to the hospital.

I don't know how she knew, but Mum was right.

I wasn't *fine*.

While the surgeons took care of me in theatre, Mum was speeding up the freeway. Mum's urgency did not stop once she reached the hospital, and she barely stopped to wait for admission into ICU.

Please let her be alive.

Before Mum reached my bed, she was stopped by a calm young Turkish woman with dark curly hair, olive skin and dark eyes.

'Ms Rackham? My name is Dr Georgiana,' she greeted her with a gentle, relaxed smile.

'Dr Georgiana, my daughter's in trouble,' Mum gasped, scanning the ICU for my bed. Dr Georgiana guided Mum gently towards it with a confident and serene manner that caught her by surprise.

'Hmm. The nurses told me you called,' she said, as they approached my bed. 'You must be psychic.' Mum looked at me, lying peacefully in the bed. As always, I was a mess of bandages and tubes. Only now, there was a new tube inserted into the front of my throat.

Another tube...

Mum turned to Dr Georgiana, panic rising again. 'What...?'

'Earlier today, around the time that you called, Sarah suffered respiratory obstruction ... her throat closed up. We have inserted a tracheostomy tube into her throat to help her breathe. She's okay. She's stable now.'

Stable. That was a good word. Better than good, it was sacred. *Stable* is the type of word that families will feast upon for days in ICU, because it means 'not getting worse'. Not many doctors had used that word about me. In fact, no one had.

'Sarah's strong. In a few weeks, this will all just be a memory.'

A few weeks. That had never been said before either. No one had ever spoken about a world beyond *tomorrow*. This doctor not only thought that I might be *alive* in a few weeks, but also that I would be conscious and have memories, and be well enough to understand the trauma of the tracheostomy.

A few weeks ... it's a dangerous phrase to use in the ICU.

Abi

I remember in the first few days when Sarah's condition became 'stable'. I thought of this like a level of recovery: clear, distinct.

> Stable was good.
> Stable was an achievement.
> Grateful.
> I updated our home voicemail machine to tell callers that Sarah was still in ICU, but she was stable. Mum gently explained to me that it wasn't an appropriate voicemail greeting.

Slurp. Suck. Whoosh.

Three weeks pass.

Mum had just come home from a visit to her own mother in hospital, and was planning to stop for a brief lunch before coming up to Monash to visit me.

Her mobile phone rang and she recognised the number – it was Monash Medical Centre. *What has happened now?*

Terrified, Mum answered, hoping for the best but expecting the worst.

'Good afternoon, Dee.' Mum recognised the voice as being one of the nurses from ICU.

Surely nurses only call in case of emergency?

'Hi Janet. What has happened?'

'Dee, I have some important news for you. I think you will be glad. Sarah took a breath on her own today. She is back on the respirator now – but she breathed by herself. I thought you'd like to know as soon as it happened.'

Mum was speechless. There were no words. After a moment's pause, she realised she must say *something*.

'Yes. Yes. Thank you, Janet. Thank you.'

'Will you be coming in this afternoon?'

'Yes. Yes, I will. I'll see you then.' Absently, Mum hung up on Janet.

One breath. On her own.

Mum sat on her bed and cried.

Part Two

**Immediate Aftermath
(2003–2004)**

Chapter Five

Wake Up

My earliest memories of hospital are ugly and strange. I have constant dreams about that period. Maybe they are not dreams, maybe they are real memories.

Back in those days, I was not sure when I was awake and when I was asleep.

In my most vivid dream, or memory, whichever you choose to believe, I was surrounded by bars and tied down on a bed. There appeared to be an endless sea of people in similar beds around me. We were all restrained and unable to move. We could not talk to each other. Or didn't, for some reason. Our bed sheets were white and crisp. I didn't know who changed them. Or when. Or why. But they were always crisp.

There were machines – lots of machines. *Slurping* and *whooshing* in a hypnotic tone that I am sure kept most of us asleep. Occasionally, a machine gave a high-pitched shriek that beckoned people in white coats. Our trance was broken. Movement and noise invaded the endless sea of beds, as the people in white coats spoke loudly at the person in the bed with the screaming machine, using words and sounds I could not comprehend.

Then, suddenly, everything was silent again. The soft *beep* and *buzz* of machines continued.

I was scared of the people in the white coats. They were doing experiments on us. In my dreams, that made sense. They had attached tubes all over my body: my arms, legs, throat, chest, and they covered one of my eyes with something, and strapped something over the top of my head. There were wires on my chest and stomach that were attached to the buzzing and beeping machines. I was sure that they have something to do with that.

When the people in white coats approached, I tried to close my eyes and pretended I was asleep, praying they didn't notice that I was awake. But they knew. Somehow they always knew.

They would stalk over and talk at me, their mouths making sounds that I didn't recognise. They played with the machines, spoke to each other in a language that I didn't understand, and then disappeared.

It's always the same dream. I think it is about ICU.

On 21 January 2003, I was discharged from ICU and moved to the high dependency unit (HDU). The only real difference between ICU and HDU was that in ICU there is one nurse per patient, and in HDU there is one nurse for every two patients. Family members are allowed to visit in groups rather than one by one. Everything else is the same.

Effectively then, HDU is an intensive care unit with fewer staff and more visitors.

For my family, this felt like a graduation. Proof that I was getting better.

Sarah needs fewer staff to look after her. She must be getting better, right?

Sort of.

I was *stable,* but in every other respect, I was still broken.

My family had the magical word *stable*, but that was all.

During the first week in HDU, with fewer staff watching over me, Abi, Greer, Mum and Dad came and sat by my bed daily, talking and waiting for me to wake up.

> ## Abi
>
> The first part of Sarah's recovery was a surreal blur. An intensely surreal blur. A mash-up of pain, relief, grief, gratefulness and waiting.
>
> Days blurred together. Mostly, they blurred because of the painkillers that doctors kept offering me. Panadeine Forte is a great painkiller, but it's terrible for everyday functioning. It kills your memory and your capacity to find words. The instructions were to take one tablet every six hours: four a day. I quickly confused that, and it became one tablet every four hours, or six a day. That was right, wasn't it? Soon after, it became one every four hours and one every six hours, just to be safe. I didn't want

to feel, and these tablets were helping me do that.

My boyfriend took over dispensing my painkillers. But I had more. I always had more. Doctors would give me one script, and one sheet of pills 'for now'. I didn't have to ask. They just gave them to me. 'For your broken finger,' they would say. But I suspect I looked a mess and they wanted to numb the grief.

The grief.

Intense grief paired with gratefulness and guilt. The grief was the most intense and relentless emotion I had experienced in my twenty years of middle-class, entitled, sheltered, life. My best friend was gone. More than my best friend – my other half.

Imagine yourself as multiple parts. Imagine one part that is reasonable, sensible, logical. The part that helps you through difficult times, helps you find solutions, calms you down when you get worked up. That voice in you that sees through people's bullshit when you are most likely to fall for it. That voice that calls life like it is. Separate it from yourself, if you can. That was Sarah.

I remember a doctor talking with the family early on, explaining to us how slow the recovery would be. He drew a matrix: the x-axis was time, and the y-axis was recovery, or perhaps – functioning. Along the axes, he drew a logarithmic curve. He explained: at first, her recovery will seem dramatic. We will see changes in her and celebrate those changes. But over time, the changes will be smaller and smaller, and she might not ever get back to the level that she was before the accident. These first few days, these are tough.

He explained, in a few months' time, things will be tough in a different sort of way. We will be waiting for changes, and they might not come. Or, they might not come to the level that we want them. He wanted us to know that the recovery is a long and slow process, and not always satisfying.

> I was thankful for his candidness and warning about that, but on reflection, I disagree. It wasn't a logarithmic curve, it was a roller coaster. There was recovery, and decline. There was remission, and new complications.

Slurp. Suck. Whoosh.

Richard Loiacono came to visit me in HDU. He wasn't sure what to expect. He certainly did not expect the girl that he saw. I was a long, frail, bruised and broken body who was barely conscious. My hair had been shaved, and my head and right eye were bound in bandages.

He saw the tracheostomy tube, and listened to the respirator as it breathed for me. While it was true that I had breathed a few simple breaths on my own, I was still on the respirator most of the time. I had fewer tubes than I had had in ICU, but Richard had no way of knowing or appreciating that. He had not been permitted into ICU. When Richard came to visit me in HDU, he saw a mass of tangled tubes that delivered nutrients, painkillers and medicines to a body that had no way of protecting herself. She did not look like the confident girl who approached him after lectures or spent so much time in his office planning out her honours project.

My position in Richard's lab was never questioned. But for that very brief moment, sitting by my bed in HDU, Richard wondered how long it would be before this body became a person, and if that person would be anywhere near as remarkable as Sarah Brooker had been.

Slurp. Suck. Whoosh.

At the beginning of the third week in Monash, Greer sat nestled between the ventilator and my bed, holding my hand and talking. Greer didn't bring in news from the outside world. *What good would that be in here?* Instead, she was doing what she does best. She was trying to make me laugh.

There is no one in the world who can impersonate people as well as Greer does. Around the time of the accident, she had perfected Donkey from *Shrek*.

And so there, in HDU, that's what she did.

'What you gonna go do a thing like that for? You think I'm some kinda fool? Well I can tell you right now...' and on it went. Rambling in a voice she hoped I'd recognise. Praying that somewhere in my unconscious state, I was laughing.

Mum and Dad sat on plastic chairs at the end of my bed and listened to her quiet monologue. Then Greer felt the thing that everyone had been waiting for.

A gentle squeeze.

'It happened! She responded!' Greer cried, turning to Mum and Dad. 'Sarah just squeezed my hand!'

A nurse approached.

'Greer, it may be a reflex...'

'No. No. It wasn't. She squeezed my hand.'

Greer held onto my small hand and gave it a gentle squeeze. I squeezed a reply.

This was no reflex. *Sarah is definitely responsive.*

I am unsure why Greer did the next thing she did. Perhaps to demonstrate that there was *conscious thought* behind my squeezes. Greer took my hand in a 'monkey grip', so that our fingers were curled, and both of our thumbs were upright. She then tapped either side of our grip with her thumb in time to a rhyme. 'One, two, three, four. I declare a thumb war! Touch!'

This is thumb wrestling. The point is to pin down your opponent's thumb with your own, before they get you. Thumb wrestling is a very serious sport of strategy, dexterity and outwitting your opponent. It is also a massive advantage if your thumbs are longer than your opponent's. I may have been unconscious, but I have longer thumbs.

Immediately after she declared the war, Greer made a fatal error. She paused to see how I would respond...

I pinned her thumb down to our locked fingers before she knew what was happening.

I was the *winner.*

I was *conscious.*

My lips twitched and I held my thumb up to my family.

Mum recalled the image that she had that first, horrible night that I was in hospital. The image where I smiled, not as a broken body, but as the tall proud girl that I had always been, and I had given her the thumbs up. *It's all good, Ma. I'm fine. It's all good.*

Slurp. Suck. Whoosh.

Other people who have come out of a coma report that it is peaceful. *Like waking from a dream ...* If it is, then I woke from nightmares.

I didn't understand where I was, or what all the tubes that were attached to my body were for. Scared and confused, I constantly tried to pull out tubes. The tracheostomy tube was the worst. The long thin tube that had been inserted into my throat made no sense whatsoever.

The nightmares that I have of this phase of waking up are as confusing as they are terrifying. In the worst of them, I am bound to a bed, or being held down against the mattress by countless hands. I am gagging and cannot breathe.

A mad scientist leans over me. He is not really more than a white lab coat and a white face mask ... only his hands are blue ... and rubbery. I can never figure out why his blue hands are rubbery.

In the nightmares, I feel the rubber hands brush past my chin, and the mad scientist forces a long tube down my throat.

'I know it's uncomfortable, Sarah. No, don't pull it out.'

I struggle to fight the blue rubbery hands. I can't reach them. I can't push the mad scientist or his invasive hands away. More hands appear from nowhere and hold me down to the bed.

I don't understand what he wants me to do. I think he wants the tube half up *and* half down my throat. That doesn't make sense. I can't half swallow a plastic tube. Either it all goes down to my stomach, or it all stays in my mouth.

'Relax, Sarah. Just relax.'

I continue to gag and choke, hands hold me to the bed. I can't go on fighting.

Suddenly, it's done. The tube is in.

The mad scientist smiles an evil smile behind his mask. He is proud of himself.

'There you go. It wasn't so hard was it? Now leave it in.'

He runs off to tell his mad-scientist friends of his victory. The other hands release me.

I start pulling at the tube. It doesn't belong inside my throat.

I am gagging again. I cannot breathe.

The nightmares may vary a little, but the fear and the confusion are always the same.

Slurp. Suck. Whoosh.

Some scenes in hospital are hard for even the most inured families. By the time that I was in HDU, Mum, Dad, Abi, and Greer may as well have been a part of the furniture, but even that could not prepare them for the scenes they were confronted with as I woke up. It turns out that the worst part of my reoccurring nightmares was true.

One morning, Abi, Greer and Mum came to visit me in HDU. The last time they had seen me, I was a heap of broken bones and bruised skin, hiding among bandages and tubes, fighting for her life. But on this particular morning, I appeared to be the mummy of a criminal, shackled and unable to move.

Each of my wrists was tied to the sides of the bed with a leather belt. My ankles were similarly shackled to the end of the bed. Braces had been fastened over my hips and shoulders, and appeared to pull my whole body into the mattress.

I was barely conscious and unable to move, tied down to my bed in the place that was meant to be trying to keep me alive.

Abi, Greer and Mum were horrified. Surely there could be no logical reason for such restraint.

Mum rushed to my side and started to untie one of my hands.

'Quick, girls! Help! Get her out of this!'

Abi and Greer, who had been too shocked to move, suddenly came to life and set to work on the belts around my legs.

'Excuse me, what are you doing?' A nurse ran over to try to stop my family, who were frantically trying to undo work that had taken her and her colleagues a good thirty minutes earlier that morning.

'She's not a criminal. Why is she tied down like this?' Mum demanded.

'Sarah's arms need to be tied down at this stage,' the nurse replied, desperately trying to re-tie the knot that Mum had just stepped aside from.

'What do you mean? Look at her!' Mum gestured towards my entire, limp body. 'She's unconscious. She's sick. She's not dangerous at all. She can't even move! Why have you tied her up?'

'Every time she starts to wake up, she tries to pull her tubes out,' the nurse explained.

'Then put them back in again!' Mum snapped back.

This of course was not an option for the nurse. It took four nurses and a doctor to put me back together each time I pulled the tubes out. They simply didn't have the manpower in HDU to keep up.

My bedside became a battlefield. Mum was fighting with the nurses, Abi and Greer were fighting the belts, and I was fighting for my life.

The battle between the nurses and Mum was resolved by a lose-lose treaty. The nurses 'lost' because they conceded to Mum's request to untie me during the visit. Mum 'lost' because the nurses requested that I was tied up again when Mum left ... and Mum was the one who had to do it.

What is worse than having to shackle your own, unconscious daughter to a bed?

I understand it now though. The nurses needed me to keep still so that they could keep me alive. Sedated and tied down, this induced coma lasted another week.

Beep. Beep. Beep.

Once I started to gain lucidity, my interpretation of the world became far more pleasant.

The mad scientists who shoved tubes down my throat seemed to disappear. The blinding bright white lights faded away. My immediate world (and therefore my *only* world) was sterile and white.

I was protected by the long white curtain along the side of my bed, which shielded me from the noise and bustle of nurses on the other side. Daytime and night time differed only by whether lights were on or off, and by the number of nurses present.

I breathed in rhythm to a ventilator that *whooshed* and *hushed* somewhere out of my vision. I could only see out of one eye (I wasn't aware that the bandaged eye even existed).

For the most part, I was so highly medicated that I didn't feel much. Food, medications and waste were delivered and removed by any one of the multiple tubes that came out of my body. Any pain I felt was removed by drugs that felt cold as they entered my bloodstream. I was completely oblivious to fact that my bruised and swollen face *should have* hurt; or that the steel frame that held my leg in place *was not* normal.

People came into my room to fill it with gentle smiles, quietly whispering their best wishes and prayers ... *wishes* and *prayers* for what, I didn't know.

I didn't know there had been an accident.

I didn't know that I was in hospital.

In fact, I had no idea who I was.

I was a person in a bed with no identity.

Abi

Once Sarah woke up, my entire life was focused on her recovery. Not just the daily tasks, the travel to hospital, the waiting, the holding of Sarah's hands ... but emotionally and cognitively as well.

It was all about Sarah.

In my stoned and groggy mind, there wasn't room for anything else.

Dad said to us at one point that he was grateful that we could be together, that he could tell us that he loved us, and that he still had time to hold us. I remember immediately deflecting all of that – changing his words in my mind as he said them to be about Sarah: we could all be together *with Sarah.* We loved *Sarah.*

> We could all hold *Sarah*. Because that was all I could do.

I saw different people come and go from my room and classified them based on their function. There were three different types of people: nurses, visitors and doctors.

Nurses came to visit me at all times of the day. They came to say good morning and ask me if I knew what my name was, what day it was, what month it was, and how old I was. They relied on me to tell them that sort of thing, and came in several times a day just to ask. I was not always sure what the answers were, but I knew they didn't know either. I liked the nurses because they were always smiling. I didn't have the heart to tell them I didn't know the answers. So, often, I made them up – with gestures at first, then, as I got better, in messy scrawl on a notepad. At the time, I thought I was a convincing liar. The truth is that I didn't fool anybody.

Visitors weren't really like the nurses. They only came once a day. I liked them too because they told stories. I loved hearing their stories, even though I didn't understand them.

Doctors were a funny group of people. They were not quite nurses, but not quite visitors either. I knew that they worked at the hospital, just like the nurses. But they only came to visit me once a day, sometimes less, just like visitors. They didn't come with stories though, they asked questions, just like the nurses. Their questions were harder too. I didn't even understand most of them.

Somewhere along the way, someone must have suggested to my family that mementos and photos from home might make my room more comfortable. Mum and Abi were well aware that the *one* thing that made me comfortable was neuroscience. So, my neuroscience textbooks were brought into my hospital room. The books *were* able to provide comfort, but only because I could refer the doctors to them.

Groups of doctors would huddle at the foot of my bed and speak some sort of mumbo jumbo about the brain. I frantically searched for the answer in my head, unsure whether I should smile and nod or frown and shake my head. When neither option felt appropriate, which was often, I would frown and point towards my neuroscience textbooks or the clipboard that hung on the end of my bed.

That was the other odd thing about doctors. They loved clipboards. They were fascinated by them. I didn't think that I had ever seen a doctor who was not carrying a clipboard or in search of the clipboard.

So, I was confused by the role of doctors. They were not quite nurses, but not visitors either. The best that I could decide was that they are a group of people that worked there, wherever 'there' was, and they didn't know very much.

But I liked them anyway.

As misdirected as it was, my understanding of doctors and nurses gave me my first clue about my own identity. They visited me often and were always asking questions. 'Do you know what day it is?' 'Can you count down from ten?' 'When was the last time you ate?' 'Do you have any pain?' 'Can you wiggle your toes?'

The nurses' questions served a purpose. When they asked questions, they responded to the answers. If I signed *yes* to pain, they gave me painkillers. When I showed them how well I could wiggle my toes they would smile and encourage me to do more. I liked the nurses. They always seemed pleased with my answers.

But the doctors' behaviours were far harder to interpret. With a conceited authority over the nurses, they walked into the room, clipboards tucked to their chest, and gathered at the end of my bed. When my friendly nurses had disappeared, they would begin their interrogation. They did not respond to answers, but scribbled each answer down in their clipboards.

In their early visits, they seemed to only talk to each other. I took this to be due to the fact that they were in awe of me, and too afraid to ask.

'What is her intracranial pressure today?'

'When was her last morphine?'

'How many breaths has she had today?'

As I became more coherent, and able to stay awake for longer periods, they started to direct their questions to me.

'Do you know what day it is?'

'Your mum says that you study the brain. You have had a subarachnoid haemorrhage. Do you know what that is?'

I did my best to help them find the answers. The poor things were often baffled by my responses, and discussed them in detail with each other before moving on to the next question.

I began to sense there was another purpose to the doctors' visits.

They must not know the answers! They must be coming in here to ask me, because they know I am so smart.

I confirmed for them how smart I was. I referred them to textbooks to look for answers.

'Do you know what day it is?'

'*Rang and Dale's Pharmacology* will explain the drugs I am taking. There are no drug interactions, generally because it is daytime...' In the early days, when I could not speak, this was gestured. By the time I could communicate, it was written or said out loud. The doctors' responses were always the same.

Scribble. Scribble. Scribble.

I had decided who I was.

I understood now.

I was definitely a guru, and the doctors needed my help.

Once I discovered this, I liked the doctors. It was good to have someone to talk neuroscience with. They came into my room with smiles and clipboards to ask me questions about medications, procedures and parts of the brain. I would happily answer them and discuss drug interactions. I didn't notice that we were always talking about *my* brain.

In the early days, when I had just woken up in the HDU and was still trying to figure out who and where I was, I *understood* what was being said when we spoke about the brain.

I understood *very* little else.

Chapter Six

A lesson in memory

Lying in my hospital bed, trying to piece together my identity, I was comfortable with the notion that I was some sort of neuroscience guru. Neuroscience appeared to be one of the only things I was sure of, and people kept coming to my bedside (which, to me was my whole world), to ask me about the brain.

Before the accident, I lived and breathed neuroscience. A conversation about the workings of the brain was far more appealing than conversation about pop culture, news and current affairs, fashion, cooking ... anything at all really.

When I woke up in HDU, I knew that I was going to do honours and that I was going to study Parkinson's disease. I knew every neurotransmitter that I would be studying, and the way that they interacted in the brain. These were *facts.* They were as plain to me as knowing how to hold a pen. But it never occurred to me (or anyone else) that I could not remember a single *event* from my degree. I only knew what I had *learned*.

I knew about the brain almost immediately, but it took me longer to understand who I was, or who the people around me were. I did not understand that the doctors were trying to save my life, I thought that they simply didn't know about the brain.

> We can break long-term memory into two different types: implicit memory and explicit memory. Implicit memories are memories of things that you have learned, but don't have to think about: walking, tying a shoelace, or brushing your hair into a ponytail. Explicit memories are memories that you consciously recall, such as facts, events and stories. Explicit memories can be divided into two more groups: semantic memory and episodic memory.
>
> Episodic memory is the memory of experiences (episodes) of events. Memories associated with these events, such as time, place, and

emotions combine to tell a story. Semantic memory is the memory of facts, meanings and knowledge. They have no associated emotions or stories, but rather are rote-learned things. Knowing that ice is made from water is an example of semantic memory. Recalling a time when you filled an icetray with water, put it in the freezer, and felt cold as you opened the freezer door is an example of episodic memory.

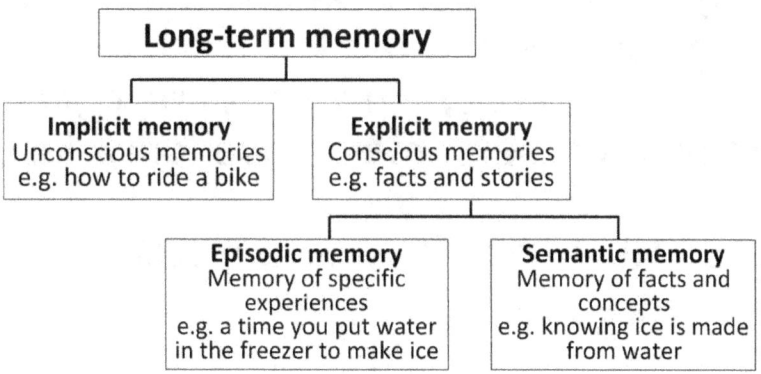

It appears that I retained semantic memories, but not episodic memories.

The reason that this is important is that it can be hard to get your head around the fact that I knew about the brain almost immediately, but it took me longer to understand who I *really* was, or who the people around me *really* were.

Before I had decided who doctors or nurses were, and before I knew who *I* was, I knew who Abi, Greer, Mum, Dad and Adam were. They were my family. I understood this and its importance long before I knew anything about anyone else about the world.

However, I don't know *when* or *how* I actually recognised them. There are no medical records or anecdotes about recognising family. Who records such things if they *don't* know that I don't recognise them?

In all reality, my *not* recognising family members may have only lasted for one day.

In HDU, one day is an eternity.

Abi

I never got the impression that Sah didn't know us. When she was conscious and learning to communicate with us, there was never a sense of confusion about who we were or what we were doing there. I trusted that she knew us, because she trusted us.

She trusted me.

Any question or instruction or comment from someone in the room and Sah would look at me or Mum or Dad for guidance on how to respond. In the early days that Sah was conscious, all she could do was write. Scribbled lines across the page that only I could understand. The moment I walked into the room she would gesture for her notebook so that she could ask questions. Not the big questions that you might imagine someone would ask, the types of questions that would have indicated a sense of continuity and self-awareness – not 'Why am I here?' or 'Will I recover?' or 'How long have I been here?' but small things that she felt she could only learn from us, like 'What is the time?' or 'Is there another blanket?'

I never got the impression that she was a different person, either. None of us did. We had no reason to think that. What had changed about Sah was that she was not the bold and independent person that we had

> known pre-accident. Post-accident, lying on the bed in ICU or HDU, or even later in her recovery, she was something incredibly valuable and fragile and in need of our protection.
> But she was still Sah.

One week had passed since I woke up.

The emotional trauma of the past month was wearing on my family. Some days, I was well, other days I was worse, the tension of waiting to find out which had been torturous.

It seemed that now that I was conscious, it was worse.

Every day was the same.

Every day, someone in my family told me about the accident.

Then I would cry.

Then I would forget.

Then it was someone else's turn to tell me. That was the part that they all dreaded.

Today, it was Dad's turn.

Oblivious to my condition, I beamed when I saw him come through the door. I was one giant eyeball, hidden between bandages, with a toothy grin. Although my tiny body was lost in the crisp white hospital gown, my bruises and scars were still very visible. A smiling, bruised, bald Smurf in a hospital gown, lying in a tangled net of tubes and monitors.

'Good morning, Sarah,' he said gently, and took a seat by my bed. Dad's shoulders slumped slightly under his neatly pressed white shirt. 'How are you?'

I couldn't understand why he appeared so sad. It was daytime. Daytime was bright and happy. *What's wrong?* I gestured by giving him a quizzical look.

'Sarah, do you know where you are?'

The nurse had just asked me that question too, so I knew the answer.

I smiled proudly. *Of course I do! I am here!* I gestured.

'Sarah, you're in hospital. Monash Medical Centre.'

Dad was always getting things wrong. *Monash* was *university.* I didn't know what Monash University had to do with hospital.

'...there has been an accident.' He continued, locking his fingers between each other and looking down between his hands.

'When?' scribbled to Abi, who was left with the task of interpreting my notes for my family

He couldn't meet my eyes.

I knew what *accident* meant. I knew it must have been a bad accident because of Dad's face.

'You, Greer and Abi were all in a car accident. It happened a month ago. You were driving back from the city, and you hit a pole on McNaughton Road. Now you are in hospital.'

Dad spoke slowly and quietly, and there was a seriousness in his voice that indicated that he spoke the truth. But I struggled to understand.

If there was an accident, and if I was here, where are Abi and Greer? Is Dad sad because Abi or Greer are hurt? Are they dead? Are Abi and Greer alright? Why did it happen a month ago? Have I been asleep so long? Why didn't anyone wake me up and tell me about this?

I looked at him again, seeking more information, but I didn't know what to ask first. Or how. He seemed to know what I was thinking, or at least some of it, because he started to answer my questions.

'They are alive. They are fine. You're...'

I didn't know it at the time, but Dad couldn't bring himself to say the last part. No one could.

...not fine.

'...You're in hospital, Sarah. You had a stroke.' Then, as if it would provide some sort of proof, he added, 'They had to shave your head.'

I reached up to touch my head, searching for hair. I knew that I should have had hair. *Everyone* had hair. But all that I felt were bandages. Someone had shaved my head! *Why had they done that? Were Abi and Greer's heads shaved? Is this what they do to you when you are in a car accident?*

Why? I mouthed, unaware that the sound did not come out. My eye filled with tears.

'You were hurt pretty badly. You broke several bones. You are recovering, but you still can't walk.'

Why would I walk? I am in a bed. You don't walk in bed.

'It was a pretty bad crash.'

There was silence. I could not imagine what a 'bad crash' was. I wished that I had been there to see it so that I could understand. I lay in bed, helpless to comfort my fragile, crying father. I didn't understand how such a terrible thing could happen in a world as lovely as mine had been no less than a few minutes ago.

I didn't notice my own tears start to fall. Dad reached out to hold my hand. He knew that I had grieved the news of the accident for the first time every day this week, and I would probably grieve it again tomorrow.

What is worse? Remembering, forgetting, or learning?

'It'll be okay, Sarah. The doctors will be around soon, and they can explain it to you. But you are going to be okay, everyone is going to be okay.'

I rolled back, closed my eye, held his hand and drifted back into a teary sleep.

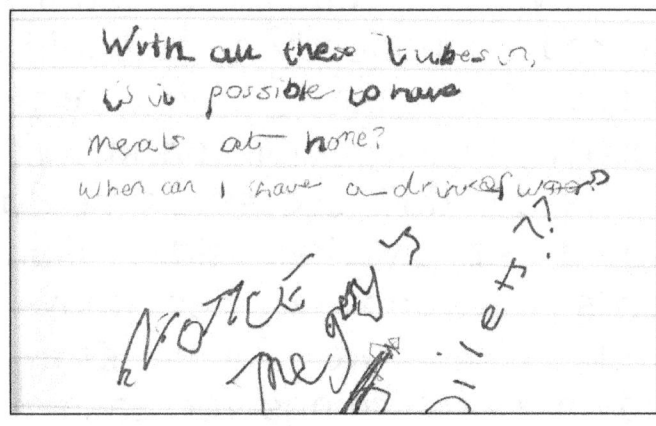

'With all these tubes in, will it be possible to have meals at home? When can I have a drink of water?' – a note I scribbled in hospital in January 2003

It was daytime. Daytime was supposed to be happy.

Abi

When Sah woke up she couldn't speak, but she could write. She would write messages to us – questions about where people were, where her car was, whether she had got into the honours program, what she would have for dinner, and for each of those questions, a follow-up question. She would look at us from beneath her eye-patch with such sincerity and trust. 'Why?' Each question, I answered as honestly as I could. My answers felt like some form of protection: letting her in on knowledge that she couldn't access on her own. I would sit by her side, lean in towards her and let her know the answer. When we were little, we would interpret things for each other all the time. Us against the world: as long as we had each other, we'd be okay. This felt the same, except it was me catching Sah up on what was for dinner, and Sah catching me up on incremental details of her recovery. And of course, it wasn't really just us two at all – there was Mum, Dad, Greer, doctors and nurses.

Our answers were building her world. Today's dinner would be

> chicken soup because we had said it would be soup. Her car was gone, not because it had been destroyed in the accident, but because we said it was gone. The nurses were trustworthy because we said they were trustworthy. In hindsight, she was learning from us the way that a toddler learns about the world. I didn't see that then. I mean, she was adorable and vulnerable we treated her like a toddler, but we didn't know that she was learning as a toddler.

I eventually understood that I was in a hospital. But I didn't have much time to pity myself, or mourn BAJ. I was too busy. My days were also filled up with important things like ice blocks and wiggling my toes.

Wiggling toes was important to practise, because it made the nurses smile. I liked making people smile. Every morning the nurses came in to do observations and would ask me if I could wiggle my toes. They would smile in appreciation of my performance and tell me that I was doing very well.

I also loved sucking on ice blocks. Not the flavoured ice blocks that children eat in summer. The plain, clear ice blocks that go into a drink.

My fascination with ice blocks started with cotton buds.

Abi, Greer, Mum and Dad were allowed to wet my lips while I was in HDU by dunking cotton buds into a plastic cup of water and running them across my mouth. They were never allowed to give me enough to drink – swallowing may damage the tracheostomy tube.

As I got 'better', they were allowed to give me an entire ice block to suck on. This was, to some degree, a sign of independence. I could suck on the block as hard as I liked, or let it melt slowly in my mouth. Ice blocks couldn't really damage the tracheostomy tube – they were too large and too cold to swallow. The idea never occurred to me anyway. I didn't realise that swallowing solid things was even a *thing.*

The point is, with ice blocks, I was in control of how wet my mouth got. It was sublime.

The confusing thing about ice blocks was that no one else ever wanted to share them with me. No matter how many times I offered, taking the melting block out of my mouth to show people the treasure that I was offering, no one seemed interested in sharing it with me.

'That's okay, darling, you have it all.'

In that first week of recovery, I knew that I was meant to be starting honours with Richard. I was conscious that I was losing time, and needed to get out of hospital, whatever 'hospital' was, and go back to university, whatever 'university' was.

I was accumulating a portfolio of facts about the world around me: I understood who my family members were; I understood who the doctors and nurses were; and I had established that I was a guru of some kind. But I still didn't really understand who I *was*.

My family all spoke to me about this fantastical girl who lived before the accident. She was a musician. She was a neuroscientist. She was the top of her class. She was a poet.

Apparently, that girl was me. *But no one could really be all those things, could they?*

I couldn't remember Pre-accident Sarah. I didn't identify with her at all. And she wasn't the only thing that I couldn't remember about life before the accident.

I explained before that I woke up with semantic memory, but not episodic memory. It appears that even the semantic memories I had were somewhat limited. I knew about the things in my immediate vicinity, but could not remember the details about anything that was not relevant to the way that things in my room worked.

For example, I understood how to hold a pen and write, because they were a part of my immediate world. I needed them to communicate. However, when nurses came around to do their observations they would ask me about something obscure, like what day it was. I had no hope at all of answering that correctly, because I didn't know that there were different days of the week, let alone what their names were. All that I knew was that sometimes it was day time, and sometimes it was night time. Another question that always stumped me was when they asked me my date of birth. I knew that I *had* been born once, because everybody had to be born. But, my memory only went back a few weeks. So I figured that my birthday had to be a relatively recent event. Which of course, was wrong, and I hated being wrong.

Stuck in this limbo, I would desperately refer doctors and nurses to my textbooks. The nurses would smile and respond with '...is that right? I'll check it out sometime.' The doctors took out their clipboards did what they always did. *Scribble. Scribble. Scribble.*

Considering my difficulty with dates and my naivety about matters in the world outside my room, it is surprising that the first thing that I 'learned' involved both.

I know the date that I first 'learned' quite clearly. It happened on Sunday 26 January 2003. Australia Day.

The nurse was just finishing her morning observations, and as usual was having very little luck with my responses to her questions.

'Okay Sarah, can you tell me what day it is today?'

I smiled broadly and pointed at the blue sky outside, to indicate that the answer was clearly *daytime.*

'Do you know where you are?'

I giggled and gestured around my room. *Surely she knows that! We are here!*

The nurse frowned, and hung my clipboard up on the end of the bed. Clearly, I had done something to upset her. I didn't like to see anyone frown. Desperately, I tried to show her that I could wiggle my toes. Surely *that* would cheer her up. But I didn't get the chance.

An older nurse stuck her head in the door, winked at me and skipped into the room.

'Happy Australia Day!' she said proudly, presenting the younger nurse with a small cupcake that was neatly decorated with green and yellow icing.

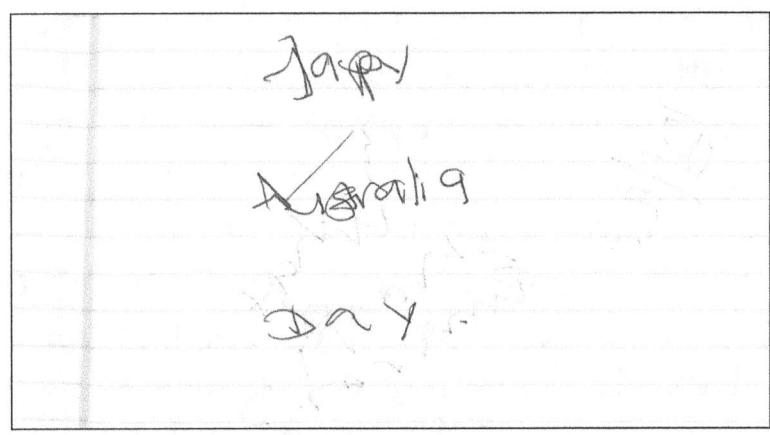

My first demonstration of memory in a note written to Greer on 26 January 2003

The young nurse smiled and squealed with delight. 'That's adorable. Thank you!'

They both left the room laughing and smiling.

Greer came to visit me late in the afternoon. She looked tired and stressed, and I wasn't sure why. I knew there was something I was meant to say. I picked up my pen and scrawled *Happy Australia Day* across the page. Greer looked at the page and tried to decipher what I had written. As she figured out the meaning of the scribble, her eyes grew large.

'Has anyone told Sarah the date today?' Greer asked the young nurse, who had just entered my room to do her afternoon observations.

'Not that I know of. But she could have heard it when Jan came in and gave me a cupcake this morning...' the young nurse suggested, not seeing the significance of what had just happened.

Despite the progress I was making, I had not held new information, unprompted, for more than a few minutes. Yet the nurse had said 'Happy Australia Day' hours before Greer's visit.

I had shown no understanding of the world outside the hospital. I did not know what *Australia* was, let alone understand its history. I had no idea that certain days had meaning to some people, but not others. I did not know what a public holiday was, because I could not grasp the concept of either *public* or *holiday.*

My world was much smaller than that.

I only understood my room. When people left the room they simply disappeared, and whatever they had told me disappeared with them.

Abi would later explain this was having a lack of object permanence. It is a phenomenon that we all experience as babies. Object permanence, or lack thereof, is the reason that you can play peekaboo so successfully with small children. When you cover your face with your hands, they cannot see it – so you no longer exist. When you reveal your face, suddenly you exist again. They squeal with delight at your magic, not understanding that you were there the whole time. This is what my world at Monash Medical Centre was like. Once Abi, Dad, Mum, Greer, or any of my visitors disappeared, I could not comprehend that they still existed. When orderlies wheeled me down the corridor for tests and scans, it was as though this world was appearing as I went passed. It never occurred to me that the hallways had always been there, or the radiology department existed after I left.

When I recalled that it was Australia Day, it was *sort of* a display of object permanence. It was a demonstration that I understood that a world existed beyond what I could see, and that something important was happening in that world. I had made reference to something that was not directly associated with anything in my room. I had no cues or clues about the date, and had no reason to remember that there was something to be celebrated.

There was only one reason why I should remember that it was Australia Day.

I had learned it.

My brain had been able to make the appropriate connections that helped me understand that *something* was happening that day, and *that* something would cheer Greer up.

Greer burst into tears.

I didn't understand what I had done wrong, and instantly wished I'd not told her. I thought I had upset her more.

Abi

Cognitive function is a person's ability to pay attention, concentrate, plan, problem-solve, learn, and remember. It's essentially all the things that a person does that makes that person that person. Sah was demonstrating her own cognitive function by communicating with us.

She could look at us, squeeze our hands, smile at our jokes, ask us questions, and respond to our questions in return. These last two things she did by miming words or by writing in a notepad, a process that was painstakingly slow for us and painful for her. When we misunderstood something, for example, she would lie with her eyes closed and start waving her hand in the air, as though she was rubbing something off an imaginary whiteboard, mouthing 'no, no, no'; then pause, furrowed her brow, open her eyes and gesture for her notepad. More importantly, Sah was remembering things.

She remembered facts about her life that were central to who she was, things that only Sah would know. She knew that she had a car named BAJ. This was important for us because it was our evidence that Sah was returning to us – that she was reconnecting with her identity.

We hadn't lost her and there was nothing to grieve.

For her, though, these memories served a completely different function. The things that she was remembering were no longer part of her identity, they had lost that meaning. They were now simply trivial pieces of information in her head. She was learning to piece together this trivial information and infer meaning from it.

Sah learned that she had owned a car named BAJ. It crashed. She was now in hospital. Her challenge was to try to link these three pieces of information together to understand her world. It had nothing to do with her identity. So – Sah's recollection was a very important task, even if it was not what we thought it was.

My strongest example of this memory game is when Sarah recited a poem. It sits in my mind as the perfect example of this bittersweet tension between us grasping to this identity of Sah, and Sah retrieving the trivial information in her mind.

It sounds like a contradiction, Sah reciting poetry. This science-focused girl shouldn't care for poetry. But Sah did care about poetry. She was a big fan of Emily Dickinson. The rhythm and melancholy of Emily Dickinson's poems was reflected in the songs that Sarah wrote. I wasn't really a fan of Dickinson. I could never remember the lines. Sah could.

Mum, Sah and I were in Sah's room in HDU. Someone had brought along a book of Emily Dickinson poetry to read to her. Mum asked me to read aloud. I flicked open to a poem on a well-worn page, a poem titled 'Nobody Knows This Little Rose'. It was one of Sah's favourites.

I knew it was about a flower.

I started reading and looked up. Sah was smiling, her eyes closed. I remember Mum sighing as she recognised the poem, swallowing tears. Sah was mouthing the words as I read, but she couldn't keep up. I stopped and told her we would start again at her pace. I started again, saying the words slowly and deliberately. Sah mouthed along, perfectly matching each sound. It was

> like some melancholy twin-ventriloquism act.
> What a poem to recite, that quiet day in HDU, as she struggled to remember who she was.

I knew that there was *something* that I could not do that people were waiting for me to do. I knew that I could not talk, and the reason that I could not talk was because of the tracheostomy tube. *Maybe that was what they were all waiting for?*

In order to talk, I had to take the tube out. The problem was that, even though I was a guru, I didn't know how to remove a tracheostomy tube. This was a terrible problem, because I didn't want to admit to anyone that I couldn't do it. If *I* couldn't do it, how on earth would it be removed? How was I ever going to talk?

In the end, it didn't matter. I didn't have to do a thing. The doctors did all the work. It turned out that they *were* clever after all.

I don't remember much about the actual removal of the tracheostomy tube. I have very vague memories of gagging and struggling as the nurses and doctors pulled the tube from my throat. But I will always remember the events surrounding my first words.

Mum, Dad, Greer and Adam were there when the tube came out. Adam had managed to get a week off work and had flown down to Melbourne, but Abi was missing.

They were all happy for me, but all I wanted was for Abi to know that the tracheostomy tube was finally out. I knew that would make her happy. I wanted her to be as happy as everyone else in the room. There had to be a way to tell her that would make her laugh...

I started to form a plan. I was going to trick Abi. It was going to be hilarious, and Abi's laughter would be *glorious.*

My idea was to have a nurse call Abi for me. Then, I would take the phone and tell her 'Sarah can talk'. She would think I was a nurse, and she would probably ask for more information about the procedure, because Abi was very professional like that.

That's when I planned to surprise her. I would tell her it was actually *me* making the call. I would tell her all about how clever the doctors were to take the tracheostomy tube out for me, and how it was easy, and now I could talk. We would both laugh hysterically at my joke and celebrate together over the phone.

She would laugh so much!

It was going to be the best news, and the best joke anyone ever played on anyone else.

Of course, my joke didn't exactly happen as planned. However, as with everything else at the time, I was completely oblivious to why it failed. Having not been able to talk for the past month, my vocal cords were very weak. I had also forgotten how to shape my mouth to make some sounds correctly, and had a terrible lisp. I *thought* that I said, in a very clear and professional voice 'Abi, Sarah can talk.'

In actual fact, Abi heard a soft whisper 'Ambi, Shah can tawk.'

'Sarah?' she replied, her voice breaking slightly.

There was a long silence, then a muffled noise. My plan hadn't worked. Abi didn't laugh. She wasn't happy. She was crying.

Why was it that every milestone I hit made my sisters cry?

Chapter Seven

Mind of a Child, Body of an Adult

Although the tracheostomy tube was out, I was still very 'broken'. I was still bed-bound and receiving food and medicines intravenously. I had a frame around my right thigh, which was held together by a metal pin. My left eye was bandaged and did not move – I still didn't even know that my left eye existed. I was bald, with a burr hole in the top of my head. And, of course, I still had problems with memory.

I was oblivious to *all* of this. Slowly but surely, I was making progress. After all, I could breathe and move my extremities independently, and all my reflexes were intact. I could wiggle my toes, suck on ice blocks, hold a pen and write words (even if they were scribble). I could smile at nurses and visitors.

I wrongly believed that now that tracheostomy tube was out, I could leave hospital and go back to university and study Parkinson's disease. All I needed to do was learn to walk.

The first step in learning to walk is learning to become 'vertical'. This is a severely underrated skill.

One morning, I was lying in bed counting my fingers, wiggling my toes and watching the ceiling when a specialist entered my room. I recognised her, but I didn't quite know who she was. I had always assumed that she was a nurse because she was not like the doctors (she did not carry a clipboard). However, she had a different uniform to the nurses. They wore light blue. She wore a white shirt with an ID badge poking out of her top pocket. She also had freckles. I liked freckles, they made a person look friendly.

During that period of my recovery, I thought *any* characteristic made someone look friendly. Curly hair, straight hair, ponytail, blue eyes, brown eyes ... With this lady, it was her freckles. So, Freckles walked over to my bed, followed closely by my family. They were all smiling with quiet anticipation.

'We're going to try sitting you up today, Sarah,' Freckles said, pulling the blankets away from my legs. I was confused. 'Sitting up' was easy: it meant pressing a button beside my bed, which raised my head above my feet. But 'sitting' did *not* need blankets to be pulled away from me.

Freckles motioned for Abi to step forward.

'I'll do the lift, but you'll have to support her from *this* side,' she instructed, directing Abi to the top end of the bed. She looked around for another volunteer, and Mum was the closest option. 'Dee, can you come to this side when she's up? You'll have to support Sarah while I bring her feet around.' I couldn't comprehend what Freckles was talking about. *Bring my feet around to where? Hadn't she noticed that there was no trolley? Why don't they just get a nurse to help?*

Up to this point in time, I had never sat up by myself. My world had been predominantly horizontal, except for the rare occasions when I raised my head above my feet in the bed. Even though I knew that *other* people stood vertically, it had not ever occurred to me that I should also be vertical.

Freckles leaned over me and put her hands behind my shoulders. She cradled me gently, and then started to pull me up towards her. A wave of panic swept over me. Too many things were changing at once, and there were too many risks.

I was terrified that she would pull too hard and that she would pull all of my tubes out. I had vivid images of my nightmare where a gang of doctors captured me and forced tubes down my throat, while I struggled and screamed in pain and fear. I did not want to re-live that dream.

'Abi, help! What...?'

'Don't be afraid, Sah, you're almost there.'

Suddenly, it was done. Freckles and Abi had folded me upright, and I had flopped into a seated position. Mum and Greer looked at me with proud smiles on their faces.

'Sarah! Well done!' Greer exclaimed.

Freckles stepped in front of me and held my hips while supporting my legs with her arms. Mum immediately stepped up to support me from the side that Freckles had vacated. Muscles that had not been required for weeks strained as my trunk attempted to hold me up. I was entirely dependent on Abi and Mum to keep me upright.

I looked into their smiling, supportive faces, feeling vulnerable, exposed and dizzy. God I was dizzy. I leaned into Mum, quietly praying that this bizarre motion would be over soon and that they would put me back down. But it was not to be. Freckles, Abi and Mum worked in unison to rotate me around on the bed. They did not stop until I had been rotated a full ninety degrees. I watched in horror as Freckles slowly released my legs.

Even though there was nothing supporting them, my legs didn't fall away-they just hung there. I had expected that without the support of the bed, they would keep falling to the floor and either fall off or pull me down with them. But they didn't do either of these things. They stayed attached to my body, which remained on the side of the bed, and dangled. It was a curious sensation. I imagine now that astronauts feel the same sense of weightlessness when they first enter space.

My head started to spin again. I thought I was going to pass out.

I didn't.

Instead, I toppled over and threw up on Mum.

She took it gracefully, and quietly smiled at me. 'Too fast, sweetie?' I was scared to try 'dangling' again. It was exhausting and dangerous. I still couldn't comprehend sitting, and did not see the purpose, other than to dangle my legs over the bed. Nonetheless, Freckles continued to visit me and try to help me up, and over the next few days, my fear started to fade away.

In the real world, a few days is not a long time. But it can be *an eternity* in hospital. Not because of boredom, but because of the simplicity of life. There *is* nothing to fill the day, so time moves slowly. Taking a few days to gain confidence 'dangling' was, in fact, a very long time.

As my confidence grew, 'dangling' became a game. I'd wake up early and wait for Freckles to come and visit, just so that I could 'dangle'. *Someday, I'll be able to do this by myself.*

I graduated from 'dangling', and learned 'sitting'. Nurses would help me into a chair so that I could practise doing 'sitting' for a while. I noticed that they didn't call it 'dangling', probably because my legs touched the floor when I did 'sitting'.

Rather than wheel me around on a trolley, orderlies started to bring a wheelchair to take me to appointments. Mum, Abi, Greer and Dad would come with a wheelchair to take me on trips up and down the corridor, into rooms with large soft chairs called 'couches'. Once I had the freedom to do 'sitting' in a wheelchair, I had the freedom to move away from my bed and visit other places. My world took on new meaning. It was more than spots on the ceiling and a blue window. It went well beyond the nurses' station that I could see outside my door.

I learned that there was a whole hospital beyond my room.

Even though my awareness of my surroundings was increasing daily, I still had no memory of life before the accident. I had only ever known a world indoors. The still air was always twenty-four degrees Celsius. I could see blue sky outside my window, but it never dawned on me that this had anything to do with light. Fluorescent lights controlled the brightness of every room and corridor. Murmurs between nurses, dull televisions and softly beeping machines made up the soft background noise that I had become accustomed to. The wheelchair gave me access to an entirely different world.

Mum was the first to try to share this new world with me. She couldn't wait for me to experience *fresh air.* She helped me into my wheelchair and proudly wheeled me down the corridor, out to one of the hospital courtyards.

The courtyard was filled with things that were so incongruent with anything that I had ever known that I barely knew what most if it was. The small courtyards had been designed to encourage staff and visitors to escape the sterile indoor environment and 'enjoy nature' over a cup of coffee. The designated spaces were lined with grey brick paving and cement blocks for chairs. This was broken up by flowerbeds, hedges and the occasional gum tree. All of this was designed to give the hospital a 'natural' feel.

It was a hot day in the middle of February, but still beautiful. A cool breeze drifted across the courtyard, making the outdoor heat tolerable. The brilliant blue sky that I loved so much from my room was made all the more glorious by the summer sun. There were peculiar white things floating across the sky that Mum would later call 'clouds'. Birds chirped happily in their trees, grateful for the touch of nature provided by the hospital, and bees buzzed frantically between the flowerbeds. People perched very happily on their cement blocks, chatting as they sipped ice drinks, stopping occasionally to listen to music that came from speakers hidden between trees.

But I saw none of this.

I saw chaos and noise. The mixture of birdsongs, music and conversation was more than my ears had ever experienced. I could not decipher one sound from another. Nor could I determine where any of the noises came from. The assault of sound did not pair up with any of the movement in the courtyard.

It was all happening too fast. I decided immediately that outside was terrible. It was cold, bright, hard, noisy and confusing.

Mum did not see or understand my distress. She wasn't to know. All that she saw was the beautiful blue sky, and the people relaxing to music, and she longed to share it with me. She was so ready, so eager to have me experience nature and feel the fresh air. How could she have understood my torment?

I asked if she had a warm blanket. She didn't. I sat miserably for the next few minutes, willing her to give up on this adventure. Wishing that she would take me back inside. I asked again if she was sure she didn't have a blanket.

She must have seen then how uncomfortable I was. Mum put down her coffee, began to undo the brakes on my wheelchair and started to wheel me back across the courtyard and into the hospital. 'Well, Sarah, that's probably enough excitement for one day. I'm glad that you got to feel that!'

I was glad that one of us was pleased.

There was another skill that I had to learn that I did not like doing at all. Eating. I didn't understand the point. Mouths were for talking and sucking ice blocks, *not* eating. I thought it was a terrible chore. And unlike 'dangling' and 'sitting', 'eating' took weeks to get used to.

In the beginning, hospital staff made the mistake of bringing me entire meals. The trays consisting of a covered plate, a drink, a bread roll and some form of dessert were far too overwhelming.

There were so many steps involved in eating. I had to sit up and pull the tray table into me. I had to lift the lid off the plate *and* find a place to put it down. I had to pick up a knife *and* fork at the same time, *and* cut the food up into even more pieces than were already on the plate. I had to choose one of those pieces, pierce it with the fork, and put it in my mouth. But the job wasn't done yet. I still had to chew until the food was a mushy pulp. This could take forever. By the time I'd done all this, I was exhausted, and I still wasn't past one mouthful. I still had to do the most uncomfortable part – I had to try to swallow. I didn't like the feeling of food going down my throat. It was confusing. There shouldn't be anything in that part of my body. Tubes didn't need to go there anymore. *Why am I letting a foreign object into my body?*

Once, Dad brought me in a bunch of fresh, green grapes to entice me to eat. He picked a few grapes from the bunch. He placed three on the tray in front of me and took a couple for himself. He put the first one in his mouth, and gave a supportive smile as he started to chew. I reluctantly picked one up and put it into my mouth. I bit down on the grape, like I had seen Dad do. It squirted out a sweet juice that was easy enough to swallow. I sucked on the pulpy mess that filled my mouth until all that was left was skin. Finally, I swallowed.

Dad smiled at me, proud that I had eaten a whole grape. 'Have another one!' he encouraged, smiling and gesturing to the two remaining grapes.

Abi came to visit me later that afternoon. She saw the bunch of grapes on the tray on my table. To her, the grapes looked untouched.

'Have you eaten anything today?' she asked.

I felt betrayed, and was furious with her.

I had already done my eating that day, and shouldn't have to do extra.

'I've already had three grapes!'

Three grapes was a lot.

It was three whole times more than one grape!

My dislike for eating went beyond *my* eating. I was disgusted when I learned that other people ate too, and that they ate *by choice.*

Abi, Mum, Dad and Greer had come to visit me on a Friday morning.

Deciding that they'd like to give me a greater tour of the hospital, they wheeled me down to the cafeteria for a coffee. I had survived the courtyard, but was in no way prepared for the overwhelming chaotic activity of a cafeteria.

A barista stood behind the coffee machine making coffee for hospital staff and visitors. He banged and tapped coffee from the jugs, before making the machine scream and gurgle as milk frothed. Somewhere, a baby was wailing. Its mother sat beside a pram, rocking it back and forth to calm the screaming infant; children ran around tables, squealing and laughing in a game of tag, unaware of the peace that they were disturbing; friends sat opposite each other deep in conversation, elbows on tables, separated by empty coffee cups; doctors passed us by with their precious clipboards in their arms, and purpose in their stride. Behind this pandemonium, Fox FM played Avril Lavigne.

    Filtering information was hard and exhausting at the best of times. If I really tried, I could almost focus on one thing at a time in a busy room. The problem was that I didn't have the ability to identify what was the most important thing to focus my attention on. I was extremely distractible. Something would catch my attention and, mid-sentence, I'd stop, pause and change topic altogether. This is a problem that I still have to manage today.

As Greer, Dad, Mum and Abi wheeled me into the cafeteria, the noise and activity were unbearable. The further in we went, the harder it was to concentrate. They remained unaware of my struggle, and were happy just to be sharing this new environment with me. My mood decreased with every step into the cafeteria. By the time we reached our table, I was exhausted, furious and had completely lost awareness of almost everything in the room.

Almost.

I was fixated on a man sitting at a table. He was *hideous.* He sat alone, with a cream bun and a cup of coffee. I wasn't sure why he had them. He picked up the cream bun and leaned over his plate. As the bun approached his mouth, he squeezed it slightly, just enough to make jam and cream spill out either side. He shoved the contorted mess of bun, sugar and fat into his mouth and bit down, making an even greater mess. It appeared to go all over his face, and as he pulled the bun away, he spilled crumbs and cream onto his plate. He put the bun down in the pile of cream he had just dropped, and chewed on the mouthful of fat and sugar that he had just put in his mouth. I watched in horror as he smeared the crumbs, cream and jam from his face with a serviette, and leaned back in his seat to enjoy his mouthful.

He didn't even try to hide the hideous act of eating. He chewed and chewed and chewed.

He reached for his coffee, lifted it to his face and took a swig to help wash down the mouthful of fat and sugar. Placing the cup down, he reached for the remainder of the bun, ready to go through the whole disgusting process again.

It was *grotesque.*

'Abi, did you see that?' I pointed at the man, furious with him for becoming *more* grotesque with every leaky bite that he took.

'What, darling?' I remember Abi's face looking so concerned by my apparent horror.

'He's *eating!*'

I was so angry. It was disgusting! It's bad enough having to put grapes in your mouth and eat them ... but to do that with a bun? With cream and jam? Voluntarily? It was the most hideous thing I'd ever seen, and I didn't like it.

She looked around. All she could see was an innocent small man in a tidy grey suit enjoying a bun and a coffee on his morning tea break. There was nothing grotesque or offensive about the way he ate at all. If anything, she would have pitied him because he had to eat it alone.

I couldn't be calmed. I glared from behind my eye-patch. Hating him as he ate his bun. The man, however, remained oblivious. He had almost finished.

'Why, Abi? Why is he *eating?* How could he do *that?*'

By this point, Mum was aware of the problem, and tried to calm me down.

'It's okay, Sarah. He's having his tea break. He's just having a coffee.'

'But it's not. And look at what he's *eating!* Why is he doing *that?*'

They couldn't answer my questions, no matter how much I demanded an answer. The best that could be done was to go back to the ward – quickly.

I don't know what happened to the man. Or his cream bun. All I know was that it put me off eating grapes for the next few days. I had decided: eating was something I was *never* going to do. Thank you very much!

One morning, I was sitting in my room wiggling my toes and playing with my ears. I had just discovered ears. I thought they were wonderful things. They were filled with so many treasures!

Sometimes they had wax, which did nothing but build up under my nails. Other times, if I was *really* lucky, there was dried blood. Blood was an excellent find, because it tickled so much when I pulled it out. It was a beautiful dark brown colour and came out in long strands. It was a rare but glorious find, and I spent hours hunting for it.

One morning, I proudly showed a nurse a piece of blood that I had just found in my ear. With no concept of social boundaries, I didn't understand that some behaviours were disturbing to others, and that personal things should remain private. I saw nothing wrong with wanting to share a piece of dried blood with a nurse. Blood and other bodily fluids were just as much a part of my world as my toes or my hands were. It escaped my notice completely that playing with dry blood made people uncomfortable.

The nurse ran off to find an ear, nose and throat specialist. At first, I thought this was because she knew he also liked to play with dry blood. But on reflection, I don't think he did. To start with, he cheated. He used tweezers, not his fingers, to pull blood from my ear. However, once he was finished pulling, he had a piece of blood that was longer than anything that I had ever managed.

I was happy for him, but for some reason, he wasn't smiling. He frowned and wiped the glorious prize from his tweezers with a tissue.

'Sarah,' he said, quite seriously, 'we are going to have to clean this ear properly. We need to remove all this blood.'

'Will there be any left?'

'No, Sarah. There won't.'

I frowned. 'Will it grow back?'

'No, Sarah. It won't.'

That did not make sense to me. Everything else was going to grow back: hair, bones, muscle ... why not blood in my ears? *If it won't grow back, why would he take it away?*

I did not understand that the blood in my ear was not meant to be there, or that it signalled potential hearing damage. The concept of 'deafness' was not a part of my world. I didn't know what it was and would not have understood it even if the doctors had explained it to me.

I didn't realise that you were meant to hear out of *both* of your ears. I was quite upset with the specialist, until I learned that he was referring me to have hearing tests done. I didn't know what a *hearing* test was, but I liked going to have tests. Tests meant that an orderly would take me on an excursion to somewhere new in the hospital, where I would meet a new technician, and I could tell them all about my accident.

For all the hype around the hearing test, all that the technician did was ask me if I could hear some sounds through a set of headphones.

Towards the end of my early 2003 hospital stay, I became preoccupied with the idea of going home, even though I didn't know where or what 'home' was

On this page, I scribbled: 'Why am I here?' 'RUN AWAY.' 'Get to shower.' 'I'm gonna run away from here as soon as I can walk in a straight line'

He tried to trick me a few times by not playing any sounds at all, or only playing sounds into my right ear. But I never fell for it.

It never occurred to me that the reason that I could not hear the sounds in my left ear was that I was deaf.

I was, for the most part, perfectly happy with my world in hospital. I was friends with all the nurses, and only have fond memories of them. Any grievance that I could possibly have had was forgotten the minute they left the room. They would return and become my best friend again. I liked the doctors too, despite the clipboards. I looked forward to their conversation and enjoyed making decisions with them about the way things worked in the hospital. Some of them even knew as much about the brain as I did.

While I had plenty of friends and visitors, they didn't live at the hospital like I did. I was not sure where they went when they left me, or what they did there, but slowly, I gained awareness of a world outside the hospital doors.

Occasionally, I'd wonder when it would be my turn to leave the hospital. When would it be my turn to leave and 'go home' or 'go to work' like Abi, Greer, Adam, Mum and Dad?

I didn't realise that it was not a matter of taking turns.

I didn't realise that I stayed in hospital because I was 'broken'. I could not comprehend that anything was physically wrong with me. The tubes, the bandages, the machines, the painkillers, the pin in my leg – they had all been there since the beginning of my 'existence'. I understood what each did on a microscopic level, and could explain each of their roles in recovery or monitoring function. But I could not comprehend that any of the machines, bandages, tubes, or pins, were necessary for my own survival. They were just there. They were just a part of *me.*

I still did not understand that I was sick. I was not in denial about everything that had happened, I just didn't understand the severity. What I did know was that I was in a place called *hospital,* and there were certain things that I had to learn before I could go home. I thought some of those things, like walking, should be easy, because everyone else could do them. I just needed the nurses to give me a chance. I didn't know how weak I was, or that I wouldn't be able to do those things for a long time.

In my world, I was as healthy as everyone else, and didn't understand why it wasn't ever my turn. In the few darker moments, I fantasised about running away. I dreamed of leaving the hospital and walking out with Abi.

But every dream ended at the front door of the hospital. I didn't see the outside world in my dreams because I didn't know what it looked like. I told Abi of my plans, earnestly looking at her through my bandage, willing her to help me escape. She never agreed, though.

I might have dreamed of escape, but escape to *where?* All I knew was *hospital.* My doctors told me I was destined for the Victorian Rehabilitation Centre. I'd never heard of *Victoria* or *rehabilitation.* They were scary and unfamiliar words.

'Don't worry!' the nurses told me. 'You will do fun things there, like walk!' This did little to quell my fears. *Didn't they see that I couldn't walk?*

My last day of hospital, 9 February 2003, came too fast. I sat on my bed, numb with fear. My family, the terrible traitors, were excited. Mum had arrived with a bag of clothes and a pair of white sneakers. *Clothes.* I knew about clothes. Other people wore them. I wore a hospital gown. Abi and Greer chatted excitedly as they dressed me and helped me back onto the bed. I sat awkwardly above the blankets, in foreign white sneakers, a denim skirt and a blue shirt. *Clothes.*

Terrified and uncertain of my fate, I waited for rehab.

'Sarah, it's time to go!' a cheery voice called. Two orderlies bounded into the room. Just like my family, they were all smiles. I felt so *betrayed* by their happy banter. They didn't seem to notice, and helped me across to the stretcher that would carry me down the corridors, into the ambulance, away from the safety of hospital, and into the clutches of the Victorian Rehabilitation Centre.

Chapter Eight

Leaps and Crashes

I was wrong.

I was entirely wrong about the Victorian Rehabilitation Centre.

In my nightmares, I had pictured dark corridors, disapproving nurses and screaming patients.

Instead, there were bright corridors, green trees and smiles.

My room contained the standard hospital bed, with crisp white sheets and pillows, but that is where the similarity with the world I had come from ended. The room was colourful, bright and inviting, and full of subtle promises about the way my life would change.

There was no drip at the head of the bed. *I won't be attached to machines anymore...*

There was a phone on the wooden bedside table. *I'll be able to call Abi whenever I want...*

There were soft armchairs in recesses along the walls. *I'll be able to sit there and read my books...*

The attached bathroom was a promise of independence. There was a small cream plastic shower chair tucked into a corner. *One day, I won't need nurses to shower me. I'll be able to sit on that chair and shower myself...*

There were also steel rails in the shower recess. *One day I may even be able to* stand *in this shower...*

My beloved university books had found their way from hospital to the rehabilitation centre. These books held one of the most important promises of all. They were a promise of how I imagined life *outside.* They were my link to university. I *knew* that I was smart and must know a lot more about the brain than anyone around me. I knew that this was because I had studied the brain, and that I was going to do honours in Richard's lab as soon as I left rehab. Honours was my number one priority.

Honours only goes for one year. It was already February, and the other students would be starting their projects soon. Those books were a promise that I wouldn't get left behind. I couldn't stand, walk, attend lectures or do mouse surgeries, but at least I could still study my neuroscience books and read journal articles.

Adam brought in a nylon string guitar and two old torn exercise books. They were filled with poems and songs that were accompanied by hand-drawn pictures of fretboards covered with numbers, like some sort of code. He told me that I had written the songs that filled those exercise books.

I couldn't remember them, but I was going to try to learn them in rehab too. Not because I wanted to reconnect with Sarah – that idea never occurred to me. I wanted to learn those songs for the same reason that I wanted to learn to walk, or tie shoelaces, or stand in a shower. I wanted to learn to play guitar because it was something that I would be able to do by myself one day in the outside world.

Rehab was full of so many promises about my future, and I couldn't wait to start...

The best-laid plans of mice and men often go awry.

My recovery, like all recoveries in the history of time, was not a direct path from *sick* to *well.* It was a deviation of many distracted little crises, sometimes resulting in progress, sometimes not. There were leaps forward, and there were crashes.

My medical records show my first stay at the Victorian Rehabilitation Centre lasted from 9 February to 16 March. That's just over one month. Apparently, in the first few weeks of rehabilitation I made some progress. I was eating, planning my honours project, and I had learned to stand by myself.

But I don't remember that.

I had been at the Victorian Rehabilitation Centre for just over a month when things started to go wrong. I became very aggressive and short-tempered. I was tired all day, and lost interest in food again. I hated Abi, Greer, Mum, Dad and the nurses for even suggesting that I look at food. That didn't stop them though. My family brought in fresh fruit or lollies. Nurses tried bringing me plates of hot food from the rehabilitation centre cafeteria. But my response was always the same. I wasn't interested and didn't want it. *How dare they force me to eat!*

I became confused and started to forget who people were. I stopped being able to finish my own sentences. I was drowsy, and stopped participating in activities around the rehabilitation centre with the enthusiasm that I had become known for. Then, one morning, I simply didn't wake up. No matter what they did, the nurses could not rouse me.

Bells and sirens wailing, I was bundled into an ambulance and rushed back to Monash Medical Centre, where I spent nine days recovering before returning to the rehabilitation centre. This is what I refer to as the second 'crash' in my recovery. But I don't remember that crash either.

Memory loss is, oddly enough, a wonderful feature of my recovery. As much as I love the brain, it isn't really that resilient. It doesn't function properly when it's under prolonged stress – say from starvation, dehydration, lack of sleep or inflammation. Imagine, for example, an explorer wandering the Sahara Desert. His arms and legs become weak with dehydration, but they still function. His brain, however, fails. He experiences hallucinations, memory loss, disorientation and cognitive fatigue. Long after this, his arms and legs give way ... but the brain always goes first.

This, I know, is a gross oversimplification of how sensitive the brain is. But it illustrates the point. The brain does not cope with prolonged stress.

It seems that in my case, whenever my brain experienced severe stress, such as in ICU or in the first month of rehab, the region of the brain required to code and store memories did not function properly. As a result, I have forgotten the events leading up to every 'crash' that I experienced.

Imagine a world where all that you can remember is the positive things. As far as my memory will allow, my recovery was a very pleasant journey. It is only through diaries, medical reports and the scars on my body that I know horrible things ever happened.

My family saw it very differently though. It was all too real, too consuming to be forgotten. During the immediate aftermath of the accident, the doctors told my family not to expect anything.

Not the best.

Not the worst.

Expect *nothing.*

How is that even possible?

After the first crash on McNaughton Road, my family would come into ICU or HDU wanting to hear news. Secretly wishing I was better. Secretly preparing themselves for the news that I wasn't. Always feeling guilty that they were expecting *something.*

My collapse in the Victorian Rehabilitation Centre was far worse. They weren't prepared for it. I was stable. I was on the mend. I was better. I was eating and learning to walk. Surely now they could just relax and watch the skinny bald girl progress?

Unfortunately, no.

I am not sure that the way I explain what happened next is one hundred per cent accurate, because this is not the way that the world works. But it is the only way I can explain the events that follow.

In my imagination, during my second stay at Monash, the doctors (clipboards pressed to their chests) stood around my bed in HDU. They were baffled by my sickness, and were coming up with long and complicated suggestions to explain why I had been doing so well in hospital and then collapsed in rehabilitation. All of their hypotheses were failing.

A young endocrinologist looked at the scans, and noticed the smallest and simplest thing. So small and so simple, it had been overlooked by everyone else.

She turned to her supervisor and said, 'Sarah doesn't have a pituitary gland.'

The pituitary gland is at the base of the brain. My subarachnoid haemorrhage was also at the base of the brain. Somehow, it escaped everyone's notice that, among all the brain damage that I had endured, I had also lost my pituitary gland.

This was the critical thing.

The pituitary gland regulates the release of hormones from all of the glands in the body. Hormones are essential for initiating processes like reproduction, converting food to energy (metabolism), body repair and maintaining homeostasis. With no pituitary gland, I no longer had a functioning hormone system. While I was in hospital, that was okay. My body had no need to convert food into sugars for energy, or nutrients for growth and repair. It received everything it needed through a drip.

Once I left hospital, my body had to fend for itself. With no drip, I had no way of gaining access to the sugars and nutrients from food. While I still had the glands that should have been able to make the hormones I needed, I did not have the 'master gland' to activate them. So, even though I was eating, I was starving.

I starved for over a month.

Eventually, my body couldn't take it. I collapsed and was sent back to Monash.

And I won't remember any of this, because the brain is not resilient enough.

After the young endocrinologist made the diagnosis of panhypopituitarism (a fancy phrase for 'no pituitary gland'), the senior doctors dropped their clipboards and slapped themselves on the forehead and began the search for the right hormone replacement therapy (HRT).

One of the hormones they had to replace was cortisol. Cortisol plays a role in the stress response and in energy metabolism. Anybody else taking cortisol at the levels that I was may start to feel stressed, agitated and angry. This is because their body is already capable of making and responding to sugar in their bloodstream. But not me.

My body had been starved of sugar for a very long time. Every cortisol tablet was like an extremely high sugar rush. If I had been bright and happy in hospital, the world was twice as brilliant now. Simply for the fact that I had the energy to experience it.

On 25 March 2003, I returned to the Victorian Rehabilitation Centre.

Life at the rehabilitation centre was simple, regimented and busy. I never knew that there was so much more to do in the world beyond wiggling toes!

At 8:00a.m., a nurse would arrive with my tablets and breakfast. Once I had eaten and taken my medication, I had to get out of bed. Then I had to choose my clothes. Then I had to get dressed. Then I had to put on my sneakers. At 9:00a.m., a porter would come and wheel me to my first lesson for the day.

No one else at the rehabilitation centre called them 'lessons'. They called them 'therapy sessions'. This made no sense to me at all. The name 'therapy sessions' was too many words for a start. They were lessons. I went there to *learn* things. I wouldn't let anyone tell me any different.

There were many different types of lessons: physiotherapy; occupational therapy; gym; speech therapy; doctor appointments; endocrinologist appointments; neurologist appointments; ophthalmologist appointments; ear, nose and throat specialist appointments; blood tests; X-rays; MRIs; and any number of other things. I never had more than three lessons in a day, and when I wasn't in lessons, I was back in my room reading uni books or trying to play guitar, or wandering the halls looking for someone to talk to.

Life was busy.

I didn't notice at the time, but rehabilitation was also where I learned to enjoy meals.

For some reason, after the second crash I forgot about my horror and hatred of food. Eating was a game. I look back now, and wonder if this was some sort of subconscious survival mechanism. My body knew that I no longer had machines to do the work for me, so it had to find a way to make me want to eat. But that might be reading too much onto it.

The point is that, all of a sudden, I enjoyed mealtime.

Every night at 5:00p.m., I sat on my bed in excited anticipation of the tray of food to come. Whether or not I had guests didn't matter. Five o'clock was mealtime. I don't remember selecting food from a menu, but I do remember the happy surprise with whatever came.

It wasn't the eating that excited me so much. It was the *exploring.*

I used to love touching the lid to see if it was going to be hot or cold. Cold lids usually meant sandwiches. These were okay, but they caused nowhere near the same level of excitement as hot lids.

Hot lids meant hot food. I liked hot food, because then there was the game of guessing *what* the hot food would be. I'd uncover the meal, and delight in all the different shapes and colours that were on my plate. Small round bright green peas, white fluffy mashed potato, brown gravy with squishy pieces of meat, and carrots sliced into small orange circles.

I would rummage through every package on my tray, delighted by the prizes inside. The big ones first: a bag with a roll in it, or a tub with jelly in it. Then the small ones: salt, pepper, sugar.

Dinnertime was glorious fun.

It never once occurred to me that something was missing. I enjoyed everything for its texture and colour. Nothing could be distinguished by flavour. In fact, in those days, I didn't even know that flavour was a *thing.*

So, what does it mean, to have lost flavour?

I can't tell the difference between a raw potato with sugar on it, and an apple.

Roughly ninety per cent of the flavour experience is made up of smell. The scent of food travels to the back of your throat, up into your nose, and stimulates olfactory receptors. The olfactory receptors send signals to a small pair of bulbs at the base of the forebrain called the olfactory bulbs. The nerves that do this must pass through thousands of tiny perforations in the bone behind the nose.

The fractures to my face and skull severed those nerves, meaning that there was no way for 'smell' to reach my brain. The subarachnoid haemorrhage destroyed what was left of my olfactory bulbs.

I had lost my sense of smell.

Of course, we wouldn't know any of that until after I left the Victorian Rehabilitation Centre.

Why would we? There was nothing really to smell.

I have no memory that smell ever existed and have a limited understanding of what it actually is. I believe people when they say that it exists, but cannot conceive of such a world.

What does it add to *your* world that I don't have?

Everyone was so excited that I was finally interested in food, nobody noticed that it was the colours, temperatures and textures that excited me – not flavours. I was eating, and I was happy. Learning to walk wasn't easy. No one ever said it would be. It wasn't just that I was weak, had no balance, and was in a lot of pain ... if walking was merely a matter of overcoming small things like that, then it would have happened much faster.

What no one ever talks about is how many steps are involved in the process of learning to walk (no pun intended).

I already spoke about becoming 'vertical'. But there was so much more to come, and with every new 'skill' that I learned, my world opened up a little more.

I knew how to 'sit' in a wheelchair. But in the rehabilitation centre, I learned to get into (and out of) the wheelchair by myself. The independence associated with that skill was astronomical. No longer did I have to buzz for someone to help me out of bed, or to wait for assistance to get into a car after an appointment. I could do it all by myself. I could even go to the bathroom by myself.

While I was gaining my independence in the wheelchair, I was also preparing to leave it. I had to learn how to stand upright in the parallel bars and then unaided. I learned to walk, supporting myself with my hands in the parallel bars, holding as much weight as I could, hoping that my physiotherapist wouldn't notice.

As my confidence in the parallel bars improved, I began my journey as a 'vertical' being in earnest. I could see it all unfold so beautifully in my head...

First, I would learn to stand, and my wheelchair would be traded in for a walking frame.

Second, I would graduate from walking frame to a pair of crutches. I smiled to myself as I imagined walking (hobbling) around the rehabilitation centre, as tall as everyone else. After two crutches, I would graduate to one crutch. After one crutch, then I'd graduate to a walking stick. After the walking stick, there was nothing. I would walk unaided. I would 'graduate' for real, and walk out of the rehabilitation centre.

There was so much to look forward to.

But of course, nothing in my recovery happened in a linear fashion.

I had barely learned to stand when I found myself back in hospital *again.*

Had I been living in the outside world, and had the accident *not* happened, I suppose there would have been a lot more panic about my third trip to hospital. But compared to the SAH, the car accident and my hormone crash, this 'emergency' was relatively benign.

To tell the truth, I thought it was kind of fun.

I had been back in the rehabilitation centre for six days and had made a lot of progress. I had gained confidence getting into and out of my wheelchair independently, and was only just learning to stand in physiotherapy.

On my sixth morning back in the rehabilitation centre, having tied a red bandana around my head and done up my shoelaces myself, I was very happily sitting on top of my bed and feeling quite proud of myself.

Dr Irena was doing her usual rounds, and came in to visit me. I was showing her how well I could move my legs, when she paused, approached the bed and gently lowered my right leg with her hand.

'Sarah, this leg is swollen, do you notice?'

I looked at my legs that now lay side by side on the white bed sheets. My right calf was twice the size of the left.

'Yeah, but I had a big brekkie this morning,' I responded.

'No, Sarah. I don't think that has anything to do with it,' Dr Irena assured me. She gently pressed down on my left leg again, watching me for a response. When she lifted her hand from my leg, there was a white mark where her fingers had been.

'Sarah, I think this is a DVT. We have to do more tests to confirm.'

I stared at her blankly. I had no idea what DVT stood for. It probably had something to do with legs. But legs are not brains, so I knew nothing about them.

'You need to keep your leg still until we know what has caused the swelling and redness. I'll call the hospital and see if we can get an ultrasound this morning.' And with that she rushed out of the room, leaving me alone, shocked and ashamed. Shocked that my doctor would stop me from doing the one thing that *needed* to be done to get better (learn to walk). Ashamed that she didn't think I was well enough to practise walking, and that I would disappoint my physiotherapist by not attending our lesson today.

Thirty minutes later, I was on my way to have an ultrasound at Monash Medical Centre. A serious-looking orderly met me at the ambulance outside the hospital and helped me into the wheelchair. Together, we made our way through a maze of hospital corridors that seemed to be designed to disorientate patients.

'This is Sarah Brooker, from VRC. Age twenty. Her doctor called earlier to arrange an ultrasound. History of SAH and MVA, possible DVT in right thigh,' the orderly said to a woman sitting behind a desk. I wondered how he knew so much about me. I hadn't had the chance to tell him anything. But then again, *everyone* seemed to know a lot about me before I met them. I was, after all, a medical marvel.

He wheeled me into a dark examination room and left me alone to wait for the technician. I decided that I did not like 'DVTs in legs' *at all*. Whatever they were, they were stupid and confusing. No one would tell me about them, and they could only be found by sitting in a dark, boring examination room. No cool EEG machines or CT scanners anywhere.

I forgot all about my dislike for DVTs in legs as soon as I met the technician doing the ultrasound. He laughed a lot and was fascinated by my story. He *ooohed* and *ahhhed* at all the right places, and even asked questions about the brain. We got along very well, and I decided I had made a new best friend.

Alas, all good things come to an end. The ultrasound was over within an hour.

'Righto, Sarah. Let's get you cleaned up so that you can see Dr Marcus.'

'Can't you just tell me what you saw?'

'Well, Dr Marcus wants to see your results. And he wants to have a talk with you anyway.'

I didn't know who Dr Marcus was, or why he had suddenly become involved in my case, but doctors always wanted to talk to me. Mostly about the brain, but sometimes about ears or eyes or food ... so why not about DVTs in legs?

I put my hands on the bed in an attempt to sit myself upright and swing my legs around.

'No, no, no, Sarah. Stay there. Someone will be in shortly with a stretcher to take you to see Dr Marcus.'

Why have I been downgraded to a stretcher? You only use stretchers if you can't sit, and I know how to sit.

But there was no argument. You don't argue about things like that in hospital. Stretchers were fun anyway.

Dr Marcus was a tall man with clear blue eyes, wrinkles, grey hair and a relaxed manner. He looked like he should be out on a farm, leaning on a gate with a cup of tea. But he wasn't. He was here at Monash, about to explain the complexities of DVTs (whatever they were) and their treatment. He sat down on one of the chairs next to my bed, leaned back and crossed one leg over the other.

'Sarah, you have what we call deep vein thrombosis. Do you know what that is?'

I didn't want to lie to him. 'Not really, no. I know that they form in legs...' I said, to help him with his explanation.

'Yes. Yes, they do. When you don't move for a long period of time, your blood flow slows down. It can slow so much that some of it starts to clot in your vein. Usually at the top of the leg – just like you have.' He paused to see if I was following. I nodded, confirming that I understood.

'So ... the danger is that it will grow big and cut off the blood?' I suggested, to prove that I could work out what the danger was.

'Well, that's part of it. The greater concern is that, now that you are moving, your blood flow will increase. There is a chance that the clot will break away from the side of the vein...'

'Oh, right!' I pitched in, excited that I finally understood what all the fuss was about. 'And then it could go up to the heart or the lungs, and block the blood supply there and kill me!'

I was quite proud of myself. Not only had I learned something new about the body, but I had also figured out why DVTs were dangerous. But, as with all my ailments, I had completely missed the point that this threat applied to me.

'Yes. That's right. That's absolutely right,' Dr Marcus replied slowly. He had a concerned expression. 'We need to do a few things to fix this, Sarah. First, we need to stop it growing any more than it already has. To do that, you'll receive daily Clexane injections. The nurses at VRC can help you with this.'

I nodded solemnly, as if to confirm that I thought that they were capable enough to be charged with such a serious task.

'You will also have to wear TED stockings. These will help reduce the swelling and support blood flow.' This did not make much sense to me at all. But I liked the look of the white stockings that he handed me. I imagined that they would suit my denim skirt and sneakers quite well.

'Finally, we need to reduce any chance that the clot will break off. No movement for the next week.' Dr Marcus sounded so serious as he spoke to me, but I couldn't see why. I'd been in trickier spots than this before. If all I had to do to recover from the DVT was have some injections in my tummy and wear some new tights, DVTs really didn't sound so bad. In fact, they sounded fun.

I chuckled to myself as I imagined how confused everyone at the rehabilitation centre would be. Last time they saw me, I was a girl who could use a wheelchair by herself and was almost able to stand. Next time they see me I'd be on a stretcher, and not allowed to move. *They will be so curious!* I would have such fun explaining DVTs and showing off my new tights, and teaching the nurses how to do Clexane injections...

Then I remembered physiotherapy, and the reality of the situation set in.

DVT meant that my great adventure of learning to walk was put on hold. *Again.*

Chapter Nine

Small Steps

Bill, my occupational therapist, sat before me with a deck of cards.

'This is Go Fish, Sarah,' he said. 'The idea is to make as many pairs as you can.'

Bill handed me a laminated A4 sheet that was filled with the combinations of pairs that we were allowed to make. 'Pairs' were confusing. Apparently, I had to find two cards that were the same number and the same colour, but not the same pattern. Two hearts could not go together, not even if they looked the same, because all of the hearts were different numbers. *How am I meant to do that?* Bill handed me five cards.

'Look for any pairs, and then you can ask me for a card that you would need to make another pair. If I have that card, I will give it to you. If I don't, you can pick a card up.'

The game didn't make any sense at all. So many things could go wrong. If I had a pair of red twos, did I need to find the pair of black twos? If I didn't have any twos, could I still ask for a two so that I *could* make a pair? If we had to make pairs from the whole pack, why did I only get five cards to start with? What if the card that I picked up did not match anything? What if Bill asked me for a card, but I needed it to make a pair?

This was not the first time that Bill and I had played Go Fish. Every time we played it, I became equally confused. I struggled to remember the rules and couldn't keep track of the different cards that needed partners. As a result, I found the game incredibly exhausting.

I always lost Go Fish. That day with Bill was no exception.

I must be a little better now though, because nowadays I play games like Go Fish very well.

I still have difficulty problem-solving and sorting new information, but I have developed strategies to help me cope. I have electronic *and* paper organisers, and two yearly calendar planners: a small one inside my phone case, and a large one that I have glued to my desk.

I am also a great fan of using colour-coded notes, mind maps, and rhymes to remember things.

I just can't solve puzzles in my head.

Even though I was terrible at card games, occupational therapy made me feel smart. I proudly read passages aloud to Bill and carefully retold stories that he read to me. I knew that I often got the story wrong and left out key points, but I made up for it by adding other things. Just like I had done in hospital. I thought Bill hadn't noticed that I didn't recall what we were talking about, just as I had assumed that the doctors never noticed that I couldn't answer their questions.

As entertaining as my new stories were, they were nowhere near the original passage that I was asked to read. Bill suggested that I take notes as we read through the text, but even then, I would add other features to link things that didn't make sense.

Once, we read *Old Mother Hubbard.* Bill asked me to retell the story. I didn't need to get the words right – just tell him what happened.

I knew that it started with an old lady. She was in her kitchen. There was something to do with her having no food in the house, so I told Bill that she was going to go down to the shops. I also remembered that there was something about her dog, but something else happened first – probably the trip to the shops – and it was also important that the dog was hungry. Then I changed my mind, and told Bill that it wasn't a dog, it was a cat or a fish or something. Then I remembered that there *was* food in the cupboard. But it didn't make sense to keep pet food in a cupboard, so I told Bill that she put the food on the bench, but since there was no other food, and the pet was hungry, and she really needed to go down to the shops. So she did, and everyone there was really friendly and helped her buy nice food. She even bought her cat a new collar that was pink. I couldn't remember how the story ended.

This epitomises my distractibility at the time and was typical of the way I'd interpret the world. I had completely forgotten the story, and became concerned with the cat (who was never in the original story).

In fact, my storytelling abilities have remained this way. I am notoriously a very bad storyteller, and often add information that is neither true nor relevant to the original story – even though it makes perfect sense to me.

Masking that I didn't understand things didn't always end well.

Bill suggested that go to a place called 'the kitchen' where I could learn to cook for myself. I thought this sounded like a fantastic idea, even though I had no idea what he was talking about. I didn't know what *cooking* was.

At that stage, I was still wheelchair-bound, and receiving food in my room. As far as I knew, food came on a trolley, hidden under gloriously different coloured lids. I wasn't quite sure how I would set the lids up on a trolley up by myself.

I imagined that food came from a bright and colourful room that was just like every other room in the rehabilitation centre. It was a place where nurses and orderlies made their usual chirpy banter as they placed the random assortment of colourful bowls and paper packages onto trays, and then loaded them onto trolleys lined up neatly against the wall.

I wondered what my job would be. *Perhaps I'll get to put cutlery packets onto trays.*

I thought that going to 'the kitchen' would be a fun social experience and couldn't wait to join the nurses and orderlies there.

It's heartbreaking how wrong I was.

On the morning that I was referred to go to 'the kitchen' for breakfast, an orderly wheeled me down a corridor of the rehabilitation centre that I had never been in before. It was cold, and I wished I had brought my red jumper. I joined six other patients who sat in silence around a grey rectangular table in the middle of a room.

A laminate bench was neatly lined with all the things we apparently needed to make breakfast. There was a packet of white sliced bread next to a toaster; margarine, jam, peanut butter and vegemite lined up behind a chopping board; and three butter knives. At the other end of the bench was a hot water urn, three jars labelled *tea, coffee* and *sugar,* and a jug of milk. In the middle of the bench, between the bread and the urn, was a clear, plastic container of muesli, and a small tower of white bowls.

I had not seen any of these items before, and had no idea what to do with any of them. Bill was nowhere to be seen, so he couldn't help me.

I sat in my chair at the back of the room and watched other patients stand up, one by one, to 'make breakfast'. One lady put a slice of white bread into the toaster and walked over to the urn. She put a tea bag into a plastic mug, and then filled it with water. Another patient stood at the clear, plastic container of muesli. He poured the muesli into a bowl, and carried the bowl to the urn. Rather than pour hot water into the bowl (like the lady had done with her cup), he picked up the milk, and poured it over the cereal. I was so distracted by him that I never saw what happened to the white bread in the toaster.

Desperate to know what the toaster did, I wheeled myself over to it and put two slices in, just as I had seen the lady do. I waited and waited until suddenly, two black pieces of toast popped out. *So that is how toast is made?* I looked around for the paper bags that toast came in when it arrived in my room. There were none to be seen. I had no idea what to do next.

I put my toast onto a plate, and wheeled over to the table, where I sat and miserably chomped on dry, cold black toast.

I knew I had failed.

It was two days before I next saw Bill. As soon as I saw him, I burst into tears.

'Bill, I can't do it! I don't know how to do it!' I admitted between sobs. 'Please can I have breakfast in my room again?' I told Bill all about the failed breakfast and the burned toast and there being no paper bags to put the toast into.

'I think you are too well to keep having breakfast in your room. But you don't have to go to the kitchen. Why don't you try the cafeteria?'

I had seen the cafeteria before. It was a welcoming, bright space with pot plants and large windows. Families went there during the day and sat all along the two long tables that ran the length of the room to drink coffee and eat sandwiches. I didn't think I could use the cafeteria because I didn't have any money.

'It's okay, Sarah. You don't have to pay for breakfast,' Bill said with a smile.

So, I traded 'the kitchen' for breakfast in the cafeteria.

The cafeteria looked different in the morning. The two long tables were empty, apart from three men who sat at the end furthest from the counter. They were talking, laughing and eating when I entered the room. They didn't appear to notice me. For the first time ever, I was scared of strangers. This was *their* space, not mine.

I was terrified that I would get it wrong and the strange men would laugh at me, and I'd be ashamed that I'd let Bill down. The old lady who ran the cafeteria looked friendly, but that just made it worse. *If I do this wrong, I'll let her down too...*

'What would you like, love?'

I had no idea what to ask for. I had never asked for anything in my life. Food just came to my room on a tray. I didn't even know what it was called half of the time.

'Um ... do you have *breakfast?*'

The crow's-feet around her eyes deepened as she smiled a reassuring smile and nodded. 'Today, it's scrambled eggs and bacon on toast.' She reached for a plate and started to serve up the hot food. 'Would you like a cup of tea? Coffee?'

I knew the answer to this. I hated the taste of coffee and I saw no point to tea. Coffee may have been bitter, but tea didn't taste like anything at all. I preferred hot water by itself.

'Hot water, please.'

She poured the water into one of the hospital mugs that usually came to my room.

Thank God. Something familiar.

'Thanks,' I said shyly, balancing my tray in my wheelchair. I was determined not to mess this up. She had been so nice. I didn't want to disappoint her.

I wheeled myself to a table. I should have been happy, even proud. I had a breakfast that I could eat and a cup of something that I recognised. But I wasn't happy. I was even lonelier here than I had been at the Breakfast Club.

The three men at the end of the table laughed out loud at something. I was scared of these three strange men. They weren't therapists, doctors, nurses or visitors. They were a whole new breed of person that I had not interacted with before.

One man was quite large, and would have been very tall if he was standing. The second man was probably my height and had short, dark hair. The smallest one of the three had tight curly hair, and a smiley face that looked like he never stopped laughing. But there was something else...

They were all in wheelchairs like me. They were *patients* just like me. I had never met any other patients before. Not without other therapists there, anyway. Suddenly, the tall one called down the table.

'Hello, there. What are you in for?'

I smiled nervously, wary of his motives for talking to me. 'I was in an accident.'

'Yup. We were all in accidents. What happened to you?'

'I had a stroke while I was driving my car,' I replied.

'Geez. You're a bit young for a stroke, aren't you?'

Talking about the accident distracted me from my fears.

'Well, actually, an aneurysm burst. But no. That's just as common in young people as old. It's just that young people's brains are more plastic. They recover better.'

I was sort of right, but wrong in many ways.

What I had was not really a common stroke, it was a subarachnoid haemorrhage. While both result in loss of oxygen and nutrients to the brain, they occur in a different manner. Common strokes (ischemic strokes) occur as a result of blocked cerebral arteries. A subarachnoid haemorrhage (which is what I had) is when an aneurysm (a balloon-like growth) bursts, and leaks blood into the space between the brain and the skull. Both of these events ultimately stop blood reaching different regions of the brain, starving it of oxygen and nutrients. They have *similar* outcomes, but are very different processes.

Pre-accident Sarah would never have condoned such a sloppy explanation. Then again, I didn't know her. Who knows what she would have thought. All I know is that I needed to find a quick way to explain what happened to me before I got distracted and started talking about something else.

'Well, I'm Tobias. People call me Toby. This is George,' he said pointing to the man with straight hair. 'And this is Robert. Wanna join us?'

They have names. They aren't scary.

I beamed through my good eye, ready to make friends. 'Sure.'

And so I met the three men who took the stress off learning to walk, and made rehabilitation the game that it was.

Toby, Robert and George were the only people in my world who were like me.

Just like me, they were patients at the rehabilitation centre.

Just like me, they had all been involved in traffic accidents.

Just like me, they needed to learn to walk before they could go home.

Just like me, they liked to laugh.

Even though they were just like me, I never really enquired about their lives. I had learned, from all previous experience, that people were only interested in *my* health and *my* accident. So it took some time before it occurred to me to ask them how they ended up in the rehabilitation centre. Even then, because I was so self-focused I didn't commit any of it to memory.

What I do remember about Toby, Robert and George is that they were extremely important in my social rehabilitation, and were probably one of the greatest joys of rehabilitation itself. But I struggle to remember the finer details of their accidents.

While we all had different backgrounds, we were all going through the same things in rehab. We were all learning to talk again, all learning about how to do things at home again, and learning to walk again. We celebrated each other's achievements as if they were our own because, even though everyone else was happy for us too, only *we* knew what each achievement actually meant.

We even celebrated each other's pitfalls.

One afternoon, Toby returned from a specialist's appointment and told us that his specialist had 'broken the news' to him that he was never going to walk again. He had been issued with a large, motorised wheelchair that he was probably going to stay in forever.

If Toby had been living in the 'outside' world, learning that he was probably never going to walk again may have been a great catastrophe. The 'outside' world is not designed for wheelchairs. There are some buses and taxis that are equipped to take a wheelchair, but many aren't. Everything has to be modified, and you become 'special', 'marginalised'. Sure, some buildings have ramps and lifts, but they are also accompanied by signs like

Wheelchairs only. You are classified as 'different'.

But Toby was not in the outside world. He lived in the rehabilitation centre with us, and there's no better place to be in a wheelchair than in the rehabilitation centre. The whole place was set up so that it was easy for wheelchairs to get around, and you were probably in the minority if you didn't have one.

Some parts of the rehabilitation centre were even *more* fun in a wheelchair. You could smuggle food easily on your lap from the cafeteria. You got to use the big taxis. You could get to places faster.

The main corridor that linked the therapy rooms and cafeteria to the wards was a long, slow incline. On more than one occasion, I raced people down the corridors after building up speed wheeling down that ramp. I was good at beating people who were running, but Toby, Robert and George were more experienced wheelchair users, and beat me every time. Now that he had his fancy wheelchair, Toby was always going to beat us – up *and* down the ramp.

Toby's wheelchair also made him the most popular person in the rehabilitation centre. We would steal walking sticks or crutches and link up behind him, making a train around rehab. Toby would drop us off at the gym or occupational therapy, or just leave us at the base of the ramp laughing.

It was small things like this, which were horrific or stupid to the 'outside' world, that taught me that life was a game.

It was how you played it that mattered.

Abi

When Sarah learned to use a wheelchair, she would burn around the corridors of her rehab centre with her friends – other young adults who had serious physical injuries and no sense of their own mortality or fragility. There is something hilarious and terrifying about seeing a group of young adults racing their wheelchairs towards you down the

> corridors of what looked to us like a hospital, but to them was their entire world, their home. To them, it was okay.

I was unaware of my social and cognitive skills improving under the guidance of Toby, Robert, and George. I maintained that all I needed to do was learn to walk.

In my head, learning to walk would be very simple. First, I needed to learn to stand independently. Then I would be taught to walk in the parallel bars. Then I would be allowed to use a walking frame. Then I would be on two crutches, one crutch, walking stick, then free.

But it was not that easy. There are so many movements that are taken for granted, and all of them had to be relearned. Just as I mastered one movement, my physiotherapist, Brooke, gave me another one to learn, all the time working towards 'walking'.

In one of my physiotherapy sessions, I watched Brooke demonstrate a new movement. The young blonde was seated with her hands resting on the top of a small desk. The back legs of the desk were propped up by a platform, so that the whole thing was tipping towards her.

'Start at a seated position,' she instructed.

Even though I had been able to sit upright in a chair for a while, a 'seated position' is something entirely different. There was no backrest, so I had to hold myself upright and pull my shoulder blades together.

'Seated position' was tricky work.

'Move your arms along the table. Really stretch out as far as you can. See if you can reach the back.' Brooke smiled at me as she threw out the challenge. 'But there are rules.'

Of course there are. There are always rules.

'You can only move from the hips, you have to keep your back straight.'

How do I keep my back straight? 'Straight' means 'upright'. How do I stay 'upright' and reach the back of the table?

But I didn't want to let Brooke down, so I nodded, privately deciding that it would just be best to copy whatever she did. *Don't think about the whole back-straight problem, just reach the board.*

Brooke leaned forward and her hips became a perfect hinge. As she folded down towards the table, her arms slid up. She appeared to reach the end of the desk without any problems at all.

Should be easy.

'Your turn.' She swung the table around so that it faced me.

Brooke called out my checklist as I got myself into position for my first attempt at 'bending'.

'Back straight?' *Check!*

'Arms resting?' *Check!*

'Feet flat on the floor?' *Check!*

'One. Two. Three!'

I pushed my arms up the table and reached the end of the desk the first time around. *Ha! I did it. Easy!*

But Brooke was laughing.

'Sarah, you have to bend your hips as well. You can't just push your arms up. This is all about leaning forward. This will help you learn to stand, not fly like Superman.'

I wondered if Brooke really *could* teach me to fly. Flying was just as likely as walking, probably less difficult too. There seemed to be fewer movements, and apparently, I did them naturally. Brooke interrupted my thoughts. 'Let's give it another go.'

Learning to walk was a complicated affair with lots of little *steps* to get right, but I was determined to get there. I don't remember the day that I put all those little steps together, stood up in the bars and took my first real step. It seems like one of those milestones that a person wouldn't forget. The honest truth was that *every day* I was celebrating another milestone. Leaning. Standing. Stepping forward. Stepping backwards. Walking along a line with my walking stick. Walking along a line without my walking stick. Stepping onto a small block. Walking up the corridor on crutches. Walking up the corridor with a walking frame. Stepping from the shower to my walking frame on a wet floor.

Which one is the moment that I was actually walking?

Once I could 'stand', I was given a walking frame. The walking frame was not only a new way of getting around, but it also came with all sorts of changes to my world. For starters, it took a lot longer to get anywhere. Not only because I was so slow, but also because I was extremely distractible. I would often stop and look at the wall, or out the window, or at a pot plant. I happily shuffled around the rehab centre at a snail's pace, while family members or therapists patiently walked beside me.

Abi

Sarah's cheeky approach to her recovery persisted at rehab, after she learned to walk. Just like her attempt to prank call me when she could first talk, she was completely unaware of how fragile her walking was. She thought it was hilarious to try and 'escape'. She would sing to herself and walk out of the room at a pace so slow that I could make the bed and still stop her before she got to

> the door. She honestly thought she was moving fast.

My next challenge was the treadmill.

Catherine, my gym instructor, knew how much I wanted to go on the treadmill. I had been asking her for weeks, and she always gave the same response.

'I need clearance from Brooke and Dr Irena that you can walk unaided. Wait until you are ready,' she tried to reassure me. 'You *will* get there.' Then she would distract me with some other new exercise in the gym. And, with the toddler-like mind that I had, I was happily distracted.

One morning, Catherine greeted me by saying, 'Got some news for you today, Sarah. You get to try practising walking.'

She looked over at the treadmills.

I looked over at the treadmills.

Thousands and thousands of squealing exclamations ran through my head. If I had been able to, I'd have jumped and clapped my hands. But I couldn't. I just bobbed up and down, dancing on the spot. We walked across the gym together. I awkwardly climbed onto the treadmill, excited that this was *finally* happening.

'First, you must clip this onto your T-shirt,' Catherine said, reaching past me to pick up a red clip attached to the front of the treadmill by a long black cord.

'If you walk slower than the belt, or if you drop back, it will pull on this lead. The treadmill will stop immediately.' I nodded solemnly and obediently attached the red clip to my T-shirt.

'Now, hold on to the bars beside you. Don't let go. They will do two things. First, they will give you something to steady yourself with. Second, if you hold over these metal grips, you can watch your heart rate.'

I am not sure that heart rate was something that I had to work on. After all, the objective of cardio-equipment in rehabilitation is restore movement, not improve cardiovascular strength. But Catherine knew I liked to gather data. I had done that since the day I first entered the gym. She knew my heart rate would give me some numbers to watch and record, even if I had no idea what the numbers meant, or how they related to my recovery.

'We are going to start at level 1.0. That should be enough for now. If it starts to get too much, push this button, and it will stop. We'll try fifty metres – see how you go.' Catherine was pushing buttons and pointing at clips and explaining how it worked. All I could think was *I'm going to use the treadmill!*

She counted me in, and pressed the green 'start' button. The conveyor belt beneath me moved. I jerked forward to keep up with it. One foot in front of the other, just like I had practised in physiotherapy.

Left foot. Right foot. Left foot. Right foot.

I was leaning heavily on my arms, unable to trust my legs without the walking stick, hoping that no one would see through my bluff, and instead believe that I was walking independently.

But, my arms soon tired and I was forced to push with both legs while I moved along on the treadmill. Catherine must have seen my struggle. She stopped the treadmill at twenty meters.

'That went well, Sarah. How do you feel?'

'Good,' I said, smiling bravely and resting my arms. 'Can I do a bit more?'

Ever encouraging and supportive, Catherine smiled back.

'Have a rest first, then we'll see.'

I didn't get back on the treadmill that day. I *was* exhausted. Twenty metres is a long way. It was everything that I wanted to achieve in the gym. It meant that I was well enough to walk.

It meant that I was well enough to go home.

Part Three

Recovery is a Pathway, Not a Destination (2004–2006)

Chapter Ten

Brave New World

Coming home from rehabilitation was a big deal.

I spent two months at the Victorian Rehabilitation Centre – that's more than two-thirds of my entire existence (as far as I understood it, anyway). The brightly coloured spacious rooms and wood-panel corridors of the rehabilitation centre made up the entire world that I knew and understood. I was safe there.

Yet, I dreamed of a place called *home.* I didn't really know what home looked like. I imagined that it was just like the rehabilitation centre, only Abi was always there, and there wouldn't be nurses or doctors.

I didn't realise that *home* was nothing like the rehabilitation centre.

My family had decided that it was best if I moved back to Mt Eliza to be with Mum. There was plenty of room in the old house, and it was where I had grown up. It seemed the most appropriate place to go. But there was a lot of work that had to be done.

Abi and Greer converted one end of the house into a replica of the unit that Abi and I had lived in before the accident. They spent hours assembling furniture and putting up my brain posters. Apparently they had done a very good job. Mum converted the office next to her room into a bedroom for me, so that she could be nearby if something happened in the night. Somehow, she and Dad had managed to squeeze a bed through the tiny office door. The giant bed fit snugly against one of the walls, but took up most of the room. Mum also installed bookshelves for my beloved neuroscience books, and made space for my guitar, mixer and four-track recorder, and a clothes rack for my growing wardrobe. I now owned two skirts, a pair of pants, three T-shirts, a pair of sneakers and two coats.

All the while, I waited at rehab, reading, playing guitar, practising walking, wheeling around corners with George, Robert and Toby, and counting the days until I checked out.

On 10 April 2003, I said goodbye to the rehabilitation centre and went home.

Mum and Dad came to help. Their 'help' was very much unwanted and unappreciated. They arrived early, and, after asking the nurses to organise a shower chair, toilet stand and tablets, they packed up my room. They threw my clothes into an overnight bag; stacked my neuroscience books into a large cardboard box; moved my guitar by the door; and put all the papers, pens and diaries that I had into a plastic bag.

To me, their packing appeared haphazard and rushed. They didn't have a list of what needed to be done – so how could they possibly know what I needed to take home? I tried to stop them, frustrated that nothing was being done in order. I didn't know what the order should have been either, but I was certain that most of the things they did were *wrong.*

They should *not* have asked for tablets before packing anything else. They should not have even *thought* about tablets until everything else was done. Thinking about tablets just took up space in your brain, and that meant things got forgotten.

They stacked my neuroscience books by size, not alphabetically by the author's surname. *How was I to know if they were all there?* They should not have put my shoes into the same bag as my clothes. *Shoes go in a different bag to clothes, or they get lost.* They should not have put my diaries into plastic bags. *Rubbish goes in plastic bags.* They should not have left my guitar by the door. It was in the way there. It should have stayed where it normally sat until it was time to move it to the car.

Of course, the way Mum and Dad tell this story is that I stood in the centre of the room bossing everybody around while they put things in bags and, like naughty school children, tried to hide their laughter.

Who knows which version is correct?

My mood got worse when we reached Mt Eliza.

We pulled up a steep bluestone driveway lined with tall gum trees. Eager for me to see the house, Mum hurried around to my side of the car to open my door. I mistook her offer of assistance as an indication that she didn't think I was capable of walking from the car to the front door.

Of course I can do that. I have had lessons in walking and steps with Brooke. I know the correct way to do it.

'I can do it on my own!' I snapped. She smiled an apology and started to unpack the car with Dad.

I swung my legs out of the car and looked around, completely overwhelmed by my surroundings. Up to that point in time, 'outside' had been the space that existed between one appointment and another. Buildings had always been large, multi-storey structures with grand entrances that ambulances pulled into with ease. The only driveways I had known had been sealed roads that led through open cement car parks. I had never noticed if there were trees.

I was completely unprepared for the natural chaos of Mt Eliza. We were surrounded by gum trees and shrubs, all of which were in flower. The narrow bluestone drive that my feet rested on appeared to have forged its way between an old white house and two rose garden beds. The house itself looked as though it had been consumed by a giant wisteria plant, the flowers of which hung from the roof and railings like giant purple stalactites. Bees buzzed around the roses and wisteria, while magpies warbled in the gum trees and crickets chirped like tinnitus in my ears.

In the distance, I could hear the hum of the cars and trucks on the Nepean Highway. A piercing school bell sounded from somewhere beyond the gum trees. This was followed by shouting and laughter from boys as they spilled out onto the oval for their lunch break. At the time, I could not have appreciated any of these details. It was far too overwhelming. To me, the warbling magpies, buzzing bees, laughing boys, colourful flowers and tall, swaying trees were all just pieces of information that needed to be blocked out.

Exhausted, but determined to prove that I was okay, I fought my way through the cacophony of activity and colour towards the safety of the house.

Left foot. Right foot. Left foot. Right foot.

I made it to the base of a set of dark-green cement steps, which led to the porch of the old white-brick house. Holding tightly to the rusty, rickety old rail with my left hand, and leaning to avoid the wisteria on my right, I negotiated each of the six steps that led to the house.

One at a time.

First Step: left foot. Right foot. Second Step: left foot. Right foot.

By the time I made it into the house, Mum and Dad had completely unpacked the car, put the kettle on, and made salad sandwiches for lunch. Dad invited me to come and sit next to him at the large dining table. But the packing, travel, and onslaught of noise had been too much.

I asked where my room was, collapsed on the bed, and didn't wake until the next day.

The 'outside' world was hard work.

I had been living in Mt Eliza for nearly a week before I ventured down the bottom end of the house. Abi, Greer, and Mum kept suggesting I go down there and look at the 'apartment' that Abi and Greer had put together, but I wasn't all that interested in seeing the replica of a stranger's apartment. I went down to see it out of respect for Abi and Greer's efforts.

The journey took nearly ten minutes. Leaning heavily on my walking stick, I hobbled out of my bedroom and into a narrow hallway with plush carpet, and set off on the arduous trek to the other end of the house, to the door of a stranger's bedroom.

Exhausted, I leaned on the doorframe and looked in.

The walls and ceiling were covered by a maze of words written in large red script. *Hippocampus, Thalamus, Orbitofrontal Cortex* ... it went on.

The words were linked by arrows that covered the walls, ceiling and window panes. Green arrows in one direction, blue arrows in another. Hundreds of smaller captions, in neat black script, were scattered among the arrows and words.

The maze was breathtaking.

I searched for the start – but couldn't find it.

Perhaps this is not a maze ... perhaps it is a map?

I let the possibility sink in, as I began to digest the meaning of the words that surrounded me.

Yes! Yes, it is! I recognise these words! I am standing inside a map of the brain! ... but there is a hole in the frontal lobe.

The arrows and labels parted in the frontal lobe to make room for a poster of Ani DiFranco. She was leaning down looking into the camera, her arms locked in front of her.

I looked into her giant eyes. 'Ani, what are you doing here?' But I already knew. *This is a woman whose music I love.* It made sense to have her here ... in the frontal lobe of what must have once been *my* room.

A black guitar case stands in the far corner. I knew what was inside without looking. A brown, solid-top Seagull acoustic guitar. She was my second guitar. Her name was Tuesday.

But why 'Tuesday'? Who named her that? And why do I have two guitars?

Leaning heavily on my walking stick, I shuffled towards the bed and picked up a photo frame from the small bedside table.

Two little girls, no older than four, sat at a picnic table. They both had dark messy hair, crooked fringes, and matching red parkas with white trimming.

Who are they?

One of them was definitely Abi. Her little head was bent down and she was holding a sandwich in her hand, as though she was just about to take a bite. She had been interrupted by an identical little girl in the foreground, who was leaning across to kiss Abi on the nose.

A moment of great intimacy, caught on film forever.

Who is that other little girl?

An uneasy feeling grew in my stomach. *She's me.*

I didn't remember this. I didn't remember her. In fact, I didn't recognise her at all.

But the first girl was definitely Abi...

As I put the photo down, I felt as though something was *watching* me.

Then I saw it.

A half-built homemade microphone stand, rearing its ugly head from the other side of the bed.

Stupid ugly microphone stand.

Whoever had built it was clearly a novice. None of the parts fit together properly. Its awkward timber frame hadn't been sanded or painted. The hinges were loose and crooked, and the slender wooden arm and wooden counterbalance were covered with dried glue. Even the metal microphone clamp looked out of place, as it held on tightly to the top end of the stand.

I stared at it in angry horror, filling with rage.

The stand quietly looked at me from the other side of the bed. 'Why do you exist? What are you doing here?'

Apparently, I'd built it. Mum had told me a few days ago, when I suggested to her that I build a stand so that I could record songs as I learned them. I recalled how excited she looked when she told me that I had built one before the accident, and how proud she was when she presented me with this ... *thing.*

Stupid Ugly Thing.

I hated it. I hated everything it represents. *It represents a girl that I don't know, but that Abi, Mum, Dad and Greer are waiting for me to become. They think that just being here, I will magically turn into her.*

I won't though. I don't know how.

There had been another girl. She had *actually* existed. She built that stand. She made the brain map.

Her name was Sarah, just like me.

She had dark hair, just like me.

She played guitar, loved Ani DiFranco, and loved neuroscience, just like me.

But she wasn't me, and I wasn't her.

I didn't know her.

I felt so betrayed – but by whom, I don't know.

There was nothing before hospital. That is when I began.

I looked at her memories around the room.

I dropped the walking stick, lowered myself to the floor, looked up at Ani's eyes, and cried.

People would think that after confirming that another Sarah had existed before the accident, I'd put effort into finding out who she was. They may imagine that I would put on my detective's cap and, like Sherlock Holmes, travel the countryside seeking out anyone and everyone who knew her.

Surely you must have wanted to know her? Connect with her? Surely you grieved her?

No. I didn't. How do you grieve someone you never knew?

There really wasn't time to grieve Pre-accident Sarah. There was not enough space in my head. My world had already become too big and confusing, without having to worry about *her*.

I had to focus on learning about *me* as I am now, not as I was then.

The first week in the 'outside' world was confusing. There were so many things that had to be done, but *nothing at all* to govern the order in which I was meant to do them.

When am I allowed to have breakfast? When am I allowed to call friends on the phone? What time should I be out of my pyjamas and into daytime clothes? How much time am I allowed to spend reading a book? How do I know if I am reading too slowly? Now that there are steps at home, am I meant to practise walking up stairs every day? Should I practise walking on stones? When do my lessons happen?

The result of this confusion was that I didn't get anything done in the first few days. I wandered between my bedroom and the kitchen, forgetting the purpose for the trip in either direction. To make sense of my new world, my occupational therapist suggested I make timetables. *Timetables* were the magical things that were created by the rehabilitation centre. Timetables told me *what* to do, *when* to do it, and *with* whom. I didn't think I was allowed to make my own.

'I'm allowed to do that?' I asked her incredulously. She smiled reassuringly. 'Yes, Sarah. You can.'

I was excited to try making timetables by myself. I found an exercise book and some coloured pens down the far end of the house, among the things that Mum had said were mine. I was glad to give them a purpose, and couldn't wait to start filling up the blank pages. I imagined a new color-coded world, ruled by timetables made of red, blue, green and yellow highlighters. *This* world was going to make sense.

I sat down on the edge of my bed, leaned on the small desk that Mum had given me, and considered the steps involved in making a timetable. I started by writing the days of the week in black pen down the side of the page. This took three attempts. The first attempt failed because I couldn't fit all the days on the page. Next time around, I decided to leave Saturday and Sunday off. Abi had a timetable that only had Monday to Friday on it, so they were the days that I chose to keep. *If they are good enough for Abi, they are good enough for me.*

My second attempt failed because I spelled 'Wednesday' and 'Friday' wrongly. But I was scared that I was wasting pages, and didn't want to get in trouble. I decided to keep this attempt as a rough draft. I spent the next forty-five minutes writing down the tasks that I intended to do each day.

On my third attempt, I *really* took my time. I spent fifteen minutes carefully writing each weekday, evenly spaced, down the page. I spent another hour copying the tasks across from my draft.

Nearly two and a half hours after I had started to make the timetable, it was finished. It was an overwhelmingly full schedule of teeth-brushing, tablet-taking, book-reading, guitar-playing, breakfast-making, sleeping, and phone-call making, dotted with the occasional visit to doctors, specialists or rehabilitation. Some days had close to twenty tasks.

After finishing the timetable, I crawled back up my bed and slept for two hours.

Timetables are an exhausting business.

As taxing as my timetables were, I needed them to survive. Without them, I probably would have just continued to wander between my bedroom and the kitchen, not sure of where I was supposed to be, or what I was supposed to be doing.

This requirement for structure and timetabling is one that I still have today. Even though my morning routine is always the same, I need my phone alarms to go off at set times to make sure I am staying on track and know what I am doing next.

I am told by family members that the girl who existed before 31 December 2002 also lived by timetables. I am told that this is proof that we are one and the same – even if I don't identify with her. But I think that her motivation was different, and that is critical.

Abi once explained to me the concept of *locus of control.* Someone with an internal locus of control would believe that everything that happens to them is within their power. For example: 'I lost my job because I was no good at it'. A person with an external locus of control feels as though they have no control over the things that happen to them. For example: 'I lost my job because my boss is a jerk and has it in for me'.

Pre-accident Sarah created timetables because she was in control of her world. She started her day at university at 7:30a.m. – thirty minutes before lectures – because she loved the quiet study sessions. She finished her day when she had completed her work in the library, or after she had visited Richard. The hours in between were also hers to fill.

I use timetables to tell me what I *should* be doing. Appointment times, social events, the time I must be at work ... it is all predetermined by someone else.

It appears to me that that Pre-accident Sarah had an internal locus of control and that I have an external locus of control. *She* controlled her world through timetables, while I let my timetables control what I do.

No one around me realised that. They saw a girl who created a world of structure and timetables, just like Pre-accident Sarah had done. They had no idea that it was a different girl making them.

Sarah was alive. *Sarah* was home. *Sarah* was getting back to her old life.

I longed for the opportunity to demonstrate my independence. *I was well.* I just needed to prove it to everyone.

As far as I could tell, the main problem was that I didn't have the ability to go anywhere by myself. I didn't walk great distances. I still used a walking stick and was not very stable on my feet. Our house was in a quiet court that turned onto a busy highway. Even if I had been able to negotiate my way down the driveway, there was nowhere to walk once I got to the highway, other than an uneven dirt track that turned to mud in winter.

I was determined not to drive again because I was scared that I might kill someone else. I did not trust that I would not have another stroke and end up killing someone else's son, daughter, mother or father. But if I was going to be independent, I had to learn another way to get around.

I had to learn to use public transport.

My occupational therapist supported this idea, and we practised catching the bus together.

Catching the bus from the rehabilitation centre with my occupational therapist was a very staged affair. We waited together for the bus, then we'd both board and she would talk me through the steps while the bus driver patiently waited.

I learned to count out money so that I had it ready before I approached the driver. I learned to identify the type of information to give the bus driver, so that he could give me the correct ticket. I learned to place my money on the tray. I learned how to validate my bus ticket by tapping it against a machine on the bus. I learned to stay in my seat while the bus was moving, and not walk up and down the aisles talking to other passengers. I learned how to push the red button so that the bus would stop at the next stop. I learned to wait for the doors to open before holding onto the handrail so that I could carefully climb out of the bus. I learned everything there was to know about *how to catch a bus.*

I was desperate to try it by myself just to prove to everyone that *I could.*

But my family had other ideas.

The local transport in Mt Eliza was incredibly unreliable. Locals considered it acceptable that buses came either fifteen minutes before or after their scheduled time. They were happy to wait thirty minutes at a bus stop for a fifteen-minute bus trip. For my family, thirty minutes by myself at a bus stop was a very long time. They were not confident that I would stay focused on the task. They worried that if I got distracted, I may stay in the bus stop and miss the bus. Or worse, I could get stuck in town and not remember the bus number to catch home. Or, even worse again, I could forget to get off the bus and end up at the bus depot, forty-five minutes away. As far as they were concerned, there were too many things that could go wrong.

My occupational therapist came up with the solution, and Abi was the one to see it through.

Late one morning, Abi's old brown Torana pulled up out the front of our house. Her arrival should have looked suspicious. People don't ordinarily take a day off work and drive for an hour and a half to 'pop in for lunch'. But I missed that fact altogether. Abi drove us to Mt Eliza shopping centre, and we chose a small cafe where we could watch the people and traffic go past. Abi went inside to place our orders, while I found a table under the trees. I felt very grown-up being allowed to make that decision for us.

I did not notice when our meals came to the table. I had been distracted by a large old bus that had pulled into the stop across the road, and was watching people as they filed on and off the bus. Abi took this opportunity to instigate the plan.

'You know what would be cool?' she asked, with a glint in her eye. 'Wouldn't it be great if you catch the bus back home? We could race and see who got there first!'

By allowing me to catch the bus back home from Mt Eliza, my family could evaluate two things. First, they could see whether or not I could catch the bus and arrive at my destination safely. Second, they would know how I interacted with the driver. The concern was that I would start to tell him stories when I bought my ticket, and hold up the bus. This was very likely to happen, as I was still telling stories to everyone I met.

I was oblivious to all of this, and thought that it was a great idea the very instant she said '...you catch the bus'.

'If I run, I can catch that one!' I exclaimed excitedly, reaching for my walking stick.

'Well, no. Not that one. It's going the wrong way, and we have to have our lunch first. You can catch the next one.'

We ate our lunch, discussing how I was going to catch the bus. I promised Abi that I knew which ticket to get, and how much it would be. Just to show her how organised I was, I counted $1.10 from the coins in my wallet and stacked them neatly on the table.

The waitress came to the table to take our empty plates.

'How was everything?' she asked.

'Great!' I told her. 'Well, actually, I wouldn't know. I can't smell. That means that I can't detect most flavour either. But the sandwich looked very pretty. I had the chicken sandwich ...

you know, the one with salad in it?' I was worried that I would upset her by not knowing what the sandwiches tasted like – *because people are expected to know those sorts of things.*

'I would like to stay for longer,' I added, 'but I can't. I am going to catch the bus! Look, I have the right change.' I gestured to the pile of coins that were neatly stacked on the tabletop. 'I have to wait at the bus stop over there...' I pointed in the direction of the bus stop, as if to confirm that I knew that it was the right one. Another piece of evidence that *I knew how to do this.* The waitress shifted, balancing the plates in her hand. She smiled at Abi and me, 'Well, that sounds nice...'

'Sah, we can't keep this lady all day. Come on, we'd better get going,' Abi said, giving the lady an apologetic grin for my onslaught of exuberance. I picked up my coins, and we headed across the road towards the bus stop. Abi watched for a gap in the traffic and stepped onto the road, holding her hand out behind her. I reached for her hand, and obediently followed. This is still a routine we have when we are together today, even though I am perfectly capable of crossing the road. Green man or not. There is no discussion. Abi is always there to safely guide me across.

The five-minute wait at the bus stop seemed to take forever. Finally, the old blue bus lumbered up the main street and pulled in beside us. There was a *whoosh* as the doors slowly opened. I held on to the handrail, and made a show of being careful as I climbed the steps to meet the driver.

'One two-hour concession, Zone 3, thanks,' I said to the driver, in my clearest, most grown-up voice. I turned to see if Abi had noticed how well I interacted with him. She was standing at the base of the steps, watching me, smiling. I calmly walked up the aisle and sat down on a brown vinyl seat next to the window, determined to show Abi I could do this. As the bus pulled out, the excitement was too much. I forgot how 'grown-ups' were supposed to act. I stood up, and started waving at Abi through the window, laughing and smiling like a happy little four-year-old.

The bus made it back to our house long before Abi got there. By the time she drove up the driveway, I was happily sitting on the front porch singing, 'We are the champions!' at the top of my voice, through the wisteria.

I had done it.

On 5 August 2003, I caught the bus by myself for the first time.

I was truly independent.

Chapter Eleven

Sarah is a Little Bit Different

'Do you want to feel the hole in my head?'

My newest best friend was an elderly lady at the bus shelter, bundled up in a parka with a shopping bag at her feet. I didn't know her name. All I knew was that she was waiting for the bus. Only two bus lines came to this bus stop, and they both went to the shops. We were probably going to the same place.

I had introduced myself moments ago by explaining that I was catching the bus to the shops because I didn't have a licence, and that I didn't have a licence because I had been in an accident. *Then,* in order to prove that I was okay, I invited her to feel the hole in my head.

She looked surprised at the suggestion. I didn't understand why.

'It's okay. I don't mind. It's not a hole *really,* more like a dent,' I assured her. 'They had to drill a hole in my head to relieve the pressure, but it has mostly covered over now.'

There was a look of uncertainty on the elderly lady's face, as though she wasn't sure what the polite thing to do was. Up to this point, all she had to do was smile and nod. She tentatively extended one hand, and I reached out and guided her finger to the dent in the top of my skull. She let out a gasp.

'Feel it?' I encouraged her.

'Yes, dear. That's quite a hole,' she stammered, clearly surprised. I released her finger, and she quickly pulled away, tucking her hands into the warmth of her pockets.

'Yeah. It's only a dent now. It used to be a hole,' I bragged. 'But then they filled the hole with paste to protect my brain.' I didn't know if this last part was true, but had recently read that *that* was done in mouse surgeries, so guessed that it could have happened to me.

Out of the corner of my good eye, I saw a bus trundling up to the shelter. The lady reached down to her bags.

'What number is it dear?' she asked. I didn't have the heart to tell her that I didn't know. My eye wasn't good at reading numbers that far away, and I often had to wait until the bus stopped before I learned where it was going.

'735,' I lied, but was confident with my guess. Mum, her girlfriend, and I had recently moved to Blackburn, and I had studiously spent hours learning the timetables of all the local buses.

The bus pulled up, and there was a *whoosh* as the doors opened.

'Blackburn?' the bus driver called out through the doors.

'Yep!' I replied, a little too enthusiastically, but proud that I had guessed the correct bus.

'Oh, darn,' the elderly lady said with a sigh. 'Do you know when the 733 is coming?'

'He's about five minutes behind me. I can take you as far as Blackburn road,' the bus driver offered.

'That's okay. I'll wait.' The elderly lady smiled politely and sat back down on the bench to wait for the next bus. She watched me with a curious, uncertain expression as she clutched the bags that rested at her feet.

'Okay then. Well, it was lovely to meet you. One day, I'll stay with you and catch the 733,' I promised her as I climbed onto the bus. I swiped my ticket and took a seat next to a large man who was struggling to hold an old cardboard box on his lap. I leaned across him and gave the elderly lady a cheery wave as the bus pulled away.

'She's catching the 733,' I explained to him. 'Where are you going?'

He hesitated with his response. 'Uh ... Blackburn.'

'Wow! So am I. I'm catching the bus because I don't have a licence, I had a stroke while I was driving my car...' My new best friend shuffled the box uncomfortably. It was a long ride to Blackburn.

Despite achieving 'independence', I did not understand many social rules of the 'outside' world.

I wanted everyone to be my friend, and I believed that simply talking to someone *made* them my friend. I approached strangers at the bus stop and started conversations the only way I knew how – by inviting them to feel the hole in my head.

Some people were genuinely curious and would feel the dent in my skull; others did so in an attempt to stop me talking. But, because very few people outright refused my offer, I believed that it must be acceptable behaviour, and a good way to make friends.

It wasn't, of course. People would go back to their shopping, or get on the bus, and I would never see them again. Bus drivers, however, could not escape my attempts at friendship, and made up a large portion of what I considered to be *my* social circle.

I sat up the front of the bus and chatted happily, just as I did with ambulance drivers and the people who chauffeured me between medical appointments. When we reached the end of the bus route, I would wait with the drivers on their ten-minute break, still talking and telling stories about my accident and my recovery, before riding the bus back home.

I felt safe with the bus drivers, because they worked to a timetable. I trusted timetables. I am not sure whether or not they listened or cared about the stories I told them, but they always greeted me with a smile. They all knew who I was and where I lived. Several times, I fell asleep on the bus, and the bus driver had to pull over and wake me up to let me know we were at my stop.

There were other social rules I couldn't quite grasp. For example, I wore my clothes wrongly. I could not understand why jeans were worn with the zipper at the front, but skirts were worn with the zipper at the back. I insisted on wearing all my skirts backwards, because that is where I *knew* the zip should go: at the front. Even if it meant that the prettier side of the skirt was facing backwards. The zip always had to go at the front.

I wore a bright-red bandanna to cover the bald patches on my scalp. This would have been fine, except I also still wore an eye-patch over my right eye. This gave me the overall appearance of a pirate. A happy little pirate, with her skirt on backwards, a walking stick, and a lisp. I was oblivious to this. As far as I was concerned, I was independent, I was functioning and I was making friends. The world was exciting and full of promise.

For me, Blackburn was a much more 'social' suburb to live in than Mt Eliza. There were more buses, for a start, so I had a greater pool of potential 'friends'. In addition to that, there was a large shopping centre just up the road from our house. This became an entirely new source of potential 'friends'.

Considering that I still relied on the walking stick, the walk to the shopping centre was a long, arduous journey. The trips started out manageable enough. For the first ten minutes, I'd slowly make my way along the even cement pathways through the quiet backstreets. The next stage was a little trickier. It took me fifteen minutes to negotiate the uneven wood chips in the park, and then the soft, short grass on the oval. At the end of the oval, a little pathway that wound its way around the tea trees, up a slope and out onto the highway. This was the hardest part of the journey. The climb itself wasn't so bad, it was the hum and movement of traffic roaring up the highway at the other end of the little path that was hard for me to filter. *That* was what took all my energy.

I could never stay at the shopping centre for long. Filtering the noise and activity was an exhausting exercise. I had to contend with the colourful displays of assorted goods and bright lights flashing from shop windows. Each store blared music louder than the store next to it. Escalators hummed as they carried people between levels. Customers rushed to and fro, avoiding eye contact with sales people touting their goods from stands in the walkway.

On one occasion, as I walked through the shopping centre, a lady smiled at me from behind a perfume stand.

'Good afternoon,' she called. She was very nicely dressed in a black suit with her hair tightly pulled back. I thought she wore too much makeup, but didn't want to offend her by telling her so.

'Hi,' I replied, giving her an enthusiastic smile. 'How are you today?'

'Great. Having a wonderful day. How about you?' She probably gave the same answer to all her customers, but somehow, she still managed to sound spontaneous and genuine.

'Good, thanks. I've just come up for a walk. I live across the road,' I replied, looking at all the pretty coloured bottles she had lined up in front of her. 'There sure are a lot of bottles here.'

'Yes,' she agreed. 'That's the great thing about working here. It's not like those stalls in the department stores. We're an independent seller, so we have access to all the latest fragrances.'

I liked this lady; she was as chatty as I was. She was probably already my friend.

'Have you tried the new Curious?' she asked.

'Um. No, I don't think so.' I wasn't exactly lying. I didn't know that *Curious* was a perfume. Even if I had known that, I wouldn't have been able to try it, because I couldn't smell. She smiled as she held up the bottle. She *must* be my friend...

'It's the latest release by Britney Spears. Here, try some.'

I had absolutely no idea what she was talking about. I thought Britney Spears was some sort of pop singer. Nonetheless, I obediently offered her my wrist, then held it up to my nose pretending to enjoy the scent. I tried to imagine things that *Curious* was associated with.

Puppies. Learning. Exploration. Did these things smell too?

She must think so. She appeared very excited about the scent of Curious.

'You're in luck today,' the young woman said, smiling. 'We have a special deal going on the Britney Spears gift set. It is a three-piece set, with Curious, Fantasy and Midnight Fantasy.'

They smell, too? I wondered privately.

The lady held up a box dominated by an image of Britney's face painted in a ghastly rainbow of makeup. Beside the hideous image, there was a small plastic window that displayed three delicate little bottles inside. 'It's only $35 today. It's normally $60. The sale technically ended yesterday, but I can do it for you for $35 today,' she added casually.

I had no idea what she was talking about. She was rattling off all sorts of numbers and perfumes and talking about things that I didn't know even *had* a smell. I was struggling to keep up. But she was so happy and optimistic about her bottles of perfume, that I really didn't have the heart to tell her I couldn't smell. I was so embarrassed by the situation that I had forgotten that I wasn't actually there to buy perfume.

'But you know what?' she said, excited that I appeared to share her enthusiasm for the pretty bottles. 'I think you'd be far better off buying the gift sets...'

Two hundred and eighty-one dollars later, I picked up my paper shopping bags full of gifts for Abi, Greer and Mum. I was no longer embarrassed. I was actually quite proud. I had made a friend without talking about the accident. I was so proud of myself for making a *genuine* new friend, that I swung my bags the whole way home.

That night, I presented Mum with her gift of Versace Crystal Noir. I was careful to point out to her that I did not know what it smelled like, but that I chose it for her because the box was red and black. I knew she liked red and black because she supported the Essendon football team. Mum appeared a little embarrassed as she politely tried to explain to me that the box *was* nice, but she wasn't sure why I would go out and buy perfume. I told her it was because my new best friend at the shopping centre said I should.

I put Abi and Greer's perfume bottles in my room, but forgot to give them to them.

I don't know where they ended up.

Despite being an excessively exuberant young woman who smiled at everyone, I didn't have the ability to maintain friendships. To strangers, I was a smiley girl with her skirt on backwards, talking about the brain.

The problem was that I still had the egocentricity of a four-year-old. Everything in my life was about *me*. The only things I cared about were my research, my music, my medications, my appointments and my recovery progress. I still had very little understanding of the fact that people had other interests too.

Mum's girlfriend suggested that I buy a therapy dog. The idea was that the therapy dog could re-introduce me to the world. First, he would teach me about responsibility. I would be responsible for his training, bedding, hygiene, health and food. Second, he would get me out of the house. All dogs need walking and social interaction, so I would have to take him down to the dog park where he could run and play with other dogs. Finally, he would teach me how to interact with other *people.* When I took him to the park, I would be left to face other dog owners. I had to learn to make conversation with other people.

The thought of a therapy dog usually conjures up images of intelligent dogs like golden retrievers, border collies or kelpies.

That's why Harvey was such a surprise.

Before presenting me with the idea of getting a therapy dog, Mum needed to determine whether or not I even *liked* dogs. I knew what dogs were, and had met dogs that belonged to other people, but Pre-accident Sarah hadn't especially cared for dogs. What if I didn't either?

One morning, Mum and her girlfriend took me down to the local pet store. I assumed that the reason that we went to the pet store was so that they could play with the puppies and kittens. They liked cute things like that.

I stood in the doorway of the store, leaning on my walking stick, looking inside and waiting for my eyes to adjust to the light. I was wearing the eye-patch less often, but my left eye was still very weak and took much longer to respond to changes in light than my right eye. To compensate for this, I would close it, winking at strangers as I entered brighter or darker rooms.

The pet store was a long, narrow cacophony of movement and colour. It took every ounce of energy to filter and decipher the information before me. The front counter was littered with all sorts of paraphernalia: brochures, pet toys, magnets and anything else that the sales assistant might be able to convince customers was essential for the happiness of their pet.

An eerie blue light shone through large fish tanks that lined the walls. Fish of all sizes and colours swam among air bubbles that popped as they reached the surface, and water filters buzzed monotonously. Opposite the fish tanks were shelves of fish food, plants, little plastic castles, and fish bowls. A few birdcages were evenly spaced along the length of the store, housing a pathetically small collection of budgies and galahs. The birds were just as distracting as the fish. They banged on mirrors and danced on the spot as they squawked at each other and to customers. In between the cages there were stands of mirrors, swings, birdseed and trays.

The far wall was lined with shelves of assorted pet food, rubber rings and squeaking plastic toys, soft balls with bells, and pet leads.

Along the back of the store were four cages. The two cages to the left contained kittens that tumbled over each other, performing for potential owners. The two cages to the right each contained three equally active puppies.

A middle-aged sales assistant approached us.

'Hi, I'm Barbara. How can I help you today?'

'We were wondering if we could see some of your puppies?' Mum asked.

'Certainly.' Barbara led us past the fish tanks, birds, and cats to the two cages of puppies.

'These three have already been sold.' Barbara pointed to one of the cages. 'But all of these are available,' she said, guiding our attention to the puppies in the other cage.

Mum and her girlfriend were delighted when Barbara handed them one of two little puppies who had been wrestling at the front of their cage.

Pleased with herself that her customers were happily playing with the puppies, Barbara took a step back, and found herself standing next to me.

'Gorgeous, aren't they?' she asked.

Mum and her girlfriend may have been delighted, but I was less impressed.

I was too exhausted to humour her with a polite answer. 'Not really. I don't get the point. What do they do?'

Barbara stammered at my response. 'Well, give it time. They are smart little things. They can learn anything.'

'Humph.' I leaned on my walking stick and looked about for somewhere to sit and rest.

Mum's girlfriend asked to see the other active little puppy too and Barbara happily obliged. *Thank God they don't like kittens too.*

I was feeling the effects of filtering the noise and movement in the pet store. Angry and tiring rapidly, I hobbled to some seats near the birdcages. I slumped in my chair, snarling as I waited for Mum and her girlfriend to finish playing with the puppies.

With the other two puppies gone, the only thing left in the cage was a little white ball of fluff curled up in the corner. It turned out to be a small white Maltese Shih tzu.

Barbara picked up the white Maltese Shih tzu and handed him to Mum as a trade for the puppy that she had been playing with.

'How do you like this one?' she asked.

The white ball of fluff wriggled around in Mum's arms, and she dropped him on the floor. He shook himself off and looked at his surroundings. The world was different on this side of the cage. *So many places to go.*

He took a few steps, stumbled, caught himself and took a few more steps in my direction.

'What an odd little thing! Look at his underbite!' Mum's girlfriend said, laughing.

'Oh, don't worry about that. That's a characteristic of the breed. They all have underbites when they are this small. He'll grow into his jaw,' Barbara said, and I decided she would have made an excellent used car salesman.

I didn't know what they were talking about. I didn't know what an underbite was. What I saw was an uncoordinated little puppy-shaped mess who was in desperate need of a haircut. I watched him as he trotted down the aisle towards me. The clumsy little ball of knots hadn't quite mastered the art of walking. As he attempted to swagger past me he tripped on his front paw and fell, landing on my walking stick. I lowered myself onto the floor and pulled him into my lap to evaluate the quality of his legs and get a better look at him.

I still don't get the point of these things. And this one appears to be broken.

Two large black eyes looked up through an unruly fur fringe. The rest of the store vanished. I was no longer bothered by the fish or the birds or the cats or Barbara.

There was only Harvey and me.

Mum knew that we had found the therapy dog.

And I wasn't leaving the store without him.

I had named him Harvey after Harvey the rabbit in an old James Stewart movie of the same name. Harvey the rabbit was an imaginary, six-foot-tall white rabbit. Harvey the puppy was a tiny white dog. They were both white and would both become someone's best friend and teacher. That's where the similarity ended.

And so, the small Maltese Shih tzu puppy came into my life to teach me about the world.

I loved Harvey so much that, in those early days, he was spoiled rotten. He snarled and growled if he didn't get his way. I knew that he had to be trained, but I didn't know how. I searched the Yellow Pages for a therapy dog trainer, but there didn't seem to be anyone who could train a dog like Harvey. Eventually, I found an ad with a cartoon of an aggressive-looking bulldog and the promise 'We will come to you'.

Harvey is aggressive. I can't drive him to a dog school. Perhaps this is the dog trainer I need?

What I didn't realise was that this *particular* dog trainer taught police dogs and security dogs ... not spoiled little Maltese Shih tzu puppies with attitude problems. But I suppose after meeting me (and feeling the hole in my head, and receiving a lecture on strokes, car accidents, and the correct way to decipher ambiguous statements), the dog trainer realised that I needed help.

He agreed to take on Harvey and me as clients.

Sometimes I think we trained Harvey too well. It was more than learning *sit, come* and *stay.* It was a complete personality change. Harvey went from being an antisocial snob towards other dogs to being the most social and submissive fellow in the park.

It didn't matter who the other dog was, Harvey was eager to make friends with everyone. He would race up to other dogs and throw himself on his back in a submissive pose, as if to say: *Take me, I'm yours!*

At first, it was embarrassing. But then I realised his antics were a great conversation starter with the other dog owners. I didn't need to talk about me. I could talk about him.

When I reflect on Harvey's change, I can't help but see the similarities. I know the stories of Pre-accident Sarah. In my imagination, she was an antisocial snob. Then, in 2003, *I* woke up – smiling and waving at everyone, eager to make friends. Only, I was a twenty-year-old woman, not a puppy. Making friends as a puppy is easy. Making friends as an adult is a lot harder.

It wasn't long after I left the rehabilitation centre that I started to truly understand that I had once been someone else, and then there had been a terrible car accident. I survived. But I did not think that luck had anything to do with it.

It was the talent of the surgeons at Monash Medical Centre that saved me; and the skills of the doctors and nurses who worked in ICU that kept me alive; and the staff at the rehabilitation centre who taught me to walk again. It was the comfort, familiarity and patience of my family that kept me sane. My own effort thus far, as far as I could see, had been relatively small.

I loved everyone around me and had the constant need to tell them so. With one eye still covered with the eye-patch, I was one giant smiling eyeball, with brown spiky hair, a red-bandana and her skirt on backwards. I would smile and wave at strangers, doctors, family members and friends, and try to strike up a conversation about the accident. I had long since forgiven the doctors for always asking silly questions.

There was one group of people that I did not get to see: the people who saved me from the initial trauma. I had not been to ICU to meet the doctors who made the decisions during that first critical month of my recovery. The more I learned about the accident, and the role that the staff in the ICU had played, the more I wished to meet them.

People were surprised when I said that I wanted to visit the ICU. It apparently wasn't the done thing. I suppose they expected that it would be traumatic for me. They were scared that I would see other people who were unconscious and think *My gosh, that was me ...* That was never going to happen though. I had no memory of being unconscious. I could not identify with other patients in any way, shape or form. The only other patients that I knew were Toby, George and Robert. *They* were not unconscious.

The ICU patients were strangers. Strangers who were asleep. I was not phased by strangers. All I cared about was seeing and thanking the doctors and nurses. I knew that without them I would not be alive.

Abi, Greer and Dad took me to ICU at Monash Medical Centre. I don't know how they arranged it – ICU is not the type of place where you simply 'pop in'. I don't remember the drive there or entering the hospital. But I do remember my surprise trying to get into ICU.

Entering ICU was unlike entering any other ward.

For one thing, the doors were locked. I nervously shifted my weight over my walking stick, thinking that it probably wasn't such a good idea to go into a place that was locked up without an appointment. *We'll probably get in trouble for trying.* But the lock didn't surprise anyone in my family. Greer calmly pressed the button on the intercom.

'Good afternoon. It's Sarah Brooker and her family here, come to see Dr Danks.'

While I knew there had been many doctors involved, Dr Danks was the only name that I actually knew from the whole saga. I was nervous and excited to finally meet him.

Then it occurred to me: it had been over three months since I was discharged from ICU. They had probably had millions of patients since January. *How would anyone remember me?*

'One member at a time, please,' the voice over the intercom said. I turned to look at Abi.

'We can't all go in, Sah, it's not that kinda place. Maybe just take Dad. Greer and I will wait here.' She took a seat on one of the couches outside the ICU, trying to act casual to calm me down. Greer put her hand on my shoulder. 'It'll be okay, Sah,' she said, smiling. Dad took me by the hand, and together we walked through the doors and into the world of ICU.

There were beds all around us, and a strange, comforting sound. *Slurp. Suck. Whoosh.*

Why is that so familiar?

Dad and I approached the nurses' station, where we were met by a tall male doctor and a nurse. The doctor wasn't carrying a clipboard; in fact, he had his hands in his pockets. Both of them were smiling. The doctor introduced himself as Dr Danks. The nurse introduced herself as Anita. They were the heroes of my story, and they were smiling at me. I was as nervous and as excited as a child meeting Santa.

'Hi. You probably don't remember me. My name is Sarah. I was in here in January. I had a car accident. You saved my life...'

Anita smiled again, and threw out her arms to give me a hug. 'Of course we remember you, Sarah. It's lovely to see you!'

'Yes, Sarah, we remember you. Anita was one of the nurses working here when you were in ICU,' Dr Danks explained. 'You may not know any of the other nurses here today.' He looked around the unit for anyone else who may have known me. I didn't remember *anyone,* but I didn't have the heart to tell him.

'I just wanted to come in to say thanks ... you saved my life.'

Overwhelmed and shy, I was unaware of how often I was repeating myself.

'Well, that's fine. We don't get many people coming back to say thank you.' Dr Danks smiled. 'We never get to see people after they leave. Thanks for the thought, Sarah.'

I thought this reflected very badly on the alumni of ICU. Didn't the other patients realise that they owed their lives to these people? Why wouldn't they come back?

Dad understood what the doctors were really saying.

Very few people who had been unconscious in ICU for three weeks survived to come back and say thank you.

I was one of the lucky few.

I go to uni next week. And again, my life will have meaning. There was more I wanted to tell you, but I have no words. This is either a miraculous end or a wonderful beginning. It may even be part of the story. In fairy tales, the hero has to lose the first part of the final fight — or any of his fights, for the audience to be wishing him to win. I showed you all I was capable of winning — I did the degree. Then I had to lose for a while to keep you all on your toes.

A year on from the accident, my future felt assured

Chapter Twelve

Honourable Mentions

In April 2004, I turned twenty-two.

I had been out of rehabilitation for almost a year and was leading what I thought was a normal life. The Traffic Accident Commission (TAC) paid for my therapies, medicines, and other 'accident-related' expenses, which included a gym membership. I spent as much time as I could walking on the treadmill, watching people who were brave enough to run. Off the treadmills and away from the gym, my ability to negotiate uneven surfaces had improved, but I still needed the walking stick if I was to go any great distance. I was relying less on other people to drive me around, and more on public transport. I had learned every bus route in Melbourne and knew most of my local bus drivers.

Most importantly, I had started honours at Monash University. I was one of seven students in Richard's neuropharmacology lab. To say that I was excited would be an understatement. I was an eager student. Too eager.

I had stopped introducing myself to strangers by talking about the accident. Instead, I introduced myself by saying 'Hi, I'm Sarah. I study the benefits of nicotine on the brain. Turns out it could be neuroprotective against Parkinson's disease. But I suppose it depends on what you want: your brain or your life.' Then I'd launch into the structure of my project. I never noticed their eyes glaze over. *Surely everyone is as fascinated by this as I am?*

Richard received the brunt of my unbound enthusiasm. He was, after all, my honours supervisor. He was also the one person in the world I believed was as excited about nicotine and neurodegeneration as I was. Unfortunately for Richard, this was not the case. While it was true that Richard *was* excited about the effects of nicotine in Parkinson's disease, he also had lectures to write and deliver, tutorials to plan, assignments to mark, grants to write, and committee meetings to attend. On top of that, there were six other students in his laboratory demanding his attention. I only had my project to think about.

Many years later, Richard confessed that he had once thought that *he* was a morning person.

Then he met me.

Correction.

Then he met me on *cortisol.*

Richard *first* met me before the accident. Pre-accident Sarah. She was certainly enthusiastic and dedicated to her work, just as I was. But she was more measured. She respected his time, and only came to visit him in the late afternoon.

Post-accident Sarah. Me. I was a different kettle of fish. I appeared to have no regard for Richard's time. Not in the early mornings anyway, after I had taken my cortisol. I was unnaturally energetic. 'Exuberant' he'd said.

For the two years that it took me to complete honours, Richard could not avoid starting his day by listening to one of my excited rants. He would sneak into his office early, hoping to get *something* done before I arrived. Alas, no sooner would he sit at his desk than I would bound into his office, high on cortisol, with new ideas about the direction of the project, or something I had read, or a thought that I had on the bus.

'I think it's the α-7 receptor. The α-4 might only be short term. Do you think they work together?' I would pant excitedly. Only after I had exhausted all my ideas would he be free to go on with other work.

However, the grass is always greener...

Occasionally I didn't come to visit him. Those were *really* the times to worry. If I wasn't in Richard's office early in the morning, high on cortisol, telling him my latest plan, then I must have been somewhere else in the university, high on cortisol, seeing that plan through. The problem was that I chased new plans and ideas like a puppy chases butterflies, bouncing one way and then another, and Richard could never be certain *which* butterfly I was chasing, or how much damage would be done by the time I caught it. He needn't have worried. I always came back.

And I only ever caught interesting butterflies.

For all of my enthusiasm in the morning, eventually the cortisol wore off, and I settled into the silence of study. I spent most of my time alone at a desk in the corner of a small office that had been allocated to the postgraduate students. There wasn't enough room for a computer – just my books and their confusing words, silence and me.

Every day at 11:30a.m., my phone alarm went off. I'd pack up my articles, tidy my desk and make the long trek across campus towards the arts faculty. I'd walk wearily across the green lawns, passing undergraduate students who laughed and joked with each other loudly as they played a on campus lawns, drank at the university bars or crowded outside lecture halls. They were blissfully unaware of what a life away from university could bring.

Exhausted by *their* exuberance, I'd push open the heavy wooden doors of the Menzies building, and silently catch the lift to the eleventh floor. Without stopping to talk to anyone, I entered the Sleeping labs and collapsed onto a bed that was reserved just for me.

After ninety minutes, a second alarm on my phone would ring to wake me up. I slowly made my way back past the energetic undergraduate students to my small desk in the isolated student office in the pharmacology building, and continued my reading.

I doubt that anyone noticed I was gone.

Occasionally, the other students from Richard's lab came into the office. I never knew what to say to them. They were different to my friends at the bus stops. My attempts at conversation with people at the bus stop always involved Harvey, my project or my accident. I had never learned what to say after that, because I never saw those people again. However, the other students already knew about Harvey, they knew I had been in an accident and they already knew about the brain. What was left?

In the early days of honours, they attempted to include me in their conversations, but this nearly always resulted in failure, it was obvious that we had nothing in common. When they asked what I did on the weekend, I'd respond that I honestly could not remember, but that I probably played with Harvey. When they asked me whether or not I had seen a particular movie, I'd respond that I honestly couldn't remember, but probably not. When they spoke about food they liked, I'd respond that I could not detect flavour, so didn't really have a favourite food. When they spoke about TV shows, I couldn't follow the plots, so kept away.

I was scared of the other students. I couldn't understand how they had time to do anything other than study. *Why don't they find this hard?*

No amount of studying could have prepared me for mice.

I was terrified of them; they were small black assassins, darting about in their cages, sharpening their teeth and claws on dry mouse food, waiting for the opportunity to attack. Unfortunately, when you are investigating the effects of nicotine on the mouse brain, working with mice is unavoidable.

A responsibility that we all had was to check mice regularly. This is meant to be an easy task: look through the lid; make sure that they were all moving, had food and water; and check that the sawdust 'bedding' was in a reasonable state. No need to take them out of their cages. Just look.

One night, while doing my mouse checks, my worst fears were realised. It was late at night, I was exhausted. The mice in the animal house squeaked and scratched among the sawdust in their cages. I was certain that they were all trying to burrow out of their cages.

As I reached up to collect my first cage, two mice wrestling each other on the other side of the room kicked a plastic tunnel against the side of their cage. I did not understand the innocence of the noise, and thought that they had somehow lifted the lid of their cage.

I screamed and dropped the cage that I had been holding.

The plastic cage crashed open as it bounced on the floor, spilling sawdust and mouse food at my feet. Somewhere among the racket, a small, brown figure darted across the floor and under the cage rack along the far wall.

Every fear that I had became a real possibility.

There was a mouse under a mouse rack, ready to attack me, and I was alone.

I needed help.

I called the one person who I thought was brave enough to face a mouse: Mum. People didn't argue with Mum. Surely, mice wouldn't either?

In between tears and gasps, I relayed my dilemma to her over the phone. There was silence.

'What is it that you want me to do about it, Sarah?' Mum asked, confused.

To be fair, she was home, forty-five minutes away. And she didn't have a pass to get into the building, let alone clearance to enter the animal house. Realistically, there really was no way she could help.

Feeling foolish, I agreed, and told her I'd think of something. I hung up feeling desperate, scared and alone.

Richard lived even further away from the university than Mum, so there would be no point calling him. *Who else would have a pass to get into the animal house?*

I considered the problem while I cleaned up the mess on the floor, keeping my eyes on the corner where the mouse was hiding. *I know you are there. I know you are waiting to come out and attack me. I just have to find a way to catch you.*

Of course! Security can come and help me!

I used the animal house phone to dial security. The security guard who answered sounded just as puzzled as Mum had been. *What did I expect him to do about it?* But, as 'assisting university students in distress' was a part of his job description, he agreed to help.

My hero.

Minutes passed. They seemed like hours. I waited, listening anxiously to the rustle of the mice in their cages. Finally, the animal house door opened.

My hero entered the room.

'Righto. So ... uh ... where is this mouse?' he asked.

'I think it is under here ... but it's been there forever, and I have no idea when it is going to come out and attack us!' I whispered with earnest urgency.

'Okay. Well, we have to encourage him to come out.'

'It's a her. Girls are worse than boys when they're on their own,' I cautioned him.

'Is that so?' he asked, momentarily distracted by this new piece of information. I had no idea if this was actually true, but I wanted him to be careful. He needed to know all the risks that he was taking if he was going to approach the horrific beast.

'Well, either way, we have to get her out. I'll *shoo* her out from this side. You get ready with your cage, okay?'

I was horrified by this idea. Approach a mouse who was not in a cage? When *she* had the upper hand with her jumping abilities, claws and teeth? *Was he insane?*

Apparently.

He banged the end of the animal rack with a broom. The mouse darted out across the floor. I screamed again, and dropped my mouse cage. Luckily, the mouse was under the cage. We'd captured the mouse!

But the problem was not yet solved.

The mouse was now trapped under the cage, much like a spider under a glass. The problem was that we would not have been able to slide paper under the cage, because, unlike a spider, the mouse would fall straight through. We had to find something harder.

I reached for a plastic folder. 'Will this do?' I asked, scared that my hero might nominate *me* to slide the folder under the cage. He didn't. He smiled at me and accepted the folder.

'No need to worry, the hard part is done. We have her in the box. I'll fix this bit up.' He calmly slid the plastic under, inverted the box, and carried the whole ensemble to the bench. But the saga was yet to finish.

'We have to get the lid on, and we have to put food and bedding in there too...' I said nervously, the tears in my eyes threatening to start again if this catastrophe didn't end soon.

My hero, who had been quite pleased with himself for helping to catch the mouse, looked at me quite confused. 'What do you mean?'

'Well, I am not allowed to just leave her there like that. I have to put her into a cage that has sawdust, and a tunnel, and food, and then I have to put a water bottle on the top...'

'Can't you do that?' he asked, a little annoyed that the job was going to be bigger than he thought.

'Well ... uh ... okay. Yeah, of course,' I said, trying to sound more sure of myself. 'I should be okay now that she is back in the cage.'

I *was* perfectly capable of setting up a fresh cage. But there was no way that I was going to take the lid off a cage that already contained a mouse. Only, I didn't want to tell him that. I didn't want him to do more than he had to, and I would have liked to remain friends.

'Yeah,' I said again, 'It's okay. I just needed help getting her in a cage. You are right. Thanks for that!' I smiled to let him know I was okay. It was a fake smile, but I was good at those. He *had* to walk away happy. It didn't matter how scared I was. At that point in time, it would have been far worse to have him be angry with me. I felt foolish enough as it was.

'Okay, then,' he said, walking towards the door. 'Have a good night.'

And with that he was gone.

My hero had deserted me.

Thirty minutes later saw a mouse in a cage, full of sawdust and food and all things good, and a nervous, exhausted girl slumped in the corner crying. It took another ten minutes to work up the courage to look through the lids of the remaining mouse cages.

They *looked* fine. I picked up my bag, let myself out, and didn't look back.

I didn't go into the animal house much after that.

My memory still wasn't perfect. I forgot a lot of things, but I was too proud to admit it. To hide my memory loss, I wrote down everything that happened. In reality, this just made me work slower.

When I did surgeries on mice, I timed and recorded how long it took for each mouse to go to sleep after receiving anaesthetic and then how long it took them to wake up again. I scribbled down the exact amount of any drug given to each mouse and the speed at which drugs were administered. I stopped mid-surgery to record the exact coordinates of the burr hole I drilled into each mouse skull, along with the amount of time it took me to locate and drill it. I even made notes about how much hair I shaved off their head.

There may not appear to be any harm in excessive note taking, but if you were having brain surgery, and the surgeon stopped to record things like this every few minutes, would you think they were *more* or *less* efficient? Thankfully, my note-taking requirements did not hurt the mice at all, but it was unnecessary and inefficient.

This is just *one* example of how poorly I managed my memory. I was terrified that one day someone would ask me about something I had done, and I wouldn't be able to answer. They would find out that I was a fraud – that I wasn't the girl who had been accepted into honours in 2002. They would see how bad my memory loss was, and I wouldn't be allowed to keep doing honours.

But I don't think the university would have kicked me out of the lab for not knowing how long a mouse's tail was, or how many whiskers they had before or after surgery. But they may have questioned my abilities if they knew I *was* recording such information ... who knows?

Mouse surgeries started early in the morning, preferably before 7:00a.m.. The earlier I started the better, because I heard that this the easiest time to put mice under anaesthetic. I didn't want to test that theory.

One morning, the bus came fifteen minutes late. It was bad enough that this would put me fifteen minutes behind in surgeries, but I had been standing in the rain in the dark for nearly twenty minutes. When the bus doors opened, the bus driver was met by a very cold, wet, angry little scientist.

I wanted to let him know that I wasn't happy. Frowning my darkest frown, I slammed my walking stick onto the step before lifting my foot to climb onto the bus. My stick slipped on the wet surface and gave way beneath me. As I fell, I hit my head on the door and I jarred my neck. Hurt, humiliated, and angry, I picked up my walking stick and hobbled back home, covered with mud and cursing that I would be late doing surgeries.

Mum was shocked to see me limping up the driveway covered in mud.

She wanted me to go to hospital to get my neck looked at.

After the usual x-rays, we learned that no vertebrae were damaged. They told me at the hospital that I had to wear a neck brace for the next two weeks.

This was a disaster! I was at the end of a two-week period of mouse surgeries. I had one more day to go. With a neck brace on, there was no way I would be able to do stereotaxic surgery on mice. That would mean that the past few weeks of treatments were wasted.

It was a horrible situation to be in.

There was only one person in the world who I could trust to help me.

Greer.

Greer was a nurse. She had been in hospitals and knew how to handle blood. Surely, she would be able to do stereotaxic neurosurgery on mice...?

My darling older sister was too polite to say no. She didn't have the heart to tell me that there was a large difference between a theatre nurse and a ward nurse. Nor did she point out that there was a large difference between mice and humans. In my mind, the principles of the surgery were the same, so they may as well have been the same thing.

That night, Greer found herself at Monash University, in the neuropharmacology lab, helping me perform stereotaxic neurosurgery on mice. She stood on the other side of the lab bench, watching as I reached into the cage to pick up the first mouse. The small mouse squeaked as I turned it over and injected the anaesthetic.

'What's my job?' she asked, reaching for one of the lab coats that hung on the door beside her.

'Right, well, let's see...' I said, placing the mouse under a heat lamp on the surgical bench. I thought about all the things that needed to happen, and how best to explain them.

'Once they are under anaesthetic, you are going to have to shave their heads, because I can't bend my neck on that angle.'

Greer picked up the clippers that I had already placed on the bench. 'How do you shave a mouse's head?'

'It's easy, just shave against the grain. You'll get right down to the skin. We only need this region here,' I explained, pointing to the top of the mouse's head. Greer carried the clippers to my side of the bench and sat on a stool in front of the surgical mat. She watched the sleeping mouse.

'They aren't actually so scary when they are asleep,' she observed. 'They are actually quite cute.' Greer gently picked the mouse up. 'Look at her – she's beautiful! Her hair's so sleek and shiny!' she said.

I wasn't converted. 'Just leave her there until she's fully under,' I instructed. I still didn't trust mice. Greer did as she was told. We spent the next few minutes getting things ready for the surgery. I handed Greer medications, and she drew them up into syringes. I looked over at the mouse, who was sleeping happily under the heat lamp.

'She's asleep enough for you to do her head,' I told Greer.

Greer took a breath as she picked up the mouse again.

'Okay then, *dar-ling*,' she said, impersonating Zsa Zsa Gabor. 'Welcome to my salon. What style would you like today?' Greer held up the unconscious mouse to her ear, feigning a conversation. 'Excellent plan, *darling!* Bald is all the rage right now. Come, take a seat!' She gingerly put the clippers to the mouse's head, and pushed forwards, making a perfect bald dome on the top.

'How's this?' she asked with hesitation.

The haircut was perfect. I knew it would be. This was my big sister Greer. She was a nurse. She could do anything.

'Perfect.'

Greer smiled, proud of the job she had done. She would shave twenty more heads that night – and have similar conversations with each of them.

'What next?' she asked with enthusiasm.

'Now, I need you to get her into the stereotaxic frame. I can tell you the coordinates, and will have to drill the hole myself, but you can get her set up.'

Greer looked at me. 'Stereo what?' she asked as Eddie Murphy.

I gestured to a small surgical frame that would keep the mouse's head in position while I drilled through the skull and inserted the drugs into the brain. 'You need to lift the mouse, and put her head in that part. Greer picked up her bald little friend, and carefully manoeuvred her into the frame.

'You put your little head here now, and mind where those teeth go!' Eddie Murphy had been replaced by Mrs Doubtfire. 'There you go, possum!'

Greer sat back and let me drill the hole and administer the drugs that she had prepared earlier.

I leaned back, rubbing my neck from the awkward position I had been in.

Greer loosened the bars from the mouse's ears.

'You have to watch her now,' I explained seriously. 'She has to stay under the heat lamp until she starts to wake up. You have to make sure she is warm and breathing.'

Greer nodded solemnly as she took on this responsibility.

I picked up the next mouse to deliver the anaesthetic. Greer gently stroked the back of the first mouse.

'It's okay, lovey. You'll make it,' she told it softly. She turned her attention back to me. 'Ready for me to shave her head?'

'She's almost under. Give her another minute.' I advised.

We waited another minute or so, and Greer picked up the second mouse, becoming Zsa Zsa Gabor, and going through the whole routine again. Suddenly, she remembered the first mouse. She looked over, and saw that she *still* wasn't awake.

'No, Shrek! Stay with me!' She took on Donkey's persona. 'If you see a light, stay away from the light. Stay away from the light!' She reached over to the mouse, picked her up gently and stroked her back again, looking at me with pleading eyes.

'She still hasn't moved, and she feels cold. Is she going to be okay?' Greer pleaded. Suddenly, the mouse gave out a little *squeak* and kicked a leg – almost as though she had heard Greer's concern.

Greer, who had not yet held a *conscious* mouse, screamed and dropped the mouse on the heat mat. For the first time in a long time, I laughed in the lab. I reached over and picked the mouse up, cradling the semi-conscious creature in my hand.

'It's okay, Greer. It might just be a little startled.' I offered her the mouse. 'Here, would you like to put her into a cage?' Having recovered from her initial shock, Greer took the mouse from me, and carefully carried it across the lab to where a series of fresh mouse cages were lined up under their own heat lamps.

We powered through the surgeries. Greer was running between heat lamps, shaving heads, and dialling numbers on a machine she'd never seen before. I was drawing up medications, and slowly rolling the syringe to expel them into the correct regions of the brain, and of course, taking notes.

Once again, my amazing big sister showed me just how brilliant she is. I don't know many other people that could do neurosurgery with no prior experience of surgery, neuroscience, or animal research. But I do know that it was the first time that I had a friend in the lab, and it was fun.

That night with Greer, I realised that I *needed* people.

Pre-accident Sarah may have thrived in the isolated environment that I had created, but I couldn't. For me, research was too lonely, and I would not survive that world.

There had to be something else...

Chapter Thirteen

What Are You, If You Aren't a Neuroscientist?

I did complete honours. I loved the brain too much to do anything else. At the time, I thought that my research would change the world. Alas, Parkinson's disease still exists, and I think my beautiful thesis can only be found can only be found gathering dust on the shelves in one of the libraries at Monash ... if it was ever printed.

Towards the end of 2004, I closed the door on my dreams of being a neuroscientist, took a breath, and turned to search for another door. But I didn't know what any of the other doors looked like. *What do you do if you aren't a neuroscientist?*

I asked Mum, who was a teacher.
I asked Dad, who was a policeman.
I asked Greer, who was a nurse.

They all responded with the same loving advice that anyone would give: 'You can be anything you want'.

This didn't help. I was looking for specifics. What did other people *do?*

Abi was everything. She was a researcher and tutor, worked with homeless people and was my hero. But I couldn't do the same things she did. She was so much smarter and stronger than I was, I didn't think that I could do anything anywhere near as well as she did. Plus, it would be copying. That wasn't nice.

Greer was starting her nursing career. She got to help people, just like the nurses helped me in hospital. I thought I'd like to do that too. But she had to live in the city in a flat with her friends, and I couldn't do that. Inner-city Melbourne was far too big and busy, and I didn't have any friends to live with.

Adam drove a taxi in Queensland. I couldn't do that. I didn't have a taxi or a licence, and I didn't live in Queensland.

Mum was a teacher at a TAFE. She was very smart. I didn't think I would be smart enough to talk to people about the important things they spoke about at TAFE.

Dad was a policeman in communications in the city. As far as I knew, he had always been a policeman. I hadn't always been a policeman, so I didn't think I could work on communications.

Harvey was a puppy. He didn't have a job.

There was nothing that I could be *except be* a neuroscientist.

I didn't know how to be anything else.

The TAC still provided transport to and from medical appointments. I enjoyed this, because it meant that I got to see the chauffeurs, all of whom I considered to be my very best friends. Graeme was my favourite chauffeur. He had retired several years earlier, and drove periodically 'to fill in the time'.

Graeme already knew all about my accident, so while we drove, I chattered happily about Harvey, university or Parkinson's disease. Occasionally, Graeme told me about country music, politics, or gardening. One day, I presented Graeme with my dilemma.

'Graeme, what do you do if you're not a neuroscientist?'

'Well, I drive cars,' The crow's-feet around his eyes danced as he grinned at his own joke. I smiled in return. *Of course* he drives cars, but he wasn't a neuroscientist.

'No, I couldn't do that. I don't drive.'

'Well. Not yet. Never say never,' he responded.

We pulled up at traffic lights. Graeme looked across at my concerned face. 'You're really bothered, aren't you?'

I nodded. 'I just want to know...'

There was silence while he gave the matter some thought. His eyes, which normally sparkled blue with excitement as he turned puzzles over in his head, were grey and serious as he watched the traffic and considered my problem. The lights turned green.

'There are countless things to do, Sarah,' he said, breaking the silence at last. 'I can't tell you though. That's for you to decide.'

'I know, Graeme, that's what everyone keeps saying. But, *decide* what? How do I know what I can *decide?*' I protested.

'I tell you what...' he said as we pulled into my street. 'Make a list of all the things you like to do.' Graeme slowed as we approached my house. 'For everything there is to be done, there is someone else willing to pay for it. Look at me.' He looked across at me and winked. 'I like driving and talking to people. Who'd have thought that there would be someone to pay me to do *that* in a lovely car like this?'

Having made his point, he concentrated on turning into my driveway.

'So make your list. There will be something there.'

As soon as I got inside, I wrote down everything Graeme had told me.

Graeme usually gave good advice. I just had to figure out what he meant.

After thirty minutes of deep concentration, I finally had a list of things that I liked to do: I liked to help people; I liked to talk to people; I liked to research things; I liked to give people things; I liked to use computers; and I liked to play with Harvey.

There were only two people that I knew that got to do most of those things in their jobs: Janine and Catherine. Janine was my educational psychologist. She had been the one who had set up all the supports that I needed to complete honours. She arranged the sleeping labs, extensions on exams, speech-to-text software to help me write my thesis, and had helped Centrelink to figure out what sort of payment I should have been receiving. I wanted to help people just like she helped me.

Catherine was my case manager at the TAC. As far as I understood, Catherine was personally responsible for everything the TAC had done. In my imagination, she had organised: counselling for my family; all of my surgeries; appointments and payments for doctors, surgeons, procedures and hospital stays; reimbursements for medication; and booked the drivers and ambulances.

I didn't realise that Janine and Catherine had completely different jobs.

After all, they both *managed* the people that were involved in my *rehabilitation case.* In my eyes, the only difference was that Janine was more 'hands on', while Catherine worked in the background.

I had decided what I would be if I wasn't a neuroscientist. I was going to be like Janine and Catherine – *they won't mind if I copy them and do what they do.* I was going to be a *rehabilitation case manager.*

If I wasn't going to be a neuroscientist, I needed to leave Melbourne. Everything about Melbourne reminded me of the life that I had aspired to, but ultimately failed at. I had to choose somewhere new to live. I chose Adelaide.

From my family's perspective, my decision to move to Adelaide came from out of nowhere. But for me, it made perfect sense. In October 2005, Abi, Greer and I had flown over to Adelaide to meet Mum's new girlfriend. We stayed in a small backpackers in the middle of the city.

Adelaide was a beautiful country town with the courage to call itself a city. The only city I had seen was Melbourne, which was full of trams, cars, taxis, trains, noise, movement and people. Melbourne had hills and tiny, twisty alleyways. It had big grey buildings, and billboards with flashing lights. No matter how well I studied maps, I could never remember where I was going, or where I had been. Melbourne was chaotic and exhausting.

Adelaide, on the other hand, was organised and quiet. The CBD was set out in a grid that was a perfect little square, bordered by streets named North, East, West and South terraces. The buildings were smaller than those in Melbourne, and much older and prettier. I could see the mountains in the East from any point in the city, so I could always figure out which way I was facing.

The public transport seemed to have been designed for my damaged brain. Rather than running to and fro in all directions like the buses, trains and trams of Melbourne, Adelaide buses all ran directly to and from the city. All stops were numbered. If I could find a bus stop, I would be able to determine how far away I was from the city.

It was the most liveable place I had ever seen. It was paradise.

Harvey rested his head on his paws as he slept among the pillows on my neatly made bed. The afternoon sun shone into my bedroom, giving my room a golden glow. The scene should have been tranquil, had it not been for my boisterous squeals of triumph. I spun across the floorboards on my desk chair, laughing with glee and giddy with pride. An onlooker might have considered my dancing, spinning and laughing to be inappropriate. After all, all that I had done was write a list. But in *my* reality, I was 'discovering', and that was exciting and worth celebrating.

I had decided to move to Adelaide, but now I had to start planning how I would *become* a rehabilitation case manager. I figured I had to get some more qualifications. I didn't know what they were, but I was pretty sure that having an honours in neuropharmacology was not enough. Not if I was going to be a *really* good rehabilitation case manager.

Abi told me that I would probably need a Certificate IV in Social Work. I wasn't sure that I'd be eligible, it sounded like a degree *less than* honours. Then again, the advice came from Abi. A Certificate IV in Social Work was worth a try. It needed more research, and I was very good at research.

'Harvey, I'm the cleverest researcher in the world!' Harvey lifted his head, ears pricked up at the sound of his name. 'Come look, kiddo!' I gestured to him, pushing myself back to my desk. He jumped off the bed with the same lack of coordination that he had displayed on the first day I met him, and tumbled across the floor to my feet. I picked him up and held him on my lap so that he could see what was on the desk.

'Somewhere here,' I said, picking up two double-sided sheets of paper that were covered with colour-coded scribble, 'is the person who will help us in Adelaide!' Harvey panted, sniffed at the papers, and then lowered himself into my lap to continue the nap that my excitement had interrupted.

I had spent two hours creating a detailed list of all the organisations I believed might help me become a rehabilitation case manager. The more names I wrote down, the more excited I became.

I had very little insight as to how inappropriate some of my candidates were. I thought dog training centres could have been important, because Harvey was a therapy dog, and he had to be trained somewhere. IT training centres could also be important, because rehabilitation case managers needed to know how to use computers. Fitness training centres would be important because patients had to build strength.

Relationships Australia and the Mental Illness Fellowship of South Australia (MIFSA) may have also helped. But I wasn't too confident. *How was mental health involved in rehabilitation?* After some consideration, I decided that it didn't matter, and added them to my growing list.

I also researched details about the specific people that I needed to talk to. Educational background, sports clubs, home address, past jobs ... I didn't see anything unusual or wrong with doing this. In fact, I thought that it was quite important. I knew if I was going to have a conversation with someone, they would probably want to talk about themselves as well as my accident or Harvey, and I wanted to give them that opportunity. *That was how you made friends ... by showing an interest in the other person.* The result of my research was the two colour-coded sheets of paper, listing organisations, contact names, and personal details that I was now trying to show to Harvey.

'Pass me the phone, Harves!' I said, patting him on the head. He panted softly, his warmth giving me the comfort that I needed to calm down before making the first call. Awkwardly, I reached across his little body, over the computer desk, and tried to pick up the phone. Harvey wriggled, resisting any attempt at movement.

'Kiddo, I am sorry. I have to make these calls. Either you let me have the phone or you go back to the bed. What's it to be?' Harvey looked up at me, his large, dark eyes hiding under a mass of white knotted hair. He opened his mouth slowly, revealing his lower teeth in a Bubba Gump type of smile. *He never did grow out of the underbite. Barbara was wrong.*

After considering his options, the little white ball of fluff rolled off my lap and sauntered back to the bed. I immediately regretted giving him the option to leave. I reached for the phone and dialled the first number.

Every call I made was the same. I introduced myself to the person on the switchboard, and told them about the accident, Monash University, deciding not to be a neuroscientist, and my current plan to become a case manager. I even told some people about Harvey. *Then* I asked to be put through to the person who I had already researched on Google. Once I reached *them,* I started the story all over again.

Everyone I spoke to listened patiently, *ooh*-ing and *aahh*-ing at the right moments. Caught up in my conversation about *me,* I often forgot to use the personal information that I found on Google so that I could ask them about themselves.

Many of the training schools and colleges were hesitant to encourage me to enrol in anything. One training centre referred me to a disability employment network, saying that if I had a case manager there, *they* would help me find a job. I was confused. I didn't *want* a case manager. I wanted *to be* a case manager.

'No one seems to understand. No one wants to help me, boyo. A bit upset about that, Harvey,' I said, trying to be brave as I updated Harvey on the situation. I looked with dismay at the papers in my hand. 'No. A lot upset,' I corrected myself, screwing the lists into balls and tossing them into the bin. I straightened the coloured pens on the desk so that they were in the correct order for me to take notes properly, picked up a fresh piece of paper, and started again.

'If you want to learn something, Harves, you should really go to *university*,' I said, feeling very clever for the wisdom I was passing on. Harvey jumped off the bed and walked across to my feet, offering his support. Forty-five minutes later, I was squealing and spinning around the floor again. The University of South Australia had a course that was named after the *exact* thing I wanted to be – the Graduate Diploma of Rehabilitation Counselling. Pre-accident Sarah may have taken her time. She may have researched accommodation and employment *before* making her next move. I am told that she was meticulous like that.

I'm not.

I had found the course that I wanted. Surely now all I needed to do was meet the Program Director and ask him to help me enrol. So that is what I did.

Abi

When Sah was recovering, I was intensely obsessed with and proud and protective of her. Everything was about her achievements: her first words, her first steps, when she finally came home – all that still makes me cry. Sah was my fragile other half, and she needed protection.

Then, Sah left rehabilitation, and she started to become herself. She established her independence. She started to make decisions about her life and take ownership of those decisions.

As Sarah was gaining her independence, I could see Mum hovering over her in the same way that I did. Wanting to protect her, but hesitating, letting her try for herself. Watching Mum doing this was the first time I noticed how hard this must be for her, for anyone other than Sarah. Mum was the real protector, the real carer. Mum was the parent, caring for a twenty-something-year-old infant.

I had to take a step back and let Sah find her independence. So did Mum.

But instead of taking a step back, I shifted my protectiveness. I became fiercely protective of Sarah's independence. I saw complete logic to every decision she made, simply because she had made it. I was so proud of her for doing that, for owning her life. She wants to do her honours? Of course she does, she's brilliant! She wants to get up at

3:00a.m. every morning to go to Monash? Of course she does, that's how every honours program works! She wants to move to Adelaide? Of course she does. I'll drive her!

She wants to make friends with every person who she meets? Adorable!

I mean *every* person, by the way. She held up lines at the supermarket as she got to know the life histories of check-out people in the local supermarket. She made friends in elevators and on aeroplanes. On a one-hour plane trip from Adelaide to Melbourne, Sah once made friends with the people sitting around her and convinced them I would drive them wherever they were going once they got to Melbourne. *Don't get a taxi,* she assured them. *Abi will drive you.*

The following weekend, I packed my bags and flew to Adelaide to meet the Program Director, Professor Charlie Collins. This was the first step.

The whole expedition made me feel very 'grown-up'. I no longer relied on the walking stick and had long since ditched the eye-patch. I looked like everyone else, so I could pretend to be like them.

I understood what it was that I had come through, and how amazing my recovery had been. I laughed at myself for thinking that I had 'recovered' when I left rehabilitation. I had improved so much since then. I had an honours degree. I could manage my tablets by myself, make and attend appointments by myself, and catch a bus by myself. I even had Harvey to look after me and teach me about the world. I was researching my own life, away from Abi and Mum and everything else in Victoria.

Of course, I hadn't recovered. Not by a long shot.

I am quite sure that anyone who met me would have known that. I still spoke a lot and was fairly indiscriminate about the topic subject. I was still highly distractible, and unable to talk about the same thing or focus on the same task for very long. I still had extreme mood swings, and spoke like a child when I was excited. The only reason I thought I was grown-up was because I was being *allowed* to do things by myself – not because I actually had the ability to do them properly.

But I didn't understand that as I took my seat on the flight to Adelaide. All I knew was that I had a goal. I was going to forge a new path for myself, and the future looked bright.

I wasn't scared as I skipped through the university grounds towards Charlie Collins's office. I wasn't even nervous. I was excited. I was about to meet the man who was going to help me gain *real* independence. I had already emailed him, introduced myself and told him all about my plans. At the time, Charlie Collins may have been just a name at the end of an email, but he was the only name I knew.

Charlie's office was on the ground floor of a red brick building, with a view of a car park and a small green oval surrounded by gum trees. I imagined that it would be lovely to spend lunchtimes walking around that oval and finding a place to sit beneath a gum tree, where I could eat a vegemite sandwich. I said this to Charlie as I stood at his doorway, waiting to be invited in.

'Pretty view, do you ever eat vegemite sandwiches out there?' Charlie looked up from his desk, with a confused expression on his face, 'No. Uh ... I don't eat vegemite.' The confusion quickly changed to a smile as he realised who I was. 'You must be Sarah Brooker!'

I beamed. Forgetting I had emailed him and told him that I was coming, I assumed that he must have already heard of me. *Janine must have told him.*

'Yup. That's me. Harvey couldn't come along, he's at home,' I informed him, assuming that he knew who Harvey was too. He didn't, of course. All he knew was that a girl from Victoria had contacted him about the Graduate Diploma of Rehabilitation Counselling, and that she was coming to see him.

'So, Sarah, how can I help you?' He asked, motioning me into the room.

'I want to be a rehabilitation case manager,' I informed him, accepting his invitation and settling into a leather chair opposite his desk. 'Just like Janine and Catherine. See, a few years ago, I was in a massive car accident ... I had a stroke when I was driving my car. The had to drill a burr hole to reduce the pressure ... wanna feel it?' I offered, leaning across the desk to Charlie. Charlie reluctantly held his hand out for me to guide his finger into the dent in the top of my skull.

'It's not actually a hole anymore,' I said reassuringly. 'It's a dent.'

Charlie's finger found the dent, and he let out a small gasp. Inside, I smiled with delight that such a simple thing could shock everyone. It confirmed how unique I was, and I wore it as a badge of pride.

I explained that I had completed honours, and then decided to leave Melbourne. I told him the story of Harvey, and how he had helped me rediscover the world, and informed him, 'Now I am really good at talking to people, because Harvey taught me how.' I told him about the sad decision to leave neuroscience, and the happy decision to become a rehabilitation case manager.

'So all I need to do is get the degree, which I can do, because it's a graduate degree, and I have already graduated once. Well, I didn't go to the undergraduate graduation ceremony – because I was in a coma – and I won't go to the honours one, because I will probably have already moved here by then. But I'm pretty sure I don't need to have gone to the ceremonies ... do you think they will mind?'

Charlie, having been patiently listening to my stories, had barely had a chance to speak, apart from the appropriately placed '*ooh*' or '*ahhh*'. He appeared pleased that he finally got the chance to contribute. 'I agree. Going to a graduation ceremony is not important. Did you finish the degree?'

'Oh, yes,' I said, assuming that because he was not in the pharmacology department, he did not understand how honours degrees worked. 'They don't let you do honours unless you finish the undergraduate. I submit my honours thesis in November.'

Charlie smiled politely, as though he was not sure what to make of this strange, chatty girl.

'Well, Sarah, I am sure you'd make a great contribution, and certainly with your experiences, you have a lot to offer. But, it's not entirely up to me. You have to apply to SATAC, and you might like to look for work with a rehabilitation provider before you begin the course...'

I gave him *another* confused look, so Charlie slowly explained the process that I would have to go through, and gave me a brochure with step-by-step instructions detailing how to apply for a degree in South Australia.

Looking at the brochure and listening to Charlie, I began to get the impression that it was going to be very hard to become a rehabilitation case manager. *Everyone must want to do it, because it would be the best job in the world. That's probably why they need a whole government department (SATAC) to decide who gets to do the Graduate Diploma of Rehabilitation Counselling and who doesn't.*

'It's okay,' Charlie reassured me. 'It's really just a formality. You have plenty of qualifications, and if you follow all the steps, you're sure to get in.'

I agreed.

Our conversation ended with Charlie agreeing to see what he could do to help me get into the program. I left his office even more elated than when I arrived, and skipped and sang my way back to the hotel. I had made the right choice. I was going to move to South Australia.

All I needed now was a job and somewhere to live.

A few weeks later, I wrote Charlie a very professional and grownup email.

Hi Charlie,

I was very glad to have met with you at the UniSA open day a few Sundays back.

I am just writing to let you know that I have submitted my SATAC application to do the Graduate Diploma of Rehabilitation Counselling, and am now planning to come to Adelaide as soon as the honours year is over. If I can get accommodation, this could be early November.

During our conversation, you mentioned that there is occasionally work in the clinical rehabilitation world for people without qualifications (receptionist work etc.). I was wondering if you could please let me know if you hear of anything like that becoming available, so that I can forward an application or resume to the appropriate person.

I think it was a really good suggestion that I find work in a rehabilitation setting, because then I can get a better understanding of what goes on. Thanks for the tip.

Anyway, I would be really grateful for any help you could give me, but if it's any inconvenience then don't feel obliged, just say so. Thanks again,

Sarah Brooker

In my head, university, accommodation and employment were all a part of the process of moving to Adelaide. I needed all three. None could exist without the other two. So it made perfect sense to me to write to the head of department at the University of South Australia to ask him about employment and accommodation in

Adelaide – because as far as I could tell, he was deeply involved in the university process, so he must also be involved in the other two stages.

I had thought my letter to Charlie Collins was professional and very grown-up. I had used all the phrases I'd heard other people say, and I'd said 'please' and 'thank you'. I had gone to Adelaide and met him, and we'd spoken for an hour. In my mind, we were old friends.

Adelaide was real.

Part Four

**Adelaide
(2007–2016)**

Chapter Fourteen

Independence

The day I handed in my honours thesis, Harvey and I got into Abi's car and moved to South Australia. I rented a little three-bedroom house in a quiet street in Magill. The backyard was big enough for Harvey to play in, and we could walk down to the oval if he wanted to run around. It was perfect.

I received a small allowance off TAC. I wasn't sure why they were paying me an allowance. My case manager at the time explained that it was a 'Loss of Earnings Benefit' based on what my income would have been if the accident had not occurred. I didn't know who I was before the accident, so trusted whatever they gave me. It was enough to pay my rent, which meant I was independent. I was proud to be independent.

Everything I needed was close by. There was a small shopping centre with a supermarket, chemist, hairdresser, and vet on the other side of the university. I introduced Harvey to the vet immediately, so that they would know who he was if something ever happened. I found myself a doctor, neurologist, endocrinologist, ophthalmologist, dentist and an ear, nose and throat surgeon, almost as quickly as I found the vet for Harvey. I made appointments with each of them. I explained to them that I wasn't sick *at the moment,* but I thought it was important to introduce myself. If they were to be my new specialists, I had to get them up to speed as soon as possible.

Public transport was easy to manage. The bus stopped directly opposite my front door, and it didn't matter if I fell asleep on the bus, because the bus terminus was at the other end of my street.

I felt very grown-up and very organised. I was proving to everyone that I could make it on my own. However, before I could seriously believe that my *Moving to Adelaide* adventure was a success, I needed to achieve each of my three goals: *university, accommodation* and e*mployment.* I had university and accommodation – now I needed employment. *Real* grown-ups had jobs. CareerOne became my second-best friend, after Harvey of course. I spent hours searching through advertised positions and making applications.

'Here's one, Boyo!' I said across the room to Harvey. 'Zoo keeper! That could be me, couldn't it?' Harvey raised his eyebrows, yawned and put his head back down on his paws.

'The job description says *must be able to form relationships with animals.* I can do that. I have a pretty good relationship with you. Don't I?'

I reached out and scratched Harvey's head. After my last grooming effort, Harvey now had several bald patches across his scalp and his eyebrows were crooked. *Even with a wonky face, you are beautiful,* I thought, admiring the white ball of fluff that had brought me back to the world. Harvey lowered his head so that I could scratch the back of his neck, stuck out his bottom jaw, and gave a puppy-like smile.

I looked back at the advertisement. *Must have experience working with animals.* Ha! Well, I have that too, don't I? I did all those surgeries on all those bloody mice. That's experience!'

I continued reading down the page. The more I read, the more excited I got – the job was a perfect match. The zoo was looking for someone part-time, which I thought was a good idea because then I still had time to study. They wanted someone local. Even though I grew up in Melbourne, I lived in Adelaide ... so surely that made me a local?

It never occurred to me that, prior to seeing this advertisement, I never entertained the thought of becoming a zoo keeper. I was not suited to this work at all. I didn't understand that the 'animal experience' that I had was not sufficient and I had completely forgotten how scared I was of animals other than Harvey.

Armed with this naive enthusiasm and my ignorance of how inappropriate I was for the position, I set to work on writing an application. I was very careful to spell out how much I loved Harvey so that my future employers saw that I could form bonds with animals.

Two weeks later, I received an email from the zoo, informing me that '...on this occasion, you have been unsuccessful'. I didn't really understand why. I asked Harvey, but he didn't know either.

It didn't matter much anyway. Over those two weeks, I had submitted applications to be a sales consultant (I enjoyed talking to people, so thought I'd be good at sales), an IT support officer (I was confident using Microsoft Office and set up my internet by myself, so I *should* be able to figure out other IT-related things), a postal delivery worker (I liked to walk Harvey around the neighbourhood, and imagined that it would be fun to include him in my job), and a hairdresser (I was getting very good at using the clippers to cut Harvey's hair – surely people were not that different?).

I didn't get any of those jobs either. I wasn't sure why.

The only task I ever *had* to do was catch the bus into the city to buy a weekly bus ticket from the Adelaide

Metro office. I could have done the same thing at my local supermarket, but I liked giving the job the importance of its own special bus trip. This served a double purpose, as the Adelaide Metro office was just opposite the gym, so I could go play on the treadmills as a reward afterward.

One day in the Adelaide Metro office, I saw a leaflet on the counter for the Brain Injury Network SA (BINSA). I had seen other brochures about acquired brain injury before, but they were all information telling me how to recover. I didn't need a brochure for that – I'd already recovered.

The BINSA leaflet was looking for volunteers for their Springboard program, which helped people 'get back into life after ABI'. I knew all about how to get 'back into life', because I had achieved it myself and was living independently. I could help other people do that.

The leaflet also said that BINSA paid volunteers enough money for bus fares into and out of the city each day that they came in. I thought that was the same as being employed. To me, this meant that if I volunteered at BINSA, I would have achieved all three goals that I needed to make Adelaide a success.

This would show the world that I really *was* better.

I knew I would be a good volunteer, so I set off to tell BINSA the good news.

BINSA was in the southern wing of a grand old sandstone building in the heart of Adelaide. My sneakers squeaked along the quiet corridors as I made my way to BINSA's rooms, and I started to wonder if the businesses in this building were more professional than I had imagined. *I should have dressed like a nurse or a therapist!* I scolded myself.

I pushed open the heavy oak doors to the BINSA wing and stood awkwardly in the doorway as the joy and merriment of the people within washed over me. These people didn't *look* all that serious or professional at all. In fact, they looked like they were having fun.

People of all shapes and sizes filled the room. They chatted and laughed as they sat around a long table that was covered with sandwiches, fruit and water bottles. Some people were in wheelchairs, and used special devices to speak to their neighbours, who leaned over walking sticks or walking frames to hear better. Other people, probably volunteers because they had name badges, casually joined conversations and jokes, occasionally getting up to pass sandwiches or drinks up the table. Therapists in matching blue polo shirts sat evenly spaced around the table, also taking part in the merriment.

I watched as one old gentleman sat with a silent smile at the far end of the table. He picked up a piece of paper and wrote a few words down with a crooked, painful, slow hand. His neighbour read it out to the group, and they smiled and laughed, agreeing with whatever in-joke he had just made.

I had not seen such a happy community since rehabilitation. But, even then, this place was different to rehabilitation. The therapists were eating and sharing lunch *with* participants ... there was no separate staffroom. This was a place of total inclusion.

I approached a large lady in a floral shirt who sat at the top of the table.

'Is this BINSA?' I asked her quietly, self-conscious that I was intruding. The woman looked up from her sandwich. The crow's-feet around her eyes deepened as she smiled and welcomed me. 'Yes, dear, it is. I'm Christine. How can I help?'

I smiled, relieved she wasn't upset that I had interrupted her lunch. 'My name is Sarah. I want to be a volunteer. I was in an accident, and have an ABI, and I got better, and I want to help other people do that too.' I rattled all this off in a rush, trying to justify my being there.

Christine kept smiling.

'That's lovely, Sarah,' she responded, brushing a crumb off her face. 'Well, why don't you hang around this afternoon? Not volunteering, just seeing what we do. After that, you can decide if you want to join us.'

I didn't need to think about it. I *definitely* wanted to be a part of this community. I stayed for the afternoon and started volunteering the next day.

***

I fit right in at BINSA.

My job was to help participants through their individual programs by assisting during various activity sessions. This was fine by me, as the activity sessions were just like the things that I had done in my own rehabilitation. In occupational therapy, we played card games like memory or Go Fish, while some patients played harder games like chess. I wasn't very good at those, but I enjoyed playing anyway. In speech therapy, we played games with tongue twisters and counting. In physiotherapy, we played games like quoits. Sometimes, participants would lie on a plinth while physios like Brooke helped them move their arms and legs. During those sessions, all I could do was try to distract participants from the discomfort of moving stubborn limbs that were perfectly happy to remain immobile.

One afternoon, I sat in the speech therapy room with Kattie, a tall, dark-haired woman with partial paralysis. Kattie shared my love of knock-knock jokes and became the source of most of the jokes I told my family.

'Knock-knock,' she said slowly through the right-hand side of her mouth, while we waited for her therapist to arrive.

'Who's there?' I asked, eagerly anticipating a new joke.

There was silence in the small therapy room. I leaned forward, thinking I'd just not heard or seen Kattie respond. 'Kattie, who's there?'

Kattie stretched her mouth open, baring her teeth as she arched her neck and tilted her head to the side. She raised her right arm – a sign that she was laughing, enjoying the suspense. I missed this signal.

'Kattie, I can't hear you. Who's there? Maybe try to say the answer slowly,' I suggested. 'Or write it down with your good hand.' I looked around the room for a crayon that she could hold.

'No,' she slowly replied. 'I can't.' She bared her teeth again and leaned her head back, in pure bliss that her joke was having the desired effect.

'Why not, Kattie? What's wrong?' I felt my chest tighten. Maybe she wasn't laughing? Maybe she was choking? Having a seizure? I pushed my chair back, ready to run and get help.

'No,' she said again, eyebrow lowering and looking at me in earnest. 'I can't say who's there, because potatoes can't talk!' Kattie rocked her head back again and made a deep guttural sound as she laughed at her own joke. I smiled, relieved she wasn't in danger. Moments later, the meaning of the punchline sank in and I clapped my hands and shrieked with joy. 'Kattie! That's brilliant. I don't think I'd pull it off as well as you, but I can't wait to tell Abi!' I jumped out of my chair and went to get a pen and paper.

'Tell me again, from the top. I don't want to get it wrong!'

I appreciate now, that the knock-knock joke is neither funny nor hard to remember. But it was both for me. It had suspense and humour, and it had to be told in a certain order if you were going to trick your audience. And it involved a potato. I loved potato.

Kattie told other jokes too, but a lot of them were too sophisticated for my brain.

BINSA was full of moments like these. We would laugh, share stories, share cooking ideas, compare embarrassing things we'd done, and celebrate everyone's success together.

After two lonely years at Monash, I finally found a social circle that I fit into.

Once university started, I tried applying my new friend-making skills to my interactions with the other students doing the Graduate Diploma of Rehabilitation Counselling.

I tried sharing the jokes that Kattie had told me at BINSA, but no one laughed.

I tried to find other conversation topics, but I failed. Just like when I was doing honours, I didn't have anything in common with other students. No one else came from a background of neuroscience; no one else had a brain injury; no one else was from interstate; no one else knew Harvey. I came to the degree wanting to help people recover from accidents. Most of the other students came to the degree as professionals who just wanted to build their qualifications. They came to UniSA after a long, tiresome day at work, and just wanted the tutorials to end so they could go home, have dinner, and go to bed.

The nights tutorial had been about resources available to different service providers in rehabilitation. I had been able to bluff my way through the session, but I really had no idea what they were talking about. I couldn't figure out whether 'service providers' were the people providing the actual service, like a hospital, or the people paying for the service, like TAC. I knew that it was probably important.

'Who are the actual service providers?' I asked, as the tutorial was coming to an end. 'Do you mean the hospital or people that look after it, like TAC?' There was a snigger around the room.

'Here we go...' a well-groomed, tall blonde lady whispered to the man next to her. The tutor, who had become very patient with my questions, paused her summary. 'We are talking about WorkCover, Sarah.'

'*Ugh!* WorkCover! They wouldn't know a thing about service!' a plump woman across the room scoffed. She leaned back in her chair and crossed her arms. 'WorkCover are just out to get as much as they can. Clients aren't clients. They are numbers. WorkCover cut as many corners as they can to get to get the highest-dollar outcome!'

The plump woman confused me. She claimed to be a case manager, but she was nothing like Janine or Catherine. She was grouchy.

'But surely, if WorkCover wasn't there, none of these services would be paid for. Isn't WorkCover a type of insurance?' I asked.

'Insurance? Bah! That's a con. They are out to make as much money as they can!' she hostilely retorted.

The rest of the room was silent. Either they didn't have the energy to join in or they didn't care. It was up to me to defend WorkCover and TAC.

'No, you're wrong!' I argued back, surprised at my own boldness. The bossy woman glared at me from across the room.

'Pardon?'

'I mean, I know it's TAC, not WorkCover, but it's still the same thing,' I stammered. 'When I had my accident, TAC took good care of me.'

I looked around the room, imploring others to agree with me. 'They wouldn't have made any money at all. TAC paid for all my doctors and all my scans and everything! They even paid me a salary to make sure I was okay once I got better.' I was certain that this last piece of information would convince everyone that TAC *did* care.

'Don't be so naive! They wouldn't have paid you much,' the plump woman spat. 'Probably bottom tier, which is not where you would have been. Not after having done a degree! They probably didn't even assess your impairment rating properly. Too much paperwork.'

I couldn't believe what I was hearing. *Doesn't she understand that they were trying to help me?* My body tensed with rage.

'No. They knew exactly how well I was doing. They had all my medical records at Monash, and Catherine could have looked at them whenever she wanted!' I hadn't publicly fought with someone like this before, but she was *so* wrong in every single way, and so rude about it too. *Someone* had to defend TAC.

At the time, I believed that everyone involved in my recovery spoke to each other about how I was. In my imagination, Catherine would ask Dr Danks how I was doing, and he would ask a nurse to get my latest chart. I imagined that Catherine and Janine were old friends, who met up regularly to have coffee and discuss the merits of my honours project.

'Well then, you're one in a million,' she sneered. 'Most clients are just as bad as public insurers. How many people develop "anxiety" and "post-traumatic stress" after they have spoken with their lawyer?'

The other case managers shared knowing smiles.

A short woman with dark hair turned to face me. She rested her hand on my arm, as if she was breaking bad news. 'She *is* right, Sarah. Ever since anxiety and depression have been recognised as disabilities, heaps of clients suddenly added them to their list of symptoms.'

'But I know heaps of clients!' I protested, unaware that my face was now red and that I was shouting. 'No one at the rehabilitation centre would fake anything. Why would we add to our list of things to do? We all just wanted to get better! We all just wanted go home!'

It was true. Toby, Robert, George and I would not have faked anything. Why would we? We already had so much to relearn: standing, talking, eating, planning, doing puzzles ... why would any of us have added *anything* to that list? I couldn't recall anxiety or depression even being topics covered in rehabilitation. Toby's experience with the wheelchair was proof enough of peoples' resilience.

The room was filled with an awkward silence. The other case managers shared uncomfortable looks, unsure what to do about my outburst. The plump woman smirked. 'You're so naive. Once you get out there, Sarah, you'll see. It's not "roses" like that.'

I went home feeling quite dejected.

I also had trouble connecting with the students who *weren't* case managers. I didn't drink, smoke or go out on the weekends. I didn't have a mortgage, kids or a full-time job. I didn't understand politics, government or religion. I had no idea about the history of Adelaide. So, just like during honours, I was out of the loop in all of the students' conversations.

I tried to make friends by telling jokes, like we did at BINSA. But the UniSA students had already heard most of them, and they didn't think childish knock-knock jokes were funny. I attempted to tell one of Kattie's more sophisticated jokes: 'Henry falls over in the playground. His teacher says "Quick! Someone call Henry an ambulance!" So the children point at Henry saying, "Henry's an ambulance! Henry's an ambulance!"'

In all honesty, this joke didn't make sense to me. Surely, you had to set up that they were in a school playground, and that Henry was a student, and his teacher must have a name. Why did she think that the students would be able to call the ambulance? What were their school's phone policies? How badly was he injured that he needed an ambulance? Did he break his arm?

I modified the joke, in order to make it more understandable: 'Henry was a primary school student. One day, at lunchtime, he was playing on the swings. He swung too hard and fell off, breaking his arm so that it dangled dangerously by his side. Naturally, he was in a lot of pain. His teacher, Mrs Johns, was on yard duty and saw Henry fall. She didn't have first-aid training, but was really worried when she saw the state of his arm. She turned to the students, who had now formed a big circle around Henry, and she said, "No one is going to get in trouble. Does anyone have a mobile phone?" One student stepped forward. He was one of the tough kids, who was always breaking the rules. He wasn't mean, he was actually quite nice. His name was Jimmy. "Jimmy, quick, call Henry an ambulance." *Jimmy* took a look at the teacher, then pointed at Henry and said, "Henry is an ambulance."'

The students at UniSA didn't think this was any funnier than knock-knock jokes.

I just couldn't seem to make friends with people who hadn't experienced brain injury.

Early in second semester, I started a two-week placement with a nonprofit organisation called Arts Access SA. Arts Access SA's mission statement was to 'make arts accessible to people with disabilities'. I didn't know what that meant, and I went along to placement with the aim of finding out.

I had barely knocked when a small Irish woman opened the door. 'Sarah. Come in. Just in time!' She ushered me through the front door, closing it quickly to keep the cold out. 'We're brainstorming ways to promote *RadioCool*, follow me.' I didn't know what *RadioCool* was, who the strange woman was, or how she knew who I was, but I followed her anyway.

She led me to a small, cramped office. 'Shaun, Nate, Dom, this is Sarah. She'll be here for two weeks and will be working with us on *RadioCool*,' the strange Irish woman announced as we entered the room.

A well-dressed obese man put two giant paws on his knees and heaved himself out of his office chair, gold bracelets clinking. 'Sarah, welcome!' He said emphatically, 'I'm Shaun, I run this outfit.' I reached out shyly to shake hands, and nearly lost my arm in his enthusiasm.

A boy, swamped by his loosely fitting long shorts and oversized white T-shirt, swung around on his own office chair and waved his hand casually. 'Nate.'

'...and that's Dom,' the Irish woman said. 'He doesn't say much...' A tall, silent, boy looked up from the tambourine in his hand and nodded at me through brightly coloured glasses. 'And I'm Maeve,' she added.

It turned out that *RadioCool* was Arts Access SA's new radio program. Dom, Nate and I were to be the radio team. I felt like I was in my element, diligently preparing timetables, running sheets and scripts. Nate sourced the music. His only instructions from Shaun were to find artists with disabilities, so

Nate found a bit of everything – rap, folk, pop and even acapella groups. Dom was a DJ and was much more comfortable contending with the mixing desk than talking into a microphone. This suited Nate and me, as we both loved to talk. We were a great team, and I stayed with *RadioCool* for much longer than my two-week placement.

It was not until we did our special Christmas broadcast, in front of a live studio audience, that I understood what Shaun meant when he said that we brought '...disability and arts together through the airwaves'.

On the day of the broadcast, I lost control of the schedule. I couldn't make musicians stick to their allocated time slots. The introduction had been allocated thirty minutes, but only took twenty-five. The following act had only taken four of their allocated nine minutes. I was terrified that we would run out of broadcast material, and that the last ten minutes of *RadioCool* would be dead air.

There was nothing I could do. I did not have a script to fill in the gap. Luckily, Arts Access SA had invited a local ambassador for disability arts, Quentin, to attend the broadcast. Quentin could see my distress and came to my rescue.

'Don't worry, Sarah. There's nothing that the crowd can't fix,' he said, and calmly took the microphone. He introduced himself live on air, without a script, and worked his way around the audience, casually interviewing people about how much fun they were having.

When he approached a young girl with Down syndrome, I was mortified, thinking that surely she wouldn't be understood over the radio. But then I saw the look on her face. Interviewing her had nothing to do with whether or not her words were intelligible. Quentin had seen past her ability, and empowered her with inclusion. At that moment, she was a part of the *RadioCool* team. That was all that mattered.

I understood what the real value of Arts Access SA was. We were really bringing people together through the arts. They had done that for me, and now I was doing that for other people.

With Arts Access SA I had friends *and* I had a purpose.

At the time, I thought that people weren't aware of the effect that my brain injury had on my behaviour. I still didn't have much insight into it myself. I didn't realise that I was (and still am) highly distractible and moody. It took an enormous amount of effort to grasp new ideas. I struggled with abstract sentences and still spoke like a child when I was excited.

It was very obvious to other people that something was *not quite right.*

I suppose it was those same odd behaviours that attracted me to Alan.

Alan was my first real friend who had not known me before the accident. He did not have a brain injury, but was just as odd as I was. I didn't realise when I first met him, or even after our first few meetings for that matter, how much I needed to find someone who was like me.

Or how much of an effect that person would have on my life.

Chapter Fifteen

Alan – A Different Kind of Person

Alan and I met through my Uncle Peter.

I had heard stories about Alan before. He sounded like someone that I should be scared of.

Alan owned a restaurant in the Adelaide hills. He was a brilliant chef who also happened to be an intelligent businessman with the resourcefulness, connections and charisma required to keep his small restaurant afloat.

To his friends, Alan was a hardcore environmentalist, farmer, accountant, and a storyteller. He was also something of a practical joker. Apparently, he once convinced a young man from the city that he could talk 'sheep', and that all that nonsense about using dogs to round stock was a myth – all you had to do was ask them politely to move paddocks and they did.

One summer's night, not long after I moved to Adelaide, Peter, his partner Eddi and I were outside on the patio, enjoying the relief of the cool change. We were all waiting for Peter's friend Alan to arrive. Peter manned the barbecue, meticulously turning sausages, steaks and onions, while Eddi and I sat on lounges on the deck, making small talk and swatting away mosquitoes. At long last, a cheery British voice called through the front door. 'Hello? Anyone home?'

Eddi sprang up to let their friend into the house. There were muffled noises as she led someone down the hallway. A short while later, she appeared on the patio, admiring a bottle of wine. 'Is this from the restaurant?' Eddi asked over her shoulder.

'No. I picked it up off the side of the road,' laughed the stranger. Eddi led her friend to my side of the deck to introduce us.

'Alan, this is Peter's niece, Sarah. Sarah, this is Alan.'

I regarded him with caution. He did not *look* scary. He was about my height, with a greying beard, short brown hair, and sparkling blue eyes. He wore a pair of old Blundstone boots, with holes in the side where his bunions poked through, and a faded grey and white short-sleeve shirt, with a pair of bright pink reading glasses that poked out of his torn top pocket.

'Pleased to meet you, Sarah,' he greeted me cordially.

At that stage in my recovery, I was still unsure about how to go about making friends. I ran through my checklist of things that I was confident talking about. Alan didn't know Harvey. Alan wasn't a neuroscientist. Alan knew about my accident. The only way to converse with him must be to continue talking about the accident. So, as I stood up to shake his hand, I told him the same thing I said to most people.

'I was in a car accident in 2002. They had to drill a hole in my head to relieve the pressure on my brain. Well, it's not actually a hole now, it's a dent. Wanna feel it?' Alan obliged, and put his finger in the hole in my skull.

'Meh!' he said, feigning to be unimpressed. 'I know golf courses with larger holes than that.' Peter and Eddi rolled their eyes at the lame joke. Alan and I laughed.

The night was full of this type of playful banter.

Alan included me in jokes and laughed at the jokes that I told. He was cheeky and encouraged me to join in as he poked fun at his friends. Alan teased Peter relentlessly about (dis)abilities on the golf course, and fussiness at the barbecue. Peter laughed and teased him back about being overly cautious with money, and an extreme environmentalist. Later in the night, Alan stole Eddi's glass of wine, and gave me a wink as he hid it under the table. When Eddi playfully demanded that he give it back, he raised his hands and protested innocence. 'What?'

I did not escape the pranks. I got up from the table to get a glass of water from the kitchen, and returned to find my entire dinner plate was missing. Alan grinned at me and smiled. 'What?'

I had never been included in light-hearted games like this before. I had always been the frail girl who had been in an accident and needed protecting. But that night, Alan treated me just like any of the grown-ups in the room. I was fair game for some of his pranks, and a co-conspirator in others.

It had been almost three years since the accident, and I had never felt inclusion like this before. Previously, I had only ever found social acceptance among other people with disabilities. We understood each other's capabilities and experiences, and formed friendships characterised by innocence, safety and protection. I was an 'other' among people *without* disabilities. I didn't fit in. I didn't understand their lives, interests and opinions, and that made my otherness more apparent to them, and lonelier for me.

That night with Alan, I learned that *everyone* was an 'other' – not just people with disabilities. Alan showed me that it was okay to laugh at each other's otherness.

I met Alan again a few days later, at a golfing tournament in Adelaide. I don't play golf, and don't know much about it. From my understanding, it is the complete antithesis of my abilities.

Golf is a serious game where people must stay silent so that someone else can concentrate very hard and hit a small ball into a tiny hole that is a very long way away. I can't do any of those things. Nonetheless, Peter promised that it would be a fun day out.

I trust Uncle Peter, so off we went.

Everything about the club lounges was testament to the serenity and orderliness of golf. Sunlight streamed through the windows, making the lounges feel bright and pleasantly warm. The walls were neatly lined with trophies and plaques. Men dressed in beige and white mingled in small groups. They chatted merrily as they organised themselves into teams for the tournament.

Peter walked over to a counter to register, and I wandered over to the windows, drawn by the spectacular views. The club lounges looked out over the entire golf course, commanding a peaceful view of long, green fairways lined by tall gum trees and sporadically dotted with white sand bunkers and waterways.

It was not long before I realised that I could not see a path that led to the first hole. The only way down would be to climb down a steep the hill in front of the lounges. *Surely they don't expect us to do that?*

A knot began to form in my stomach.

Peter interrupted my thoughts when he called me over to meet his friends.

As I approached the strangers, I became self-conscious of my own attire. All the men around me were dressed in matching beige or white polo shirts and trousers, with clean white golf shoes. I had on bright-blue sneakers, a blue denim skirt with torn white lace, a bright-pink polo top and a yellow hat, which covered the blood-red bandana that held the hair out of my face.

I felt like a peacock trying to find refuge among a bevy of swans.

'Where's Pinky?' Peter asked one of the swans.

Pinky? What sort of name was that?

'Gone to organise the carts,' the swan replied.

I looked out of the window with horror as I realised what the carts were for. Golfers were going to ride them down the hill to the first hole.

Golf was not going to be as pleasant as Peter had promised it would be. I was going to spend the whole day surrounded by swans with peculiar names like *Pinky,* who were going to take those carts down the steep hill, and surely crash and die.

'All organised. I got the last two carts,' I heard a familiar voice say behind me. I smiled as I recognised Alan's British accent.

I turned to say hello and paused, shocked at what I saw.

It was Alan. Just like me, he had apparently not got the memo about the swans.

Alan was a flamingo.

Leaning casually on his golf club as though it was a walking stick, Alan smiled from underneath a bright-pink cap. He wore a matching bright-pink golf shirt, which was tucked into a pair of elasticised pink trousers. His golf shoes had clearly been coloured in with a pink marker pen. His pink reading glasses were tucked in his top pocket, just as they had been on the first night we met.

Peter later explained that Alan was known as Pinky at the golf club because *this* was his usual attire. Legend had it that one day his (ex) wife washed his golf clothes with a red shirt, and it stained them all pink. Rather than buy a whole new outfit, Alan bought a cheap pink cotton cap at an op shop and coloured his shoes in pink. Of course, Peter also conceded that it was possible Alan just wore pink to stir the pot.

I never found out the true reason. I suspect it is a bit of both.

Either way, without waiting for me to get over the shock of seeing him dressed like a flamingo, Alan smiled his wonky smile at me, 'Sah-Bear-Sticky-Bear!' he exclaimed. 'Are you with us then?'

'Yep. I guess so,' I replied, my face turning the same colour as Alan's outfit. 'How do we get down?' I looked with trepidation at the steep hill, which, in my mind, had now become a cliff.

'Roll,' he suggested. 'Or walk. Or we could use the cart.' Alan beamed at me, as though he'd reached a solution. 'You can either walk with Uncle Pierre or ride along with me!'

I didn't have the courage to tell Alan that I was too scared to get in the golf cart. Nor did I share my theories about the number of accidents that must have happened going down the cliff of death. But I would much rather stay with him than with the bevy of swans that surrounded Uncle Peter. So, I followed Alan to the row of old golf carts.

Peter had not seen us walk off together. If he had, maybe he would have stopped Alan. My family were still very protective of their little peacock who had only recently recovered from a car accident.

'You're not driving then?' Alan asked as I clumsily climbed into the passenger seat.

I looked at him in horror. I had started driving again since arriving in Adelaide, but this felt like a very different situation. *How would I know how to drive a golf buggy?*

Alan swung into the cart and sat beside me, resting his hands on the steering wheel. He turned to face me and waggled his eyebrows, his blue eyes glinting with mischief. 'I'll drive. You ready?'

'What for?' I asked.

Alan laughed again and turned on the golf cart. He steered us through the parking bay to the edge of the very steep cliff of death.

'You're not going to drive down *that?*' I asked, nervously laughing and praying that he was only pretending.

'Why not? There is no other way down,' Alan responded, dimples growing deeper in his cheeks. 'Yeee-haaaa!' he screamed, and we started to roll forwards.

Uncle Peter looked up to see Alan and me flying down the hill in a golf buggy at a speed much faster than it was ever designed to travel.

Golf was *definitely* not the quiet game that I had imagined it was. Not when Alan was around.

It was refreshing to be around someone who was as different as I was, and someone who laughed at things as much as I did. It was not long before Alan and I sought out each other's company often, and not long after that he became my partner.

There was so much that drew me to Alan – he made me laugh, he made me feel included and he didn't treat me any differently because of my brain injury. But there was something else about him that fascinated me. Alan had a glorious skill: he knew how to talk to people. It was magic to watch Alan work the floor at his restaurant. He would circulate from group to group, telling stories and jokes that made them laugh, and making people feel at home.

I couldn't do any of that.

Alan was the complete opposite to everything I was. And yet, Alan and I made the same kind of social faux pas. The difference was, Alan didn't care.

Take, for example, our sense of dress.

Ever since I had been able to dress myself, I had worn skirts backwards. I had spiky black hair that was hidden under a bright red bandana. I had no knowledge of how to coordinate colours, and could not gauge the appropriate dress code for any event. I was terrified to put a new outfit together without first consulting Abi or Greer to find out if I was wearing clothes correctly.

Alan was famous for wearing pink, no matter the occasion. He had bright pink glasses that he wore at the restaurant, and they were his trademark. He did not own a single jumper or pair of boots that weren't full of holes. He could afford far better clothes and boots, but why bother? He was comfortable.

Then there was our inability to remember jokes.

I couldn't tell a joke to save myself, and often either added too much information and forgot what the joke was about or, when I did make it through the joke correctly, I forgot the punchline.

Alan made no attempt to hide the fact that he forgot jokes. He had a list that he had written out and pinned to a notice board in the restaurant kitchen. His staff often witnessed him reading through them, laughing, and then going to entertain guests with them in the restaurant.

We were a peacock and a flamingo in a world of swans, and I was happy.

I had known Alan one month before I attempted to demonstrate my cooking skills to him.

With no sense of smell or flavour, and very little understanding of food, I was happy to eat anything I was given. Alan, is a chef *and* he is a food snob.

Alan likes 'real food'. Real food meant fruit, vegetables or meat from friends' farms. I don't think he has ever seen the inside of a fast food restaurant. I, on the other hand, lived off rice and frozen vegetables served with either tinned tuna or frozen crumbed fish. I had figured out which of these could be cooked in a microwave, and which could be done on the stove top. I was scared to use the oven, because, despite the gas detector, I didn't want to get distracted and cause an explosion. But beauty is in the eye of the beholder, and I thought I managed quite well.

So I decided to cook my speciality dish for Alan. Fried mushroom.

Fried mushroom was a treat that I indulged in once a week. I fried the mushroom whole in butter, the way that I had seen chefs do on TV. Then I'd put cheese, tomato and ham on top, and leave the lid over the fry pan until the cheese melted. To make it look pretty, I'd serve it with slices of orange and raw capsicum. It had a wonderful variety of temperatures, textures and colours, and in my mind, that made it the perfect dish.

Unfortunately, Alan did not agree, and his face dropped when I placed the dish in front of him. In my excitement to show Alan my favourite meal, I had not planned ahead to buy two mushrooms. He politely suffered through his half of the mushroom. Later, Alan tactfully suggested that we make something else to eat. 'A mushroom and a capsicum does not ordinarily constitute a complete meal,' he told me. 'Even if one does add orange slices.'

Alan didn't know me before my accident. Alan wasn't there for my recovery – those long days and nights in the ICU, those therapy sessions in the rehabilitation centre or those initial adventures in Mt Eliza. My family were though. So, while I was still a little odd, they could excuse my eccentricities because they knew how far I had come.

Everyone in my life told me that I was 'doing very well'. But I wasn't.

There were many things that I didn't know that I could not do normally. Apart from being distractible and egocentric, I didn't walk properly, I spoke like a child when excited or angry, I was excessively emotional and I had obsessive focus. Alan was frustrated that it had been three years since the accident, yet no one had pointed out these oddities to me. If I didn't know that they existed, I would *never* overcome them. If I didn't overcome them, how would I ever reach my full potential?

I wouldn't.

Alan knew this. He also knew that no one in my family would tell me these things, because they were so happy that I survived that they couldn't see them either.

> Once upon a time there was a colony of mice who lived on a small farm. Life was glorious. They had plenty of food and shelter, and their little colony was getting bigger every month. The farmer, however, did not

> want to share his farm with the mice. One day, he came home with a cat. The mice were terrified. It was said that this particular cat could catch and eat at least three mice a day!
>
> The mice held a meeting to determine what could be done. One of the little mice stood up. 'Perhaps we could put a bell on the cat's collar? That way, we can always hear when the cat is coming and we will have time to run away!'
>
> All the mice thought it was a marvellous idea. They cheered and applauded the little mouse for such a simple solution. Then it occurred to them ... who was going to bell the cat?

If the world was made up of mice, I was the cat that needed to be belled. Someone needed to tell me about my oddities.

Alan knew that if he didn't tell me, then nobody would.

Alan was going to bell the cat ... and suffer the consequences.

His first challenge was teaching me to walk properly.

By the time I met Alan, I had long since ditched the walking stick. I had done everything the rehabilitation centre had told me to do. I could move both legs at an equal pace and I didn't limp. I could climb up stairs if I held onto the rail. I had trouble walking down stairs, but attributed this to my double vision, and so had resigned myself to the fact it would continue forever. I could use the treadmill at the gym to walk or jog slowly, as long as I held on tightly to the handles. I believed that *that* was walking.

I wasn't aware that people normally swing their arms when they walk. This is done to keep balance as they shift their body weight from one side to the other. I had never been taught to do that. I had learned to walk with a walking stick that took the weight whenever I stepped forward. As I walked, I was so busy concentrating on positioning my legs, that I never moved my arms. They hung dead at my sides. This is what Alan tried to remedy.

One Saturday morning, Alan and I took Harvey for our usual walk through the forest opposite Alan's farm. Alan tried to bring up the topic of my arms. 'Sarah, do you notice that you don't walk properly?'

He stepped up over a style in the fence, and held out his arm for me to balance on.

'Of course I walk properly!' I scoffed. To show how capable I was, I shooed his arm away, and stubbornly refused his assistance. 'I'm just a little shaky climbing fences.' I stepped down from the style, catching my palm on barbed wire.

Harvey wriggled under the fence next to me, excited by his weekly excursion into the forest. 'No, you don't, Sarah. You don't move your weight properly,' Alan replied, as we followed Harvey through the paddock and headed towards the pine trees.

'What do you mean? I *do* walk properly!' I said, rubbing my hand with the inside of my jumper, hoping that Alan hadn't noticed. 'They taught me how to walk at rehab. I don't limp. I don't tilt my pelvis and I don't slouch!'

I couldn't understand why Alan would question a skill that I knew that I could do. There were plenty of other things that I *didn't* know how to do. But I *knew* how to walk. I had been taught by professionals. I decided that it must have been because Alan was a judgemental bastard who was looking for a reason to put me down.

'No, you don't walk properly, Sarah,' he said calmly. 'You don't swing your arms. It's like you're a zombie. Look, I'll show you...' Alan walked ahead, bobbing up and down with his arms dead at his sides. After he had walked a few metres, he stopped and faced me. 'When you walk, you're meant to let your arms swing. Like this...' he walked back towards me, emphasising his arm movements. 'Try it, Sarah,' he suggested gently. 'Try swinging your arms now, while you walk with me.'

Harvey, who had thought Alan was playing a game by walking to and fro, came running back towards us to join in the fun. I, on the other hand, did not see the 'game' in Alan's demonstration. Humiliated and angry, I glared at him. No one had ever said anything like this to me before.

'I don't need anyone to show me how to walk!' I insisted. 'You wouldn't know anyway. You've never learned to walk! They taught me all about it. I studied it at rehabilitation. I know I am walking properly!'

The annoying thing was that Alan stayed so calm while he talked. He has this amazing ability to *not* get emotionally involved with things. After all, in reality, it was not an attack, it was just something that he had to let me know.

I was *different.*

It was the elephant in the room.

Someone had to tell me *why* I was different, otherwise I would never change, and I would never fit in.

And 'fitting in' was really all that I wanted to do.

Alan casually picked a stick up off the ground, breaking it up as we continued our walk into the forest.

'You always do this,' I accused him. 'You always have to find something to pick on. I know that I walk properly. I studied it. I have been doing it for years. Do you think that they would have taken the walking stick away if I couldn't walk?' My voice got louder. 'I have walked Harvey every day since I first got him. How do you think I do that if I can't walk? What does "arms" have to do with it? Why are you always trying to put me down?'

I fired fresh questions and accusations at him with such rapidity that Alan had no time to answer or protect himself.

Instead, he calmly continued breaking up his stick, receiving my tirade as he quietly walked beside me, watching Harvey play around the pine trees, and waited for me to stop shouting. I was frustrated that he wasn't shouting back, and humiliated that he wanted me to practise walking. I wanted him to be as hurt by me as I was by him.

'Jesus, Alan. Stop trying to control me!'

'Sarah.' Alan sighed, dropping the last of his stick. 'Don't be a silly bugger. I am not trying to control you.' He stopped walking, took my hand and faced me. 'I am only trying to help.

You can go on walking the way that you do, if that is what you want. I am only trying to show you how other people walk.' But his words washed right over me. I didn't hear them anymore.

If he's the only one saying it, it can't be true. 'I don't need *you* to tell me how to walk. I can balance fine.'

Alan looked down at my grazed hand and raised an eyebrow. I pulled my hand away and called out to Harvey.

Harvey, who had found himself a rabbit warren underneath the pine trees and was eagerly dancing around it, looked up when he heard his name. He bounded over to me, full of excitement, ready to offer the same comfort and support that he had given since he was a puppy. Oblivious to Harvey's joy, I bent down and roughly attached his lead to his collar. I turned around and stormed back towards the house, dragging the little white ball of fluff behind me.

By the time Alan returned from the walk, I had collected my things, packed Harvey into the car, and was ready to drive home. With my poor memory, I forgot why I was mad at Alan before I even reached home. The only thing I knew was that he had done something to upset me, and I was too proud to be the one to apologise. I didn't talk to him for the rest of the day.

The second, third and fourth time that Alan attempted to teach me to walk were almost as bad as the first time. I was in complete denial of my inability to swing my arms. But soon, it started to sink in, and I started to practise walking properly. At the gym, I gave up any activities where I wasn't moving my arms. This meant that I had to give up the treadmill, because I was not yet confident walking without holding on to the rails. I took up the cross trainer instead, because it forced me to move my arms.

I hated the cross trainer. I never felt like I was never getting anywhere. There was no hypothetical distance to measure, nothing that was reasonably imaginable. I wasn't walking or cycling, I was swinging. Nobody got anywhere by swinging. Unless they were Tarzan.

I think I move my arms properly now. Alan hasn't said otherwise. Maybe he has just given up trying to bell that particular cat.

***

There have been other cats that Alan has tried to bell over the years – my propensity to act like a child, my extreme emotions, and my obsessive focus. However, one cat has been extremely hard to bell: my storytelling abilities.

I am aware that I get stories wrong, however, I never believe that they are wrong at the time. Alan has been forced to *prove* the true version of my own stories to me. When that doesn't work, he calls Abi for back-up or asks me to check with my good mate Google. And every single time I fight back, convinced that *this time* I am right. Once I spent an entire week adamant that Kim Jong-Un had called Donald Trump an astronaut. I refused to admit that the true story was that Donald Trump called Kim Jong-Un 'rocket man'.

Some cats won't ever be belled.

Chapter Sixteen

When One Door Closes...

'Put a circle on your calendar! The Disability Expo is back, for the fourth year running!'

I looked at the brightly coloured brochure, unsure what Dom wanted me to do with it.

'Is this for us to promote on *RadioCool?*' I asked. Dom beamed at me, the most animated I had ever seen him. 'Better.'

Nate looked up from the safety of his usual office chair. 'We got a stall, Sarah. *RadioCool* is going to be a part of the Disability Expo.'

The Disability Expo happens every October in Adelaide. It's a huge event. There's a stall for everything that a person could need: sports clubs, home supports, employment providers, lifestyle options, arts and crafts, animal companions ... and now there would be one for *RadioCool.*

'Shaun even says the minister will be there,' Nate continued. 'Imagine if we could get him on the show!'

'You've gotta come along, Sarah. Help promote the show. It will be fun,' Dom pleaded.

I looked down at the brochure. He was right. The team would need help.

'Sure, guys. Of course I'll come.'

In hindsight, perhaps I was not the right person or the job. From the moment I walked through the doors, I was assaulted by an onslaught of sound, colours and movement. It was complete sensory overload. My distractible little brain never stood a chance.

Every stall was decorated with colourful banners, compelling me to come try their products. There were people selling mobility equipment, patiently demonstrating the benefits of wheelchairs, plinths and hoists to passers-by. Entrepreneurs called out, inducing me to try their homegrown vegetables and plants; examine their homemade jewellery, make-up and wind chimes; and sample their cakes and biscuits. I greeted them in return, and obediently browsed each stall.

I fought hard to filter the information around me, but my energy was fading fast. I needed to get away.

Tucked away far from the music and crowds was a series of identical stalls. They were covered with brochures, application forms, business cards and case studies. Each stall had giant banners displaying photos of people wearing helmets on a worksite, sitting at a desk and smiling up at a camera or gleefully stacking shelves in a supermarket. These were the stalls of the Disability Employment Network (DEN) providers.

I had heard of these people. They were sort of like Janine. However, she had helped me get into *university.* DEN providers helped people get into *work.*

Suddenly it dawned on me.

These were the companies I should be talking to!

I approached each stand one by one. After merrily inviting them to feel the hole in my head, I told each provider the story of my accident, how I had completed honours, then moved to Adelaide to become a rehabilitation consultant. I explained that I was just about to finish the Graduate Diploma of Rehabilitation Counselling, and now looking for work.

While I spoke, the DEN providers nodded their heads politely. I believed that their glazed smiles were from wonder at my miraculous recovery, and not from wonder at this curious girl who appeared from nowhere to tell them her life story. Each 'conversation' ended the same way. They took my name and number, gave me a brochure about their organisation and said they would be in touch.

My enthusiasm must have impressed someone at the Disability Expo.

In early November 2006, I received a phone call.

'Hi, Sarah. It's Angela, I work with a DEN provider. I met you at the Disability Expo. Are you still looking for work?'

I didn't remember meeting an Angela, but that wasn't a surprise. I wasn't good at remembering names.

'Hi, Angela. Umm, right now I was going to take Harvey for a walk. It's sunny outside, and I thought I'd take him down to the oval. But I *was* going to look for work this afternoon,' I informed her.

There was a pause as Angela digested this information. 'Yes. Well, that sounds good. Has anyone called you about employment yet?'

'No, not yet. But I'm still applying everywhere,' I told her earnestly, scared that she thought I was lying about looking for work that afternoon. 'Subways is hiring, and there is a DEN provider who's looking for consultants to work in the city. I could work there, because it's close and I did a placement with them in Mount Barker.'

I briefly considered asking Angela if *she* knew of anyone else that the DEN provider could also employ, because they had several positions, but didn't get the chance.

'I see,' Angela said slowly. 'Look, we're hiring too at the moment too, Sarah.'

'Oh,' I said, disappointed that Angela probably *didn't* know anyone that I could refer to the other DEN provider, and now *she* would probably want me to keep an eye out for Case Managers for *her* too.

Angela continued, 'I was very pleased to meet you at the Disability Expo. I think you'd make a great member of our team. I told our CEO about you, and she'd like to meet you. What are you doing tomorrow?'

'Nothing yet,' I replied. 'I haven't checked the weather, so I'm not sure if Harvey and I will go out to the oval again...'

'Well, okay then.'

I agreed to meet with Angela and her boss the next day, hung up the phone, and excitedly went searching for Harvey to tell him the news.

Finally, I was going to be like Janine and Catherine. I was going to help people. Now, I was a properly *normal* grown-up, with a real full-time job – and I had done it all by myself.

I couldn't have been prouder.

Angela and her boss offered me a position as a Career Consultant. My role was to help people with disabilities find meaningful employment. They stressed to me that, even though my clients had disabilities, I was to help them find 'open employment' not 'sheltered employment'.

It struck me as odd, that I wasn't allowed to look for work indoors, but happily I agreed, because I could think of lots of outdoor jobs: postal delivery, gardeners, builders, traffic controllers, farmers...

A few weeks later, Abi explained to me that 'sheltered employment' referred to supported employment for people with severe disabilities. 'Open employment' referred to mainstream employment. This could be anything from stacking shelves in a supermarket to working as a clerk.

I am glad that I didn't ask Angela or her boss. That sounded like something that I should have known.

This is just one example of how unprepared I was for my new job. I may have completed two degrees, but I still had very limited understanding of the real world. I did not understand finances, or job suitability, or wages, or employer needs. The only thing that got me through was that, thanks to my naivety about professionalism, I was never afraid to ask questions. I asked clients about different career industries; I asked employers about the best and worst aspects of their jobs; I asked colleagues about Centrelink; I even asked my psychologist about treatments. And, as has happened at every stage of my recovery, my world opened up a little more.

This time, I learned more about people.

I came to learn there were two types of clients. The first type came to appointments on time, résumés in their hands and dreams of employment in their minds. They were excited that *someone* in the world thought they were capable of working – that *they* could be just like everyone else.

Miss X was a middle-aged woman who had never had a job, had a learning difficulty, and was overcoming social anxiety.

'Sarah! Sarah!' she panted, collapsing awkwardly in her seat. 'I found it. I found the perfect job!'

Before I could say anything, she explained that Coles supermarkets were looking for staff, and she was sure to get a job because she was friendly. She assured me that her psychologist had commented that she was getting better at talking to people. She had even been practising what she would say if a customer asked her for help.

'Look, look, look,' she said excitedly. 'Ask me where the vegemite is ... or where the milk is ... I bet I can tell you!' I hesitated for a moment too long. 'What's wrong?' she asked. 'Don't you think I should do it?'

She squinted her eyes closed, as if to hold back tears. 'Don't you think I'm ready to work anymore?' Miss X opened her large brown eyes, and looked forlornly at the floor.

I responded as quickly as I could, desperate to avoid the tears. 'Yes. Yes. Of course I have faith. You *will* find a job. Let's give it a try...'

She did try. She tried very hard. It took Miss X four two-week unpaid work placements across four different supermarkets before she met the manager who was willing to give her a *real* job. He found her a position working with a small team stacking shelves after hours. This suited her very well because, despite the progress she was making with her psychologist, customer service in a busy supermarket would have been too confronting.

The second type of client was less enthusiastic. They had no intention of searching for employment. They came to appointments because Centrelink *made* them. Mr X was perfectly capable of work. He lost his job when the Holden factory closed. Somehow, he had been given a pension, referred to DEN, and hadn't looked back since.

In our fourth meeting, I offered him a sheet of paper that described a job opportunity.

'Can't,' he said, before even looking at the job description in my hand.

'Why not?' I asked, still holding the paper mid-air over the table.

'Don't drive,' he said, letting out a feigned sigh of resignation. 'Can't very well get to work if I don't drive, can I?' He stretched his arms out behind his head, and leaned back in his chair. *Game. Set. Match.*

I, of course, was the wrong person to offer this challenge to. Not because I necessarily wanted him to accept the role that I had in my hand, but because he dared to suggest that not being able to drive was a meaningful barrier to employment. Which of course, it wasn't. Not in Adelaide, which in my mind, had the best public transport system in the world. The bus network was cheap, reliable, and easy to navigate. I explained all this to Mr X. I even offered to pay for a bus ticket. Mr X dismissed the idea with a wave of his hand. 'If I work enough to pay for bus tickets, Centrelink will cut off my payments. Goodbye, pension! Bus tickets will be too expensive. Find something where I *won't* have to catch a bus.'

Pre-accident Sarah would have handled Mr X very differently. Of course, I can't be sure, but from all accounts, I imagine that she would have told him to get off his backside, put some effort in, and stop wasting her time. But I didn't do that. I went in search for jobs where he didn't need to catch a bus.

I quite liked the part of my role that involved job search. It allowed me to meet new people and learn about jobs that I didn't know existed. I loved the afternoons that I had put aside for canvassing: going through my list of potential employers, pen poised and ready to take notes. 'Good afternoon. It's Sarah Brooker from the Disability Employment Network here. Who can I talk to about potential employment opportunities?'

Unfortunately, many employers found reasons for why they couldn't employ someone with a disability. But occasionally I'd come across one – just one – who would be willing to take the chance. It only takes one person to change a life. I found that *these* employers were the best thing about being a rehabilitation consultant.

I don't think Pre-accident Sarah would have enjoyed canvassing. She fought for truth and justice. I'm not sure how she would have responded to the hundreds of employers that said 'no' after hearing the word 'disability'. I imagine she would have behaved in a manner that her own employers would have frowned on. I believe in truth and justice too; I just don't have the courage to fight for my opinions like she did.

Two years of unmotivated clients and evasive employers wore me down though. I learned that the world was not as supportive as I had supposed it to be. Many people I met were afraid of the word 'disability' and took it to mean 'other'. 'Other' was scary, and to be avoided at all costs.

So, I packed up my desk and left the DEN, ashamed that yet another career that I had aspired to had not worked out. I was not a scientist. I was not a rehabilitation consultant.

What was I?

At the end of 2008, I went back to Victoria to visit Abi. While I was there, I called in to Monash University to see Richard. As always, Richard was his delightful self.

'Sez! How wonderful to see you!' he exclaimed as I stood at the door of his office. He stood up momentarily and smiled. 'Of course you're good. You look great! Here, take a seat!' Richard motioned towards a chair before sitting down himself.

I had barely settled in my chair when Richard leaned forward on his desk. 'I have some news for you!' he exclaimed with a proud excitement. 'You left so quickly after you finished, that we didn't get a chance to tell you, and I don't have your email address. Are you on email? You won the Alan Boura Prize!'

I didn't want to offend Richard. I didn't know what the Alan Boura Prize was. But I won't ever be any good at poker, because my face said it all.

'You got the highest mark for the research component of the year, Sarah! Congratulations!'

My face was still blank. 'You got the highest mark for your honours project, Sarah,' Richard repeated, waiting for it to sink in.

I wasn't sure. All that time alone, all those mistakes, all that uncertainty. If only he had known how scared I was of mice. Surely, he knew that I needed my notes for everything. The other students did it all so naturally. They must have all seen that I wasn't smart enough for neuroscience.

Yet, Richard believed that it was true. I was nauseous with guilt and terrified that he would find out how bad my project actually was. Surely, it was not *my* project he was talking about. I was certain I had made many errors through honours. I was *definitely* certain that I wasn't smart enough to do science as a career. *How could I dux the year level?*

Richard had no idea how much this news affected my identity.

I returned to Adelaide in a bewildered state. *Had I misinterpreted my abilities?* I knew that, unlike the girl that existed before 2003, I loved talking to people. I had thought that meant that I was supposed to be around people. I dreamed happily of a job where I helped people the same way Janine and Catherine had helped me. Yet, my attempt to be a rehabilitation consultant had failed. I had been miserable, because no matter how hard I tried, clients and employers didn't want my help.

Yet, the isolation of honours was equally soul-destroying.

I thought back to Graeme's advice all those years ago as he drove me home from rehab. *Make a list.*

Perhaps it was time to make a new list. I knew that I still loved the brain. It was like a reliable friend, comforting and familiar ... but I had been so lonely in the labs. Once upon a time, there was a girl who would argue that my predicament was a no-brainer. Loneliness didn't matter. I loved neuroscience, and was clearly still smart enough, so why wasn't I a neuroscientist?

Sarah Brooker was always going to be a neuroscientist. But I wasn't her, and she isn't me. The lonely hours completing honours had been so painful. But then again, I was lonely as a rehabilitation consultant too. I continued to make my list.

I knew that I loved asking questions, researching and finding answers. I knew that I loved talking and presenting ideas to people. Only one person in the world got to do all that. Abi. Abi had just completed her masters, and was starting her PhD. She studied psychology, and asked all sorts of questions, researched the answers, and presented them to the world at conferences.

I wanted to do that too. I decided to try to be a scientist again, just like Abi. *Perhaps I won't be lonely this time.*

Perhaps the students at Monash were just the wrong scientists?

Not long after making this decision, I heard that CSIRO was offering a PhD scholarship. The project was going to use a mouse model to look at the effect of diet on DNA damage in Alzheimer's disease. I asked Harvey for his opinion. He wagged his tail, picked up one of my socks, and ran under my bed. I didn't know if that was a good sign or a bad one.

I phoned Abi and asked her. 'If that's what you want to try, chicky, then go for it,' she said in her ever-supportive manner. So, I did.

I must have been the only applicant.

At the beginning of 2009, I started my PhD scholarship at CSIRO.

The first few weeks of my PhD were overwhelming. There were a lot of people at CSIRO. I couldn't remember their names and didn't understand their roles. There were laboratory managers, students, research assistants, receptionists, business managers and animal house staff. They all greeted me with a smile if I entered the lift with them, or held the door for me if we were passing at the same time. But no one seemed to want to talk to me about my project. I couldn't figure out who my supervisor was.

I didn't even know which laboratory I belonged to. In the genetics research laboratory, I was the only student who didn't have a background working in genetics or cell cultures. In the animal laboratory, I was the only one using mice and the only person doing behaviour studies.

I didn't know how to make friends with the other students. Their desks were all in the student office. My desk was tucked away in the corner of an unfamiliar laboratory, several floors up, on the other side of the building. The others knew who their supervisors were, and where they fit in, and were heavily involved in their own projects. They didn't have time for the girl in the red bandana who was trying to find her place.

I didn't even have friends outside work. I had lost contact with my friends at Arts Access SA and BINSA when I first became a rehabilitation consultant. Even if I had wanted to return to either organisation, I couldn't. I simply didn't have time.

It was exactly like honours had been. But now, I didn't even have the support of a supervisor like Richard, and I didn't understand my project. Once again, I found myself in a world I didn't fit into, and I was alone.

It took almost twelve months of preparation and arguments with the ethics committee to get the behavioural studies started. For the next four and a half years, I was in the animal house twelve to fourteen hours a day for three out of every five weeks.

I would arrive in the animal house at 6:15a.m., and with just squeaking mice and the radio for company, I would stay there until 7:30p.m.. When I wasn't testing the mice's learning and memory skills, or ability to smell, I was weighing them, washing cages and making mouse food. The only people I spoke with were the animal house staff, who would usually knock on the door for lunch. By the time I left, the building was silent and deserted. I'd put my headphones on and listen to *Conversations* with Richard Fidler on the radio as I fell asleep on the bus, travelling back to my car. Two hours later, I'd walk through the back door of the house I now shared with Alan, tired and angry after another lonely day.

Alan was always there to greet me when I came home. But it was hardly ever pleasant for him. On a typical night, he would have dinner waiting in the oven. As soon as he heard my car pull up the driveway, Alan would flick the kettle on to make me a fresh cup of coffee.

I was so tired and self-absorbed that I didn't notice any of this. I'd walk through the door, angry and offended that he looked so calm, throw my bag down and sit at the table.

'How was your day, darling?' he'd innocently ask.

'How do you think it was?' I snapped in response. 'My studies won't ever reach *significance* because I don't have the right numbers, and it will all have been a waste of time! But I guess *you* had a nice day.' It was hard not to notice the sarcasm in my voice. Then

I would eat the dinner he had made me and go to bed.

One night, after such a tirade, Alan finally snapped. Rather than put my dinner on the table, he opened the window and threw it outside. 'Take your anger outside. I don't want it here.' Then he exited the room, leaving me alone at the kitchen table.

I spent most of my days feeling stupid, lonely and tired. And I was driving away the people I loved. Once upon a time there was a girl who would not have minded the long, lonely hours at CSIRO. I understand that she lived for neuroscience and cared very little for her peers. To spend most of her hours in a lab with mice, studying and researching the complexities of the brain would have been ideal for her. But I wasn't her, and she wasn't me. And I didn't cope with it very well.

While Alan bore the brunt of my bad moods, it was Abi who I turned to for comfort. Even though we were miles apart, Abi and I accompanied each other home every night on the phone, offering each other support and encouragement. I phoned her as soon as I got to my car. She used my call as her cue to start packing up and headed home too. We listened to each other's tears and cheered each other up, knowing that each one of us needed the other to keep motivated to finish the projects we started.

I had Abi. Abi had me. Nothing could go wrong.

Abi

Sah and I spoke at least once every day throughout our PhDs. We would call each other to help think through ideas, vent about our days, share our experiences. We don't bother with small talk. The conversations often start mid-thought, like turning to someone who is standing next to you. We are always in each other's thoughts, always together in that sense. So why not start a phone call mid-conversation? Sometimes I'd answer and Sah would be singing a song. Other times it would start with a question: 'Guess what my mice did today?' or 'I was thinking...' or 'Can you help solve something between me and Alan?'

Sarah was frustrated through her PhD, but I think in many ways Sah's distractibility helped her through her frustrations. She would be crying to me on the phone about another mouse that died, or data that had been lost, or about feeling bullied by the ethics committee, and then something else would pass her mind and she would be okay.

The best example of this was one particularly bad day, when she was driving home, crying down the phone to me that she would not be able to continue one of her studies after fifteen months of work. All the darkest emotions of a PhD were building up: failure, isolation, imposter syndrome, mistrust, uncertainty, defeat. Suddenly, she squealed with laughter and pulled her car over. 'Ha! Abi! You'll never guess what just happened?'

'What?'

'A chicken literally just crossed the road! Just now! In front of me! Why?

> Why did it do that? Why did it cross the road?' She was hysterical. I laughed, relieved to hear her tears turn to excitement. Sarah was so entertained by the joke she forgot all about the tears, and spent the rest of the car ride trying to think of reasons that chicken had crossed the road at 9:00p.m. on a Thursday night.

Eighteen months into my PhD, I had a major breakthrough. It turned out that the 'poor diet' that I had designed for my mice was an excellent model for diet-induced obesity. This was unintentional, but I suppose it should have been expected. It was a high-fat diet that was deficient in essential vitamins and minerals. It was roughly the equivalent of only eating fast food. So, it really should not have been a surprise that my mice who were eating the 'poor diet' were four times fatter than mice eating the 'healthy diet'.

Thrilled by what I'd discovered, I presented my findings to the genomics laboratory at CSIRO. My colleagues weren't as excited; they were not very interested in pictures of obese rodents, and spent a good deal of my presentation playing on their phones. Only one pair of eyes, and one brain, stayed alert for the whole lecture.

As I was packing up, a post-doctoral student named Cass approached me. 'Sarah, this is amazing,' she gushed, holding a manila folder tight to her chest. 'Do you realise what you have here?'

Deflated by the lack of engagement from the rest of my audience, I was wary of her enthusiasm. 'Twelve fat mice?'

Cass laughed. 'No, it's more than that. This is a fantastic model for diet-induced obesity,' she said excitedly. 'Are they all healthy apart from the weight?'

'Well, they have Alzheimer's disease...'

Cass smiled again and tilted her head. 'Yes, but apart from that?'

I nodded.

'How would you like to present it at an obesity conference?' Cass encouraged, searching through her folder for an application form. 'There's one coming up, and if you hurry, you might get your abstract in on time...'

I had never thought of my project in terms of diet-induced obesity. Even though my mice were fat, I was obsessively focused on Alzheimer's disease and DNA damage. Cass's enthusiasm for this new branch of my project was one of the best things that could have happened for my confidence. With Cass's guidance and support, I travelled around Australia, presenting at conferences on obesity and nutrition. I won awards for the best student presentation and best poster and best student research. At our third conference, Cass introduced me to a tall, dark-haired man.

'Sarah, this is Justin,' she said casually. 'I've been telling him about your mice...'

I nodded. I knew who he was. Justin did not need an introduction. He was one of the leading obesity researchers in Australia and ran a very progressive lab.

'Yes. I saw your talk, Sarah. It was very interesting.' He smiled as he picked up a paper coffee cup from a nearby table.

'Thank you,' I said, excited that he was interested in my work.

'I understand why the diet you made is the way it is,' he said, and took a sip from his coffee. 'And I love the effect that it is having on your mice. I am curious,' he looked directly at me, as if to emphasise the weight of his question, 'what do you think it *really* suggests about metabolism?'

I couldn't believe it. Here was a leader of the field asking for *my* opinion? I was reminded of the early days in hospital, when I believed that the neurosurgeons were coming to me for my advice and ideas. Now it was happening for real. I happily launched into a series of hypotheses about fat metabolism. Once I finished, Justin nodded.

'That is the beauty of science,' he agreed. 'You never know anything until you test it.'

Once upon a time there was a girl who would have been horrified at this thought. She would have been even more horrified that I *dare* suggest *anything* to *anyone* without researching it first. Pre-accident Sarah believed in facts and in the truth. I don't believe she saw room for speculation.

I love that I talk to people. I have often thought that talking to people is one advantage that I have over Pre-accident Sarah. I cannot picture her approaching strangers at a conference, or happily forming hypotheses on the spot. She may have even been offended when audience members had questions, and assumed that they could not keep up with her thoughts. This is pure speculation, of course, because I never knew her. Occasionally I wonder though, would her aloofness have hindered her ability to advance in science?

For all the excitement that conferences brought, after they finished, I was forced to return to the solitude, silence and uncertainty of my research at CSIRO. I told myself that I loved it. I loved my mice. I loved my research. I loved reading on the bus.

But the truth was, I was not coping. I was exhausted and missed contact with humans incredibly. I was scared of the other people at CSIRO because

I did not know how to fit in with them. Alan did his best to provide the social support that I needed, but often, I was too tired, too angry, to appreciate his friendship. On top of this, I knew that, inevitably, the only friends that I *did* have – my mice – would die, and I would be the one who had to kill them. Then I would *really* be left alone.

Towards the end of my PhD, it became clear that I really did not have the personality that could survive neuroscience. I felt as though I had spent years in a world that I did not belong, and I didn't want to die 'in the name of research' like all my friends (the mice) had.

For the second time in my short life, I came to the devastating conclusion that I could not be a neuroscientist. I was *smart* enough for neuroscience. But I was not like the girl who existed before 2003. I did not have the strength to live in the isolation that I needed in order to achieve.

In 2014, ashamed, embarrassed and unsure of who I was, I closed (and locked) the neuroscience door, and turned to look for the next door that opened.

Chapter Seventeen

Teacher

I had failed as a rehabilitation consultant. I had failed as a neuroscientist (twice). What would I succeed at?

Remembering Graeme's advice all those years ago as he drove me home from Rehab, I sat down to write another list. I loved learning. I loved asking and answering questions. I loved sharing knowledge.

There *had* been a place where I had been able to do all those things. But it took me a while to realise that I could do them as a career. Teaching.

Early in the PhD, before the behaviour studies started, I had worked as a tutor at Flinders University. Most PhD students do this to supplement their scholarships. I taught Foundation Maths to a small class of mature-age students. During the early days of my PhD, teaching at Flinders was a respite from the loneliness and confusion of the lab.

Twice a week, after a long, lonely day at my desk, I made the bus trip to Flinders University. I'd reach the teaching rooms just as the sun was beginning to set. As the last of the sun disappeared over the edge of the campus, students would begin to appear. One by one, they'd dribble into the classroom, nodding or smiling at me as they took a seat next to their friends.

Just like the students who I had studied with at UniSA, these students came to class after a long day at work. They were just as tired and exhausted as I was. However, unlike the UniSA students, my Foundation Maths class showed very little disdain for the subject content. Numbers might be difficult for some people to understand, they may even be tedious to others. But you can't argue the outcome of an equation. One plus one will always equal two. Maths is beautifully reliable like that.

The students in the Foundation Maths class were learning simple statistics. Evenings were spent calculating averages, drawing graphs, and making tables. The students were learning that numbers were dependable. There was no reason for anyone to scoff at anyone else's opinion, because all we did was play with numbers.

My confidence grew immensely in that tiny classroom. These students *wanted* to learn, and I was able to answer their questions. I was so proud to find a place where I was useful to *someone.*

Once the behaviour tests started, I didn't have time to teach at Flinders. I felt this loss terribly. I had lost the *one* place in my world where I felt valued, and replaced it with a place that was confusing, belittling, and lonely.

A few months later, I had my second experience with teaching. Once again, I found a sense of joy and purpose that was so obviously missing in my life.

A neighbour of mine had a son who was struggling with maths at school. She had heard from Alan how happy I had been when I was teaching at Flinders, and so she asked if I could help her son. I think she underestimated *how much* I enjoyed teaching.

On our very first session, young Alex arrived with an A4 pencil case packed full of textas, pencils, erasers, sharpeners, calculators, rulers, protractors and compasses. It was as though he had brought Mary Poppins's bag of stationery. He also carried a giant Haese *Mathematics for Australia* textbook, and a much smaller notepad. I quietly noted this arsenal as he sat down at the table, and wondered how much of his schoolwork he expected to do.

'I know you're here to catch up in maths work. But, the first thing you will do, if nothing else, is learn to love maths,' I told him. 'Even if you get nothing else from our sessions.'

I love numbers.

You can tell any story you want with numbers, so long as you fold them the right way. My favourite example of this is the saying 'the glass is half empty or half full'. The number that you use is the same – half. But the story is completely different. It depends on which one you focus on. And the beauty is, both are true.

I think, at times, maths is a glorious joke that can be used to play all sorts of tricks. I try to encourage students to feel the same way. Unfortunately, kids are taught that maths is dull. They never see the joke. Most students do not see the joy in numbers. They see maths homework as a boring, confusing chore. So, they aren't motivated to learn what the letters and numbers on the page actually mean. They never see the joke.

It is crucial that students learn not to hate maths.

'Pick a favourite number,' I instructed Alex.

'What?' he looked perplexed. He and I both knew that 'favourite numbers' were not going to be on his next test.

'Well, we are going to do thousands of sums. We may as well do ones you like. So, what's your favourite number? We'll use it as much as we can.'

Sixteen is *my* favourite number. It fits nicely into most of my favourite examples. It's four squared. It's two times eight. It's one-quarter of sixty-four, and half of thirty-two. There are songs about the number sixteen, and it's the age when most children make the first step into adulthood and get their learner's driving permit. Not many numbers can claim that sort of fame.

It turns out that sixteen is also Alex's favourite number. I don't know if that was a good thing or a bad thing for him in the end. It meant that I had a million and one examples ready for him. If he had chosen seventeen, I wouldn't have been anywhere near as prepared. Apart from the fact that it's a prime number, I think seventeen is rather dull. But I am happy to be convinced otherwise.

After a few puzzles to get his brain into 'maths mode', I asked what he had been doing in maths at school.

'Teacher started algebra today,' he said, opening up his textbook. He was keen to *finally* get on with what he came to my house to do.

'The teacher did, or you did?'

He acknowledged my correction with a shake of his head. 'Yeah. Okay then. *We* started algebra.'

'Okay then. So that's where we start,' I sat next to him. 'Tell me what you know.'

'She gave us this list. It's a bunch of words we have to know,' He fished around in the Mary Poppins bag, and pulled out a crumpled piece of paper.

'Great. Excellent. A list of words. Why did she give you that?'

Alex frowned, and gave the sheet of paper a bored stare. 'Dunno. She said we have to learn it for homework.'

'Okay,' I replied, taking the sheet off him to study it. 'It's a little more important than that. Let me tell you why.' I put the paper down on the table between us and picked up my own pen, but didn't write anything. 'I'll let you in on a little secret.' I leaned closer to Alex with a smile. 'Algebra isn't maths!' I whispered. Alex looked at me, blank faced and confused.

'Maths is numbers,' I continued. 'Algebra is numbers and letters. It's a whole new language.' Alex's confused expression didn't change as he looked back at the sheet of paper.

'Think about it. Up to this point in time, maths has only been numbers.

One plus one equals two. You have always known the answer. Algebra is different. You won't know the answer. Not until someone tells you what the letters mean.'

I tapped the paper with my pen.

'This list will help you learn what to do with the letters. It's like when you were learning where full stops and capital letters went back in primary school. These are the full stops and space bars. Once you know how to recognise them, you can read the sentences.'

Alex rested his chin on his fist as he tried to make sense of what I had said. The penny started to drop.

'So ... these are the rules?' he asked.

'Exactly!' I exclaimed, proud that he seemed to understand what I was saying. 'I reckon, in class, your teacher would have tried to explain it to you differently. But that's pretty much all it is. So, let's play a little.'

I reached for a scrap piece of paper and started writing out some new sums. Alex soon learned that we were *never* going to rely on a textbook. He could do that in his own time. Alex and I worked through an equation for each of the terms on the list his teacher had given him. I made him do three more examples for each item, just to make sure he understood. It was nearly 8:30p.m. when he looked up at the clock. 'Sarah. We have to stop. It's half past. We've run overtime.'

I had been having so much fun giving him equations and watching him work them out that I had not even thought to look at the clock. 'Ah. Sorry, mate. Okay then, let's go.' Reluctantly, I let him repack his Mary Poppins bag and collect his textbook from where it had been discarded on the other side of the table. I drove him back home, apologising to his mum for keeping him out so late.

'It won't happen next week,' I promised, before pulling out of their driveway.

But it did happen the next week. And the week after. And the week after. It was not that Alex took a long time to grasp the content. He was quite bright. The reason we ran overtime was that I was too enthusiastic. I loved playing with numbers, and I was happy that I finally had someone else to play with.

While Alex was not always as enthusiastic to keep playing as I was, he was grateful, and never said *no* to a sudden challenge or test of his abilities. He came to me with questions, and we'd solve them together. Once again, I was useful, and I was happy.

Even though I completed honours at the top of my class and I have a PhD, I must not be very bright. I had been happy teaching Alex and the Foundation Maths students, but it wasn't until *after* I finished the PhD and I sat down to write a list about the things that I liked, that the idea of becoming a teacher even occurred to me. And even then, it wasn't really my idea. It was Alex's mum who suggested it.

'When Alex was younger, he went to an education centre,' Ruth told me one morning, as we sat in my kitchen having morning tea. 'The place was like a school for kids who struggled with maths and spelling.'

I took the lid off the teapot and stirred the leaves, while she continued the story.

'The man that runs it is great. He was great with Alex anyway,' she reminisced.

I nodded my head. 'That would have been good for Alex,' I agreed.

'The man there is a lot like you, Sarah.' She smiled and played with her teacup as she recalled my enthusiasm for her son's homework. I put the lid back on the pot and passed it across to her to pour. 'Really?'

'Oh, yes.' Her blonde hair swung about her face as she nodded her head. 'Reg is really passionate about what he teaches.' Ruth smiled as though she had an idea. 'Say, you should give him a call. See if he has some work for you. I'll see if I have his number at home...'

Ruth did have Reg's number. I phoned him and, after a little telephone tennis, met him for an interview. At least, I thought it was an interview, but my 'interview' with Reg was unlike any other interview I have ever witnessed.

Reg was a seventy-something-year-old man who had been teaching all his life. He was far more passionate and knowledgeable than I could ever hope to be. But, while I love maths and numeracy, Reg loved language, and he was passionate about teaching it *properly*.

I know that I'm a poor speller, and I barely know the difference between nouns, adjectives and verbs. I am clever enough with words to have written both an honours and a PhD thesis, but I know nothing of the theory that explains how words go together. This horrified Reg. Nonetheless, he took pity on me, and patiently opened up the doors of grammar, punctuation and spelling. There was almost *nothing* about the English language that Reg couldn't explain with a story or a joke. After one hour of listening to Reg talk about the wonders of English, he handed me a key. 'Can you start on Tuesday?' And so, I joined the team at the education centre, and I learned how to teach from one of the best teachers in South Australia.

Students loved Reg. He treated them like people. They would silently come into the education centre after a hard day at school, walk down the hallway to get themselves a drink and a biscuit, then walk back to find themselves a desk. Reg was amazing to watch. He would juggle the activities of multiple students at a time, wheeling between them on an old office chair, greeting them as he slid up to their side.

'Where are *you* up to, sir?' he'd ask over a student's shoulder. The student would lean back and show Reg his work.

'What? What's that?' Reg would exclaim, in mock horror of a minor grammatical error. 'No, no, no, my lad. That's not it at all. Let me explain...' Then before he'd start, he'd call up to an older student who sat quietly at the other end of the desk. 'How are you doing up there, Doctor?'

'Fine thanks, Reg,' the older student replied, looking gratefully at his mentor.

'Where are you up to?'

'I'm just about to start the comprehension activities.'

'Right. Good. You read through the text. I'll be up to show you what to do in a few minutes. Just let me finish here with young Tom and the mysteries of plurals.'

Reg sat with Tom for the next five minutes, explaining the many types of plural, and how to know when to use them. And then, true to his promise, he'd roll up to 'Doctor' and guide him through his comprehension activities.

I didn't think I'd ever be as good as Reg. *How does he keep track of everything that the students do?*

'Don't look at their curriculum – they should cover that at school,' he once advised me. 'Look at the *student.* What do they already know?' Reg gestured towards the countless folders of worksheets on the shelves above his desk. 'We develop their program based on what they need to *learn.*'

Three nights a week, I made my way to the small school in Littlehampton, where I taught literacy and maths to primary school students. I worked with students who had somehow made it to Year 4 but didn't know how to write their alphabet. I had one younger student who was so far 'behind' that she thought that *elemeno* was a letter of the alphabet. She was quite surprised when I explained to her that it is actually four different letters: *L, M, N,* and *O.*

Ruth had been right. I loved teaching. I felt like I had finally found a job that I was good at *and* had purpose. With Reg there to help me develop programs, I was able to teach students the things that they needed in order to achieve at school. I watched students gain confidence and fall in love with learning. Tutoring was something that I could do, and I was happy to have finally found a role that I fit into.

After two years teaching with Reg, I advertised for my own students in the local post office. I figured this was okay, as I lived too far away from Littlehampton to risk poaching any of Reg's potential students. I owed him a lot, and I didn't want to do wrong by him.

One day, I got a call from a local man with a son named Dillan in Year 1. Usually by this age, students can form letters, spell simple words and write sentences. However, Dillan could not even recognise letters of the alphabet.

When I first met Dillan, he resisted all my attempts to lure him into doing schoolwork. He knew that I was there to help him learn to read, write and count. But he also *knew* that he couldn't do those things. His teacher had told him so. He got in trouble at school for not guessing the shapes of letters correctly. He was terrified that I would yell too. Dillan refused to sit at the table or hold a pencil, because he *knew* couldn't do it. The way that the other kids held pens didn't make sense to him. *I know how you feel, buddy. I've been there too. But we'll go slow, and you'll see yourself grow.*

At the time, Minecraft was a computer game that all the kids were playing. Dillan didn't quite understand the strategy component, but enjoyed making different forts and structures. During our first few sessions, Dillan and I fell into a routine taking turns to teach each other something. He would let me show him how to draw a letter or a word, and I would let him show me how to build another structure in Minecraft. Eventually, his structures became more complicated.

'Dillan, can you make them any shape that you want to?'

'Yeah. Of course,' he replied proudly.

'Can you make one that says a letter?'

'Probably.'

'Give it a go. Please show me how it would look ... Could you try a *D* for Dillan?'

And so, through Minecraft, Dillan learned his alphabet and how to build and recognise his name. But he was still too scared to try writing.

***

One day, Dillan was outside playing in the mud when I arrived for our lesson. His dad went to call him in.

'Leave him there,' I said, dumped my bag on the table and walked out to join him in the mud. When I reached him, Dillan was squatting on a log beside their dam. His knees, shorts and T-shirt were dark brown with mud. His face and hands were covered with scratches and dirt. He looked like a street urchin. Dillan barely noticed though. All of his attention was focused on the small pile of stones he was trying to balance on the sloppy mud that surrounded him.

'Whatchya building, Dillan?'

'A fort,' he said, quite seriously. 'I have a pet frog called Chase, and he needs a fort.'

'Righto. A frog-sized fort,' I said, kneeling down beside him. 'Can I help?'

'If you want,' he replied, looking around for another digging stick that I could use. 'You can help dig the moat.' We worked together in silence for a while, me scratching at dirt and Dillan stacking rocks.

'Ya know, mate, your dad wants us to do some writing today as well.'

'Can't,' he replied matter-of-factly. 'iPad is flat, and I left my charger at Mum's.' *Oh no buddy, that doesn't mean that you'll get out of work. Your books are still here. You can write.* I had to think of another reward.

'Well, it's a nice day out here. Why don't we work outside?'

'Can't. It's muddy here, and I'm not allowed to get my books dirty.'

'We don't have to write on books. People were writing on things *long* before they were writing on books. We can write letters and rhymes in the mud as we build the fort.'

Before there was any time to argue, I drew the letters *a* and *b* in the ground with my stick. 'Can you fill them with rocks, and figure out what letters they are?'

Dillan did as he was told, and quickly identified *a* and *b*. I repeated the task, making a big thing of ensuring that he wasn't looking as I wrote my letters in the mud. I always used vowel–consonant combinations, because he knew them. I hadn't actually taught him about blends or four-letter words yet.

'Your turn,' I said, covering my eyes. 'Try to make it tricky. Make a word.'

Dillan had been practising three-letter words, so I knew he'd be able to spell them.

'You'll never guess it,' he said proudly as I uncovered my eyes. I looked down at a very squiggly *d o g* written in the mud. The game continued. I had never had Dillan so engaged in writing. I wanted to stretch him further.

'Hey, Dillan,' I said with my eyes covered. 'What would happen if we wanted to put Chase's name on his fort? Or even, if we just tried *frog.* How could we do that?'

I looked through my fingers at Dillan. He looked at me, betrayed.

'But I don't know how to make those sounds!' his lip started to tremble. I hate to see tears. That is the *worst* thing about working with children. *Anything* can make them cry, and it seems that I can *never* guess what that thing will be. But I put on a brave face, and tried to reassure him.

'Nah, mate. I bet you do. We can figure it out. I haven't seen it written down yet either, so we can figure it out together.' I wasn't *completely* lying. I had not seen the word *frog* or *Chase* written in the mud before.

'*Frog.* What is the first sound?' I asked him, handing him our writing stick.

'*Fffffff,*' he said. 'But I don't know that. Not when it's in the front of *frog!*'

'*Fff,*' I repeated, pretending to think carefully about the problem. 'Isn't *fff* the start of *fat?*' I eventually asked.

'How did that letter go?' Dillan giggled. *Fat* was one of his favourite words to read. 'Fat Dog.' 'Fat Rat.' 'Fat Pig.' 'Fat Cat.'

He happily scratched *f* into the ground. 'What's the next sound?'

'*fff-rog*. I don't know the letter for *rog!*' He looked at me in panic again.

'Hmmm. *Rog* sounds a bit big for a letter. What about *rrr*? Think about all of the words we read. Which ones have *rrr* in them?'

'*RAT!*' he shouted excitedly, banging the stick and dancing on the spot. He scratched an *r* next to his *f*.

'FR*rr*-OG,' he said aloud. I kept quiet, watching him problem-solve the next part of the word. 'FFR*rr*-OG,' he whispered over and over. He leaned over his word and drew a giant ring.

'*O*', he said, and puffed out his chest. Dillan was writing, spelling, and learning. And he was proud. 'Does that look done? Does it say *frog* yet?' I asked, feigning ignorance about how to spell.

'No,' he said, quite seriously. 'I think there might be more. See, here we have *fro* ... We need a *ggg* sound. *Ggg*.

Ggg,' he said, tapping his chin. He leaned forward again, drew a *d,* sat back to admire his work.

'*D* is for *Dillan* or *dog,*' I reminded him. 'What's another letter, that looks kinda like that one?' I was terrified that he'd forgotten the relationship between *d* and *g,* and that I would burst this magical moment. Dillan looked seriously at me for a while, his chest deflated. He scratched his head while he thought about it. He wasn't going to give up. Slowly, he leant down, erased the *d* and replaced it with a *g.*

'I was just testing you!' he said, laughing, and with that he stood up and ran into the house calling, '*Fff-Rrr-Oo-Ggg!* I wrote *FROG*. Dad, come look! Come, look. *Dad!*'

I was the first of Dillan's teachers who had made writing fun and accessible. Writing didn't have to be on paper to be meaningful. It didn't need to be done at a table. Dillan could write anywhere.

I know I can't take all the kids to the sandpit, but that is the kind of magic I want in a job. That's why I left science to become a teacher.

Chapter Eighteen

Student

Throughout the PhD, and even when I was working with students, things were not good at home. At work and at university I was still a bright, happy and exuberant person. I still spoke to strangers on the bus and in shopping centres. I still laughed with Abi on the phone. I had an odd sense of humour and was distractible. I was overly enthusiastic when people asked about work, but harmless enough. To strangers, I was mostly all smiles.

At home, I was a very different creature. Alan never knew what was going to come through the door. I could be a small child, skipping and laughing at the day I had. Or I could be a dark, angry woman, who was looking for a fight with the first person she saw, which was always Alan. Only occasionally did the Sarah he loved come through the door. She was an intelligent woman who made him laugh. And it was in his search for *her* that

Alan and I made one of the greatest discoveries about my world.

I knew that I was difficult to live with. I was ashamed that there were things that I could not manage. I couldn't control my emotions, which meant that Alan and I got into fights about almost everything.

It would start innocently enough. I would bring up a topic of my research, to bounce an idea or a hypothesis off him. When he gave an opinion that was not the same as my own, I took it as a personal attack, and would yell back at him. I accused him of belittling me, and not respecting that I was smart too. I accused him of not understanding the research I was doing. After all, what had *he* ever had to do with the brain? *I knew about the brain. I researched the brain* and *I had even dealt with the consequences of brain damage!*

But it was worse than that. I had a low opinion of myself, and I blamed that on Alan too. I was ashamed that I couldn't complete simple household chores. I would start one task, then become distracted by another, then another, then another. I couldn't wash the dishes without cleaning the whole house, because I would forget what I had done or what the original task was.

I was ashamed that I couldn't even remember to feed Harvey in the morning before I left for university. He was my best friend, and I was even letting *him* down.

Alan could do the dishes. Alan could feed Harvey. Alan could do everything that I couldn't. That just made it worse. We knew that we weren't coping as a team. Something had to be done.

In 2012, Alan and I approached the TAC for some sort of help. We just didn't know *what* sort of help we needed. The TAC was in a bit of a bind. The accident had happened nearly a decade ago. Ordinarily, TAC settles with a client five years after a car accident, and both parties go their separate ways. People don't normally come back. Yet, here I was, nearly a decade after the accident, asking for help.

In order to show TAC that Alan and I *did* need assistance, I went to Dr Koopowitz, a clinical neuropsychologist. After the usual scans and IQ tests were done, he requested an appointment with me. He suggested that I bring a loved one. There were only two people I would have had at that appointment: Alan or Abi. Abi lived in Melbourne, and was not available. Alan was desperate to have someone confirm that I was not okay and that I needed help, so he came with me to meet Dr Koopowitz.

I thought it was going to just turn into a gang-up-on-Sarah event. And I was right.

We arrived early. The receptionist greeted us warmly and suggested we take a seat in the waiting room. It didn't look like a waiting room to me ... it looked like they had stuck some plastic chairs, some out of date magazines and a water cooler in the hospital foyer. It was patronisingly calm. Music played gently from invisible speakers and other patients sat quietly in the cheap plastic chairs, softly murmuring to each other as they flicked through the magazines; occasionally, the electronic doors opened quietly, letting a soft breeze through as a doctor or another patient entered.

I hated everyone there for appearing so *at ease,* while I was so nervous. To my horror, Alan picked up a magazine and took a seat. He joined them. He left me alone, and joined the other people in the waiting room. *Traitor.*

We were meant to go somewhere quiet, where we could get our story straight. I didn't want him to go into one of his rants about how difficult it was to live with me ... my self-esteem was low enough as it was without him broadcasting it to the world. I didn't realise at the time, but that is exactly what Alan needed. No one else had witnessed my bursts of anger or saw me when I acted like a baby ... He needed to feel heard. But we never got the chance to discuss this before the meeting. Not with Alan sitting in the waiting room with his head stuck in some stupid magazine.

With nowhere else to go, I followed him and sat in one of the plastic chairs beside him, silently apprehensive about what the appointment might bring. The longer we waited, the more desperate I was to talk to Alan. I was sure that he would humiliate me and try to encourage Dr Koopowitz to gang up on me. It wouldn't be hard to find something to complain about. I looked down. *I'm not normal anyway.* I hated Alan for that, and was angry he was there. I was certain that he was going to make a fool of me.

Dr Koopowitz appeared at the door, and with a calm smile and a patient manner, he led us down the corridor to his room for our first consultation.

'Welcome, Sarah. Welcome, Alan. Take a seat.' He politely motioned to two chairs in front of his desk. It felt so alien, being in this doctor's office. For the first time, I was faced with a doctor who might *not* be my friend. *He may side with Alan.*

I looked across at Alan. Alan the *Traitor.* He didn't look like the man that I'd fallen in love with. *This* Alan wore a *proper* shirt that didn't have holes in it, and *clean* boots. I didn't know Alan owned clean boots. He didn't even have his pink glasses with him ... I was scared.

It started with the usual chit-chat. Dr Koopowitz asked questions to confirm his understanding of our background and get a bit of an idea about our lives. Alan answered confidently for the two of us. I stayed quiet and played with the straps on my bag.

'What effect do you think this is having on you?' Dr Koopowitz asked Alan.

I stopped playing with my bag and looked up.

Why would that matter? I was the one with the brain injury.

'It's hard,' Alan replied. 'I never know whether Sarah will be a small laughing child or an angry screaming woman when she comes home. I've learned to just close my mouth,' Alan held up his hands. 'I'm not sure how long I can last though.'

The attack had begun. The fears that I had were coming true. We had known this doctor less than five minutes and Alan was already telling him what a horrible person I was. *What a betrayal!*

'It's as though no one else sees it but me. Not her family, not at work ... She is nice to everyone else. She is all happy and smiles. But no one else lives with her 24/7. *I* am the one that sees the angry side. *I* am the one who has to deal with it.'

'No one else sees it, because it's not true!' I butted in, furious that Alan would make such accusations about me in front of a stranger. A *doctor,* no less. *How humiliating!* I wanted to hurt Alan and have him feel as embarrassed and ashamed as I did. 'You're just as stubborn, just as hard to live with. You have no idea how hard this is for me!'

Through frustrated, angry tears, I told Dr Koopowitz that I was struggling at university and that Alan thought I was stupid too, but I really wasn't stupid.

'It isn't about whether or not you are smart, Sarah. You have a brain injury. You have difficulties. You can be difficult. And you need help,' Alan insisted. I hated him. This *stranger* who was making me feel like a fool in front of a *doctor. Why does he try to turn people against me?* The betrayal was unbearable. No one understood how alone I was, or how hard it was to do anything. And now, here was Alan, the person I had brought with me for support, ganging up on me with Dr Koopowitz. It felt like a bad session of couples' therapy. And I suppose, in a way, it was.

Humiliated that yet *another* person would find out that I was a fraud, I started to cry. Both Dr Koopowitz and Alan stayed calm through my tears. Alan had heard it all before, and Dr Koopowitz was forming hypotheses about what might actually have been going on. He stood up and handed me a box of tissues over the desk. I pulled out half a dozen, and went about blowing my nose – making a show of it, to prove that *I* was the victim here.

Dr Koopowitz flicked on the light box that hung on his wall. He put an image of a human brain up on the light box. I adore the brain. It is my pacifier. There seem to be new discoveries every day, and I love hearing the views of different specialists. I was always ready for a neurological conversation. Alan, for his part, was leaning in too. Of course he would – nothing was beyond Alan's understanding.

'This is a normal adult brain,' Dr Koopowitz started. 'It's an image that I use for teaching.' I smiled to myself. *Of course it's a brain. I am far more familiar with these than Alan is. I might gain some ground here ...*

'But your brain, Sarah,' Dr Koopowitz continued, as he reached for a second image, 'looks remarkably different.'

Dr Koopowitz put the second image on the board. I was astonished. I knew that I had a brain injury. I also knew that, as I had no pituitary gland, I must be missing a section of the base of my brain. What I didn't know was how much of the brain I was missing. In the image that Dr Koopowitz put up on the light board, there was a vacant space about the size of a golf ball in the middle of the frontal lobe.

The part of the brain that I am missing is a region at the base of my frontal lobe called the orbitofrontal lobe. The frontal lobe is the part of the brain where logic, reasoning and higher-order thinking occurs. The temporal lobe is on the sides of the brain, on the other side of the skull to the ears. It is responsible for emotions and memories. The orbitofrontal lobe – the part I'm missing – *connects* logic and reasoning skills with emotions.

I still have the region of the brain required for logic. I still have the region of the brain required for emotions. But I have no physical connection between the two. The consequence of this is that one cannot help regulate the other.

This can be demonstrated with the simple act of stubbing a toe.

If a 'normal' person stubbed their toe, they may initially have an emotive response. 'Gee, that hurts!' There may even be anger or frustration with the pain. But very soon after, logic takes over. 'I still have nine other toes that don't hurt. The other toe, even though it hurts, is still there. I still have ten toes.' The person may remain upset for a short while, but it is no great disaster. There would not be tears.

If *I* were to stub my toe, no such reasoning would occur. I would undoubtedly be upset that my toe hurt – but with no logic to calm me down, my response would get progressively worse until my stubbed toe was one of the greatest catastrophes known to mankind. I would cry and carry the pain with me for several hours. I may even look for an ice pack to put on my foot.

I would continue to cry long after I had forgotten what the initial trauma was. Once emotion starts to take hold, I lose control of logical thought and I lose all insight into my behaviour.

By the time Alan and I met with Dr Koopowitz, my life was a series of stubbed toes. Tiny daily traumas were made infinitely worse by the fact that I had no logical way to calm myself down. I was most emotional when I was tired at home, which is why I was taking it all out on Alan. It was also a no-brainer that I couldn't identify with Pre-accident Sarah. The emotions and the memories of *that* girl physically didn't exist anymore.

Dr Koopowitz said this was called *orbitofrontal syndrome,* as that was the name of the piece I was missing. It had a *name.* The memory loss, the distractibility, the young-girl behaviour, the hyperactivity, the tears, the shame ... it no longer fell under the broad umbrella of *acquired brain injury.* It was no longer a list of *peculiar things about Sarah* that would never go away.

It had its own name. That meant other people experienced it too. I wasn't alone. Alan wasn't either.

The monumental task before me now was learning to identify my emotions, assess them, and determine which were real and which were distorted by my brain injury.

This was much more difficult than learning to walk again. Walking was easy. I had a very well prescribed series of steps to follow and no evidence or idea that any of those steps could fail. I was *always* going to learn to walk again.

Learning to identify my emotions infinitely harder. For one thing, I didn't have the region of my brain that was required to do this. That is the equivalent of learning to walk without legs. Secondly, throughout my *whole* neuroscience training, I had learned that neurons don't grow back. Once you lose them, they are gone. It's not like legs. I can't get a prosthetic orbitofrontal region. My original brain cells wouldn't know what to make of it. So, I went into this thinking that there was *every* chance of failure. I was not able to replace what was lost, and there was no way to connect the two regions that needed to be connected.

Thirdly, it is extremely difficult to develop awareness of whether something about yourself is genuine or distorted reality. Imagine being excited and happy, singing and clapping your hands in joy, and then being told, 'It's not all that exciting. All you did was butter some toast.' How do you accept that *that* wasn't real joy? Or, accept that it is *joy,* but not at a socially acceptable level?

Fourthly, I was in a mentally unstable place. I had an extremely low opinion of myself, and constantly questioned my abilities. I knew that I was odd, and was self-conscious that other people held this against me. That's why I found it so hard to make friends.

Now, not only did I not know Pre-accident Sarah, but I also couldn't trust the emotions of the girl I *had* known for the past ten years.

Learning to manage my feelings was a two-step process. I had to learn to be aware of my emotions, then I had to learn how to assess whether or not they were appropriate. There was no way in the world I could do this alone. *How did you see something that you didn't know was there?*

As Alan was my partner and the person who saw me most often, I asked him to take on the challenge of telling me when I *was* letting my emotions take control.

I was asking him to *bell the cat.*
Again.

Alan was good at logic, not emotion. He did not know how to speak in a language that I would understand when I got excited. Alan could not expect me to understand the sentence: 'Sarah, this is your brain injury. You aren't actually this happy.' But that was the only way that he knew how to say it.

Initially, Alan would ask 'Sarah, have you had your tablets?'

Such a simple question. Those five little words contain no malice at all, and were intended only to make sure I was okay. But, to me, they were extremely offensive. It always started a fight.

'Of *course* I have. I *can* manage my own medication, you know!'

Often, I had forgotten my tablets, but I was too proud to admit it. I was certain that my behaviour was not odd, and that Alan was using his new role to undermine me. I had no idea how unusual my behaviour actually was.

Asking me whether I was 'okay' using conventional words had clearly not been successful. It was Alan who came up with the new term.

Golfballing.

'Sarah, you're *Golfballing*'.

Golfballing is a way of referring to the brain injury, by terming it something simple and harmless. It also refers to the actual size of the piece of brain that I am missing.

Golf is not offensive. It is not associated with stigma and inability to do things. Golf doesn't imply that I am out of control. Golf is a rather calm and logical sport. In fact, it is probably the exact opposite to what the term *Golfballing* means.

Golfballing is the signal between Alan and me that my brain injury is affecting my behaviour. It may be that I am reacting inappropriately to something that's been said – either excessively excited or dramatically upset. It may be that I am acting like a small child. It may be that I have become aggressive for no apparent reason.

Initially, even this benign term caused Alan a lot of grief. Believing my emotions to be real, I would yell more and remain incredibly frustrated. But it was nowhere near as dangerous as asking if I had had my tablets. He tolerated it well, knowing that I had to get past my tirades one day.

There has been a lot to learn.

I think I am over the worst of it.

I am a good student, but the lesson isn't over yet. I am still learning to manage my moods and monitor my behaviour. I will be a 'student' for the rest of my life.

In 2016, I became a formal student *again.* I enrolled in the Postgraduate Diploma of Education at Adelaide University.

On the very first day, I sat in the middle of the lecture hall, surrounded by other students. We were the future educators of Australia. What a mix we were. The hall was filled with every stereotype of student I could imagine. This time, though, I didn't worry about fitting in with them. I was excited about what I was there to learn. I was there to learn to be a *real* teacher.

I understand that the girl who lived before the accident *also* cared more for her lecture material than she did for her peers. But I think in *this* case, our similarities are justified. We were *both* at university to learn about something we were passionate about. She was there for the brain. I was there for teaching.

As I sat in that lecture hall, I imagined all the wonderful knowledge that the lecturer would impart to us, and fantasised about how amazing it would be to use that knowledge to teach students in a classroom of my own.

So, like the girl who lived before the accident, I wasn't there to make friends. I was there to *learn.* I sat. And watched. And waited.

I did my teaching placements in a college in an up-market Adelaide suburb. My students were hardworking, thoughtful and respectful in every single way. They entered classrooms calmly, and were engaged in the lessons. They didn't interrupt each other, and put their hands up to speak. They asked questions and offered answers.

Suffice to say, while I learned a lot about content delivery, marking and lesson planning, I learned *nothing* about behaviour management. Unfortunately, this meant that I was in *no* way prepared for my first teaching role.

My first teaching contract was in a low socioeconomic area. My classes were loud, noisy and disorganised. The students showed little respect for their teachers or for themselves. They were not interested in learning; school was just somewhere they were meant to be from 8:45a.m. until 3:30p.m. Most didn't even bother turning up to class.

Yet, there was a strange sense of community. Every teacher knew every student – what their home life was like, what their interests were, which subjects they were/weren't passing. Staff meetings were spent discussing specific students and their needs, and there was constant support to help each other manage classes.

None of my students envisaged an academic future. The 'smart' ones left early to get apprenticeships. Everyone else assumed they'd be on the dole for the rest of their lives. Could you imagine growing up in a world where no one expects that you'll amount to anything? Where you didn't have the opportunity to *be* anything, simply because it never occurred to you? I longed to change their mentality. The way I saw it, the only way I could do that was to teach students at the very beginning of their schooling career. Instil in them from day one that there was a future *beyond* Centrelink. I had to become a primary school teacher.

However, I wasn't primary school trained, and was therefore, very unlikely to get a contract position teaching in a primary school. The only way to *become* a primary school teacher was to take up relief work. My plan was simple: introduce myself to *everyone* (I was good at that) and hope that someday someone would call me up.

Becoming a relief teacher was the best career move I have ever made. I accept work from everyone: high schools, primary schools and disability units. Every day, I wake up and I don't know who I will be. Some days, I am in a primary school, teaching anything from the alphabet to physical education. I laugh on these days. I was learning to walk at the same time that my students were, yet they are so much better than me at sport. There are other days when I am a high school teacher, teaching anything from maths and sciences, to English, foreign languages, dance, food sciences or metal tech.

But my favourite days are when I am teaching in disability units. On these days, I work with teenagers with the mental intellect ranging anywhere between that of a three- to ten-year-old. In these lessons, the students may learn how to catch a ball or make sandwiches; they may learn to match pairs; or they may even be able to count, add or subtract. But they are all learning *life* skills. They are learning to communicate and to share.

Some days are hard. In the disability units, students have meltdowns, or seizures, or fall and hurt themselves. In the mainstream schools, students may argue back or refuse to work because their *real* teacher isn't there.

But, no matter which school I am in, every day is magical, because there is always that *moment* when a student smiles or laughs as they learn a new fact from a stranger, or when a student can be proud of something they achieved. And I get to be a part of that. No matter what sort of subject I teach, or what sort of teacher I am, I get to be there, watching and learning myself.

Even though I am a teacher, I will always be a student at heart.

Chapter Nineteen

It's Not a Wedding, It's a Barbecue

Alan and I had been together for seven years before we were married and, naturally, for us, the wedding was not what you would call conventional. Alan had already done the whole 'walk down the aisle' thing twice before. Neither of those relationships worked out. Not wanting to jinx our relationship, he suggested that we don't do the same thing. I am not a *wedding* kind of person, so I agreed. No aisle.

We agreed to simply go to the births, deaths and marriages office, sign the paperwork, and then have a huge barbecue to celebrate. But it wasn't a wedding. It was a barbecue.

We each needed a witness for the registrar's office. It was easy to choose *my* witness. I flew Abi over from Melbourne. Dad was also staying with us at the time, so he came along too. I didn't encourage Mum or Greer or the rest of my family to come over. Who would want to watch two people sign a couple of pieces of paper? Mum and Greer always supported my wishes, so they relented.

Alan's choice of witness was his best friend, Graeme. There would have to be a joke. There always had to be a joke. That's just the kind of couple we are. Graeme was going to be the victim of our joke.

Alan did *not* tell Graeme about going to the registrar's office. Instead, he told Graeme that he needed help collecting something in the city, and as a thank you, Alan promised to take him to the casino afterwards '...so you had probably better wear something nice.'

Abi, Dad and I caught the bus into town, and got to the registrar's office long before Alan and Graeme. The registrar overheard Abi and I laughing that '*Graeme* doesn't know...'

When they came through the lift and saw Abi, Dad and I there waiting – and me wearing my finest jeans and sneakers – Graeme's mouth made a perfect O, and his eyes shone when he realised what was going on. Alan and

I laughed at our glorious joke. Graeme laughed along, ever a good sport and proud that *he* was Alan's chosen witness.

Alan and I were taken to a small room to sign paperwork in the presence of the registrar, who appeared to be more than a little concerned when he saw that Alan's middle name was *Graham.* Knowing that someone called *Graeme* didn't know about the wedding, and witnessing our light-hearted nature, he was not too sure that Alan knew why he was there.

'You *do* understand the seriousness of what you are doing, don't you?' he asked.

'Yup,' replied Alan, eyes twinkling.

'Marriage is a very serious business.'

'Marriage?' Alan turned to me, eyes wide, full of mischievous conviction. 'You said we were here to register a puppy!'

The poor registrar didn't know what to say. It took a little convincing and reassuring on our behalf to calm him down.

But Alan wasn't finished.

As we were finishing signing papers, Alan asked, 'Do you do divorce as well?'

We both fell out of our chairs laughing.

No one told me that, after the signing, I had to do the whole walk down the aisle thing at the registrar's office. I thought all we had to do was sign papers! We knew we were partners. We knew we were married. Why do all the ceremony? But they still made me do it.

Worse than that, Alan was wearing the jacket I hate.

Worse than *that,* he was laughing at me the whole time.

The registrar was reciting the vows I had to repeat. He had his back to Alan.

Big mistake.

Alan started pulling faces at me. He was contorting his mouth and crossing his eyes, looking down his nose and poking out his tongue. I couldn't keep a straight face. Every time the registrar looked back at Alan, Alan looked at him with large, solemn eyes, protesting all sorts of innocence. 'She gets like this. She has a brain injury.'

This bothered the registrar even more.

He told me that I really had to take this seriously. I protested, and said that I was, it was Alan who was stuffing around.

He turned to Alan so that Alan could say his vows.

And then it was over without too much more excitement.

Graeme didn't ever get to go to the casino, but I don't think he remembers that promise.

One month later, Alan and I sent invitations out to our friends. Not for a wedding. For a barbecue.

I was a little scared when we started to make this list. I had always considered myself socially clumsy, and thought I'd have few people to invite. But as Alan and I considered who we would send invitations to, I found myself thinking of all the people who had encouraged me as I started my teaching career – our neighbours, Alan's family and friends – and I realised that with Alan at my side, I had built a large network of people I cared about.

They were all invited. *But it was not a wedding. It was a barbecue.*

Abi flew over again from Melbourne. She got to the farm early, and helped me make salads and desserts. She kept insisting that I go and take a shower before the guests arrived. I was adamant that I had to get all the salads done, and then get signs up to direct guests to the right paddock to park their cars. *Having a shower can wait.*

I just felt so guilty going and having a shower and putting on fresh clothes when there was so much to be done. Ten minutes before guests started to arrive, Abi finally made me go have a shower. 'Sarah, go. You'll regret it if you don't.'

I think I may be one of the few brides in the world who had to be convinced to go have a shower before the guests started to arrive. But then again, I wasn't a bride, and this wasn't a wedding reception. *It's not a wedding. It's a barbecue.*

We had our own beef, and someone gave us a leg of ham and a lamb for a spit. Alan made sure we had at least a million potatoes, because they are my favourite food. We had salads and sausages and beef patties and bread.

Friends who liked to cook brought salads and desserts. Friends who didn't like to cook came and ate.

Abi

Sah vehemently rejects things that are stereotypical and expected. She revels in watching other people's happiness, and repels when the attention is reciprocated. Her wedding (forever known as the 'barbecue that was not a wedding') is the perfect example of this.

Sarah didn't wear a wedding dress, or dress up at all for that matter. For her 'barbecue that was not a wedding', Sah opted for a pair of blue jeans, old sneakers, and a new short-sleeved olive-green button-up shirt that she had recently bought from Target. She wouldn't have it any other way.

When I arrived at Sah and Alan's house, Sah was making a giant fruit salad, roasting potatoes, and planning signs for the paddock-cum-parking lot. Alan was building a spit roast for the lamb and clearing the paddock. Sah and Alan spent their 'not-a-wedding' day catering for their guests, preparing the salads, fetching drinks, and manning the barbecue and lamb-spit. I spent the afternoon getting to know the work friends and neighbours who I had heard so much about on the phone, but had never met in person.

It was a weird thing, talking with Sarah's friends. They spoke to me as though they had known me forever, because I look so much like Sarah, and they had heard almost as much about me as I had about them. They made in-jokes – most of which I understood because Sah shared them all with me. They acted as though they were spending time with Sarah.

These days, Sarah jokes that I was her stand-in at the barbecue. I was doing something that she could not do for herself, and that was celebrate Sarah.

I'm very good at celebrating Sarah.

There needed to be a surprise at the barbecue. Something different. It was, after all, Alan and me.

Early in the afternoon, our friends were happily sitting in the shade of the gum trees that line the hayshed paddock, full and content. Alan suddenly remembered that he had to collect 'something' from Strathalbyn, which is thirty minutes' drive away.

Alan asked his brother if he would accompany him on the ride. 'I'll need a hand to get it into the car', he explained. He never told his brother what 'it' was.

Forty-five minutes later, a helicopter crossed over our farm. It circled once, and then came back again. Helicopters are common in our area during summer, because we live directly opposite a pine forest with high bushfire risk. But *this* helicopter circled our farm with the same interest that the flies showed towards the lamb-spit. And it got lower, and lower, and lower.

Alan's cousin was the first one to see Alan in the front passenger seat of the helicopter.

'What? What? What's Alan doing?' she cried, as she pointed him out to all of the other guests. Surprise and joy spread across our friends' faces, as one by one they realised that Alan and I had booked the helicopter for chartered flights for the afternoon.

For the next three hours, anyone who wanted a ride was buddied up with other guests, and had a ten-minute joy ride over the forest.

Abi

Alan and Sah didn't get to share a helicopter flight at the barbecue.

They couldn't.

They had a farm full of guests. Alan was needed by the helicopter, calculating a list of people (Sah had arranged them by height and weight) for rides in the helicopter. Sarah was needed in the crowd of people, fetching each pair, negotiating with Alan about who could go up a second or third time. When the helicopter rides were over and the pilot was due to return to base, there was one last flight to take. With everyone else satisfied, Sah finally agreed to take part. She would fly with the pilot back to base, to bring back the car that Alan had used to get there earlier in the day.

I was the lucky one who got to share that flight with Sah.

She was her usual extroverted self: sharing jokes and stories with the pilot about the weather, helicopter licences, the geography below. Finally relaxed, she switched between enjoying investigating his life history and pointing out histories hidden in the land beneath us. Where I saw pine forests and farms, Sarah saw friends' livelihoods. She pointed at a property: 'I taught Dillan to read by that dam down there! Somewhere down there is a rock with the word *frog* on it!' She then pointed at another one, one hundred metres below. 'Look there! That's Harvey's favourite walking trail! See that tree? The one with the wiggly yellow top branches?'; or 'There's the high school. You can see the trampoline in the unit courtyard!' Sah's entire life

> was mapped out beneath us. The people and places she loved, helped and taught. I was so proud, listening to her chatting about the life she had established, from this special view. She was so excited to share her whole world with me from up in the helicopter.
>
> That day, I got to celebrate Sah with her friends at the farm, and celebrate her life with her in the helicopter.

I am not sure that there are too many weddings where the bride and groom get to spend three hours bossing guests around – making them weigh themselves, and form queues and 'buddy groups'.

But then again, ours was not a wedding. It was a barbecue. But I wouldn't trade our barbecue for any other way to celebrate.

Now You Have Read My Story, You can Decide

It's been eighteen years since the subarachnoid haemorrhage and the accident.

Eighteen years of rehabilitation, discovery and reinvention. Eighteen years since I was a broken blue body of a girl in HDU, who won a thumb wrestling contest and made her sister cry. But I am still broken.

I have come to accept that I must keep confirming with the world that I have a disability. Every twelve months, I ask my doctor to fill out a Medical Fitness to Drive form. When Alan and I travel overseas, my doctor provides a letter explaining why I am carrying so many medications in my carry-on luggage. Even the TAC requires an annual letter confirming that I still have a brain injury.

Every time I start a new course or job, I tick the boxes that say *epilepsy, asthma* and *other.* I always smile to myself as I try to fit all of my *other* disabilities into the tiny little space provided: 'acquired brain injury (ABI) resulting in anosmia (no smell), partially deaf, panhypopituitary (no hormones) and orbitofrontal syndrome'. I find it even more amusing when I'm asked to list 'any medications'. I usually attach a fresh page.

I accepted these procedures as part of my life, but that all changed during one of the earlier lectures of my teaching degree. The class received a visit from a disability liaison officer. Though her speech was rehearsed, I am not sure that the large woman meant to be as condescending as she sounded.

'The university is here to help you through the degree,' she told us, with the sort of smiling sincerity that any well-practised speech may achieve. Then, as though she were our conduit to salvation, she added: '*We* are here to help you through the degree.' The tall Disability Liaison Officer waved a small pile of forms. 'We encourage you to register if you need help. Of course, we won't disclose your disability to anyone. We are *very* discreet.'

I had never had a problem with paperwork before. But as the tall woman stood before us with the forms in her hand, for the very first time, I was outraged. What hurt was that I was asked whether or not I was comfortable with the Disability Liaison Unit *disclosing* that I have a disability in order to access support.

I have never thought of it as *disclosing.*

It's not as though it's a secret.

To treat any condition as 'secret' is to propel ignorance and promote stigma. 'Brain injury' does not mean 'entirely incapacitated'.

Without the *disclosure* that this woman thought was so precious, people will never learn. I got myself so worked up over the word *disclosure* that I decided that I needed to tell to the world. I probably *Golfballed* a little ... okay, maybe a lot.

Where does one *start* to contact the world?

I am a big fan of *Conversations* with Richard Fidler. Richard and his guests had kept me company for the past few years. Whether I was alone in the animal house doing behavioural tests, or trying to stay awake on the long bus trips to and from university, or waiting for clients and employers to meet me at a work site, *Conversations* with Richard Fidler was always in my earphones.

If I was going to reach Australia, I trusted Richard Fidler to do it properly. I wrote him an email, describing my frustrations, and explaining the story of the car accident. I had no idea what would happen as I hit the *send* button. I could only hope that he would receive it and be interested. I doubted it though. Surely the people that went on shows as big as *Conversations* had something to sell?

What did I have to sell?

I had a story.

Within a few weeks, Richard's producer responded to my email. She explained to me that, unfortunately, Richard only came to Adelaide once a year, and I had missed my chance to do an interview in 2016. However, he was interested.

We agreed to meet when Richard returned to Adelaide.

On Friday 10 March 2017, I met with Richard Fidler and told him *my* story. I was excited and nervous as I entered the studio and prayed that Richard wouldn't notice my sweaty hands. If he did, he didn't say anything. Richard was calm and well prepared. He and his team had worked hard in the build-up to this interview. We had many conversations where they listened and re-listened to my story, and double-checked information.

Richard did his best to keep my distracted mind on track during the interview. This was no small feat. When I am excited by something, I am still the same puppy chasing butterflies I was during honours.

Early in the interview, Richard asked me to describe my injuries. I listed them: cracked C1, fractures to the face and skull, deaf in one ear, loss of smell, fractured hips, dislocated pelvis, broken my right leg ... I was so focused on accurately remembering *all* of my injuries, that I forgot to mention the main reason I was there.

Richard remembered though. After patiently listening to my exhaustive list, he guided me back to the purpose of the interview: '...You had an aneurysm as well, and that had flooded your brain with blood and destroyed a part of it. Had you lost a chunk of your brain as well?'

'Oh! Yes! That's probably the biggest thing,' I gushed with excitement. And so it was through the whole interview. Richard patiently asking questions, and me becoming distracted in my answers. It was over so fast, I wasn't sure what I had said, or whether I got my message across. But it didn't matter. I had fun and had trusted that Richard Fidler *was* the person who could best help me tell the world about ABI.

The aftermath of the interview had very little impact on my own life. I lived in a small town on the outskirts of Adelaide. I doubted that anyone there even knew. Occasionally, a neighbour said 'Oh! By the way, I heard you on the radio the other day. I had no idea!' But that was about all that happened.

In 2018, the producers of *Conversations* contacted me to let me know that they were planning on re-airing my conversation with Richard Fidler. They were very enthusiastic.

'We had a huge response to your conversation last time,' they told me. 'Many people hear the repeat who didn't hear the first time around, so I'm sure we'll get another avalanche of wonderful emails!'

I received an email too. One that would set up my next adventure in educating the world about acquired brain injury.

It was from a publicity manager from a publishing company in Melbourne. She had heard my interview with Richard Fidler, and wandered if I'd thought about writing a book.

I hadn't.

I asked Harvey. He yawned and rested his aging head on his paws. I suppose he hadn't thought about a book either.

I asked Abi. Ever supportive, Abi pointed out that there was no harm in meeting Grace and her boss, Martin, and hearing them out. A few weeks later, I went over to Melbourne and met with Grace and Martin to discuss the possibility of a book. I took Abi with me.

Abi was rational, and professional, and knew all the right questions to ask. Grace and Martin did their best to explain what they envisaged. I did my best to demonstrate that I was well enough to write a book.

I *do* have a story to tell.

Once upon a time there was a girl.

She was smart and passionate about facts and the truth. She was a neuroscientist.

There was a subarachnoid haemorrhage and a car accident. Then she ceased to exist.

I woke up in her place.

I was a girl, in a bed, who had a family she loved, and no identity of her own. I said my first words in hospital, making my sister cry as I whispered them down the phone. I took my first steps in a rehabilitation centre, while my friends raced around corridors in wheelchairs.

I fell in love with a white ball of fluff, who rescued me from the confusion the outside world.

I married a man who, when he wasn't pulling faces at me and getting me in trouble with the celebrant during our wedding, rescued me from an undiagnosed disorder that had taken the sense out of my world.

I completed honours and a PhD, then a graduate diploma and a postgraduate diploma. I spent nine years studying formally, but will always be a student learning about her own abilities. In my quest to find me, I have been a counsellor, a consultant, a neuroscientist and a teacher.

Now, I know who I am. I am a woman with an acquired brain injury and an odd sense of humour. I am a twin, a relief teacher and a wife.

I am Sarah Brooker.

Once upon a time, I may have been someone else.

I struggle to imagine whether she would act like me.

But I said I'd let you decide.

Acknowledgements

A little over a year ago, I started to write this book.

In the beginning, I aimed to provide insight into life with an acquired brain injury (ABI), beyond what people see in the movies. I wanted people to understand that living with an ABI *is* hard, but it is nothing like what Hollywood would have you believe. Not for people like me, anyway.

While writing this book, I learned so much more about ABI, the accident, the people involved in my recovery, and myself.

This is no longer just *my* story. This is the story of my family, doctors, therapists, specialists, teachers, students, chauffeurs and friends ... and somehow, in this Acknowledgements, I must find a way to thank you all for the roles you have played.

So here goes...

First, and before anything else in the world, and although he cannot read, I must thank Harvey. You saved me, kiddo, and without you, I'd be trapped inside my own little egocentric world.

Second, thank you to everyone involved in the accident and my recovery.

Thank you to every single doctor, nurse and orderly who worked at Monash Medical Centre, not just on 31 December 2002, but every single day that I was there. You saved my life.

I also want to thank the two ambulance drivers who appeared from nowhere and took me to the hospital, and the doctors who looked after my sisters, because I don't know what other platform I will ever have to tell you.

Thank you to the specialists who have monitored my health and kept me alive for the past seventeen years. A special thank you to Dr Les Koopowitz. You made the most debilitating part of my condition bearable. You have no idea how much sense you made of the world, simply by giving it a name. Thank you.

Thank you to all the staff and patients at the Victorian Rehabilitation Centre, for the role that you played in my physical and social recovery.

For that matter, I want to thank every single chauffeur at Alternative Chauffeured Transport and every bus driver who listened to my stories. You were my first regular friends, and beautifully supportive in your own way.

Thank you to my TAC case managers, especially Catherine Cole. You guided my family through a very difficult time, and looked after them when I could not. I am in your debt for that.

Thank you to Janine Farrelly. You made the big 'outside' less intimidating.

Thank you to my honours supervisor, Richard Loiacono. Your faith and support during my first lonely attempt at neuroscience will never be forgotten. I can only hope to be half the teacher that you are. Thank you to all the other supervisors and colleagues in every career I have attempted since then as well.

Now onto the book...

Thank you to everyone at *Conversations* with Richard Fidler. Your hard work and dedication to producing a brilliant interview kick-started the adventure of producing this book, and I am forever grateful.

Thanks must go to everyone at Affirm Press, especially Martin Hughes. The wisdom you imparted and professionalism that you maintained as you navigated me through this whole publishing process have been invaluable. Thank you for your patience as I rejected cover after cover, edit after edit, and photo after photo. You learned quickly that the phone calls and emails of excessive exuberance and/or angry tears were not those of a prima donna who needed to be put in her place, but of a woman with an ABI who had a story to tell. You took a deep breath and accommodated me as best you could. I appreciate that. I know there must have been times that you regretted taking me on ... but I am glad you persevered, and I am proud of what we have achieved.

Thanks must go to my editors – Cosima, Freya and Jess. I think you are insanely brave to take me on as an author. It must be incredibly scary to tell a stubborn young lady with a Golfball missing that her story didn't make sense in parts. I am glad that you did though, because there were many things I just assumed people knew. A special thanks must go to Jess, for taking on the incredibly hard task of helping me to 'find puppies to kill' and build a structure that tells the story well.

Thank you to my husband, Alan Rochford. You are a rock. Your ability to put up with my tirades and tears and laughter and obsession with this book is phenomenal. Thank you for helping me find words and knowing when to pull me away from my laptop. Thank you for taking me to Thailand where I could be left alone in peace to write the book while you 'took one for the team' and went and had a massage. That must have been *very* difficult, but I love you for it. Thank you for accepting that for the past twelve months, I have had very little else to talk about, and that often, even though you are the only one in the room, you are not a part of the conversations I am having ... Thank you.

I would like to thank Mum, Dad, Greer and Adam for your support and love. Thank you for facing demons and reliving a horrific period of your lives, as you bravely tried to answer my naive questions about death, survival, fear and loss. Thank you for the grace that you showed as you learned more about this accident from my perspective, and the patience you showed as I tried to learn it from yours.

Finally, thank you to my twin sister and hero, Abi. There is no other word for what you are to me. You are my hero. I love you and appreciate your laughter, wisdom, tears and stories. I love your honesty in writing and your infinite wisdom about a world that I find hard to understand. You are my 'phone a friend' and inspiration. Without you to cry to, or laugh with, none of this project could have been achieved.

To those that do not see their names here specifically – I have not forgotten you ... just me.

Back Cover Material

A double-pronged freak accident hijacks your brain and robs you of all memory. How do you find yourself again? Or do you choose to become someone entirely new?

Sarah Brooker was an ambitious young woman studying to be a neuroscientist. She had the world at her feet. Then an almost unbelievable series of events changed everything: an aneurysm in Sarah's brain burst at the exact moment she was in a devastating car accident. Weeks later, Sarah woke from a coma with no idea who or where she was. But thanks to an extraordinary quirk of the brain, Sarah *could* remember neuroscience. In fact, when doctors came to visit her during the many weeks she spent in hospital, Sarah assumed they were consulting her as the brain expert, not tending to her as a patient.

While her loved ones waited for the 'old Sarah' to emerge, she herself began exploring the world anew. Like a newborn, full of wonder and curiosity, she learned how to speak, how to walk, and how to touch and feel as if for the first time. Sarah was given the chance to start again and what she achieved in the years following her accident will astound you. In a way, the aneurysm was the luckiest thing that could have happened to her.

My Lucky Stroke is an extraordinary memoir, full of warmth and humour, insight and drama – a story about rebuilding a life from square one that you won't easily forget.

www.ingramcontent.com/pod-product-compliance
Lightning Source LLC
Chambersburg PA
CBHW071432300426
44114CB00013B/1399